RETENTION, PERSISTENCE, AND WRITING PROGRAMS

RETENTION, PERSISTENCE, AND WRITING PROGRAMS

Edited by
TODD RUECKER
DAWN SHEPHERD
HEIDI ESTREM
BETH BRUNK-CHAVEZ

UTAH STATE UNIVERSITY PRESS
Logan

© 2017 by the University Press of Colorado

Published by Utah State University Press
An imprint of University Press of Colorado
5589 Arapahoe Avenue, Suite 206C
Boulder, Colorado 80303

  The University Press of Colorado is a proud member of
The Association of American University Presses.

The University Press of Colorado is a cooperative publishing enterprise supported, in part, by Adams State College, Colorado State University, Fort Lewis College, Metropolitan State College of Denver, Regis University, University of Colorado, University of Northern Colorado, Utah State University, and Western State College of Colorado.

The paper used in this publication meets the minimum requirements of the American National Standard for Information Sciences—Permanence of Paper for Printed Library Materials. ANSI Z39.48-1992

ISBN: 978-1-60732-601-4 (paper)
ISBN: 978-1-60732-602-1 (e-book)

Library of Congress Cataloging-in-Publication Data

Names: Ruecker, Todd Christopher, editor. I Shepherd, Dawn, 1971– editor. I Estrem, Heidi, editor. I Brunk-Chavez, Beth, 1970– editor.
Title: Retention, persistence, and writing programs / edited by Todd Ruecker, Dawn Shepherd, Heidi Estrem, Beth Brunk-Chavez.
Description: Logan : Utah State University Press, [2017] I Includes bibliographical references and index.
Identifiers: LCCN 2016035663 I ISBN 9781607326014 (pbk.) I ISBN 9781607326021 (ebook)
Subjects: LCSH: English language—Rhetoric—Study and teaching (Higher) I College dropouts—Prevention.
Classification: LCC PE1404 .R446 2017 I DDC 808/.0420711—dc23
LC record available at https://lccn.loc.gov/2016035663

Cover illustration ©hxdbzxy/Shutterstock.

This collection is dedicated to all the students striving to achieve a college education despite odds often stacked against them, as well as the often underpaid and overworked teachers of writing working with them.

CONTENTS

1   Introduction: Retention, Persistence, and Writing: Expanding the Conversation

Todd Ruecker, Dawn Shepherd, Heidi Estrem, and Beth Brunk-Chavez   *3*

PART 1: WRITING, RETENTION, AND BROADER POLICY CONTEXTS

2   Retention ≠ Panopticon: What WPAs Should Bring to the Table in Discussions of Student Success

Rita Malenczyk   *21*

3   Beyond Coordination: Building Collaborative Partnerships to Support Institutional-Level Retention Initiatives in Writing Programs

Ashley J. Holmes and Cristine Busser   *38*

4   Big Data and Writing Program Retention Assessment: What We Need to Know

Marc Scott   *56*

5   The Imperative of Pedagogical and Professional Development to Support the Retention of Underprepared Students at Open-Access Institutions

Joanne Giordano, Holly Hassel, Jennifer Heinert, and Cassandra Phillips   *74*

6   How Student Performance in First-Year Composition Predicts Retention and Overall Student Success

Nathan Garrett, Matthew Bridgewater, and Bruce Feinstein   *93*

7   "Life Gets in the Way": The Case of a Seventh-Year Senior

Sara Webb-Sunderhaus   *114*

**PART 2: WRITING PROGRAM INITIATIVES
THAT MATTER**

8   Absolute Hospitality in the Writing Program

   Pegeen Reichert Powell   *135*

9   Retention, Critical Pedagogy, and Students as Agents: Eschewing the Deficit Model

   Beth Buyserie, Anna Plemons, and Patricia Freitag Ericsson   *151*

10 Reconfiguring the Writing Studio Model: Examining the Impact of the *PlusOne* Program on Student Performance and Retention

   Polina Chemishanova and Robin Snead   *167*

11 Retention Rates of Second Language Writers and Basic Writers: A Comparison within the Stretch Program Model

   Sarah Elizabeth Snyder   *185*

12 The *Kairotic* Classroom: Retention Discourse and Supplemental Instruction in the First Year

   Sarah E. Harris   *204*

13 Enhancing Alliances and Joining Initiatives to Help Students: The Story of How We Created Developmental Learning Communities at Texas A&M University–Corpus Christi

   Susan Wolff Murphy and Mark G. Hartlaub   *219*

14 Undergraduate Mentors as Agents of Engagement: Peer Advocates in First-Year Writing Courses

   Michael Day, Tawanda Gipson, and Christopher P. Parker   *237*

15 Afterword: Navigating the Complexities of Persistence and Retention

   Linda Adler-Kassner   *257*

   About the Authors   *271*
   Index   *275*

RETENTION, PERSISTENCE, AND WRITING PROGRAMS

1

INTRODUCTION
Retention, Persistence, and Writing:
Expanding the Conversation

Todd Ruecker, Dawn Shepherd,
Heidi Estrem, and Beth Brunk-Chavez

"Colleges are Failing in Graduation Rates." "It's Bonus Time for Arizona University Presidents." "Keep Students, Earn More." These headlines have something in common: higher education's increased concern over student retention and graduation in recent years, a concern that has impacted colleges and universities in ways we could not have predicted a decade ago. For example, the majority of states now have funding formulas in place that weigh retention and graduation rates in determining funding allotments ("Performance-Based Funding for Higher Education" 2015). Perhaps not too surprising, university president compensation is now often partially based on reaching and surpassing retention and matriculation benchmarks. And in an interesting and perhaps somewhat predictable move, at least one institution, Coastal Carolina University, has implemented a new policy that directly links faculty salary compression raises to improved student retention rates (Mulhere 2015). The logic goes that with more students staying around to finish their educations, postsecondary institutions can maintain their enrollment and share a portion of the tuition dollars that go along with them. These are three examples, but one would be hard pressed to find a single state, even a single institution, that isn't "gravely concerned" about retention and graduation rates and is in the process of developing a range of strategic plans, action plans, programs, initiatives, and metrics to keep students enrolled and graduating in a timely manner. We wonder, however, how involved academic programs and their faculty are—or should be—in these conversations?

DOI: 10.7330/9781607326021.c001

As teachers and scholars interested in improving student success at our institutions, this increased attention to retention and persistence is welcomed. As teachers of writing in postsecondary institutions, the four of us have been increasingly concerned about students in our classes who show up for a day, a week, or even a few months, and then disappear, sometimes because of unexpected family obligations or simply because they fall behind in the coursework due to an inflexible or overwhelming work schedule. We have explored how to work with students as individuals while thinking of ways to improve success rates across our writing programs. We are not alone. A search through the Writing Program Administrator's listserv (WPA-L) archives shows retention to be an ongoing interest of the composition community, a community who tends to teach small classes and has the opportunity to get to know the students who disappear. However, with the exception of work by Beth Brunk-Chavez and Elaine Fredericksen (Brunk-Chavez and Fredericksen 2008), Pegeen Reichert Powell (2009, 2014), and Todd Ruecker (2015), and some scholarship in basic writing (e.g., Baker and Jolly 1999; Glau 2007; Hagedorn 2012; McCurrie 2009; Peele 2010; Seidman 2012; Webb-Sunderhaus 2010), there has been very little published work that explores the ways writing program instructors and administrators can be involved in discussions of student retention and success and affect change not only at the programmatic level but also at the institutional and state levels.

But what is it that we mean when we enter conversations about retention? As you read this collection, you will notice that a variety of terms are used to talk about issues concerning this subject. When we discuss and analyze issues related to the retention of students in higher education, we use words like *success, persistence, retention,* "*drop out vs. stop out,*" and others. The title of this collection captures two of the most prominent terms, *retention* and *persistence.* As editors, we use *retention* deliberately because it is the key term most often used in the popular media and in our own scholarship. Retention is an institutional approach—and one that perhaps too often loses sight of student learning, interests, and motivations while focusing on the statistical and financial importance of each retained student. Student *persistence,* though, is in many ways the mirror opposite of retention. This term is most often identified with Vincent Tinto's work; it situates agency differently than does retention and assumes that students have a variety of reasons for continuing in higher education, or not. Using both these terms, as we do in the title, reflects our belief that that continued student learning and engagement in college is a mutual responsibility that involves actions by both institutions and students.

Other terms commonly associated with retention/persistence discourse are involvement, engagement, and integration. Wolf-Wendel, Ward, and Kinzie (2009) define involvement as "responsibility of the individual student," (425) focusing on the energy they put into participating in the classroom and in other aspects of campus life. In contrast, engagement centers on the work that administrators, faculty, and staff do in "creating campus environments that are ripe with opportunities for students to be engaged" (425). Finally, "Integration (or what Tinto might now call 'sense of belonging') involves a reciprocal relationship between the student and the campus . . . a student must learn and adopt the norms of the campus culture, but the institution is also transformed by that merger" (425). As we discuss below, institutional considerations of integration have often emphasized the need for the student to change as opposed to the reciprocal obligation for the institution to change. Consequently, it is perhaps unsurprising that Tinto himself has been quoted saying, "I don't use the word integration anymore—haven't used it in decades" (Wolf-Wendel, Ward, and Kinzie 2009, 423).

This collection aims to unsettle and complicate these terms via chapters that explore how retention efforts at the institutional level impact writing programs, how writing programs can impact retention efforts at the institutional level, and how these efforts may or may not affect student persistence.

STUDENT RETENTION AND PERSISTENCE: A BRIEF HISTORY

Discussion around student retention in higher education expanded largely through the work of Vincent Tinto, whose 1975 piece "Dropout from Higher Education" synthesized existing research while introducing a model of student dropout that remained largely unquestioned for a few decades. Basing his theory of dropout on Emile Durkheim's theory of suicide, Tinto argued that students' likelihood of success at college was based on their integration into the system, namely

> that the process of dropout from college can be viewed as a longitudinal process of interactions between the individual and the academic and social systems of the college during which a person's experiences in those systems (as measured by his normative and structural integration) continually modify his goal and institutional commitments in ways which lead to persistence and/or to varying forms of dropout. (Tinto 1975, 94)

Tinto explained that academic integration included engagement in classrooms while social relations meant involvement with students and professors outside the classroom as well as engagement in various extracurricular activities. He briefly referenced additional factors that positively correlated with retention, such as coming from a higher socioeconomic class background with educated parents and strong high school achievement, but he did not study extensively how students from different racial or ethnic backgrounds fit into his theory.

In later work on retention, Tinto (1988, 1993, 1997) expanded his theory of student integration into academic settings by drawing on Van Gennep's *The Rites of Passage*. Tinto's work here helped influence others who have also used Pierre Bourdieu's concepts of habitus, capital, and field to make similar arguments that explore the disconnect between particular communities and academic communities and how this disconnect may promote high dropout rates. According to Tinto, "Individuals who come from families, communities, and schools whose norms and behaviors are very different from those of the communities of the college into which entry is made face especially difficult problems in seeking to achieve competent membership in the new communities" (Tinto 1993, 97). As a result, Tinto popularized the idea of establishing learning communities within institutions by arguing that creating a stronger community in the classroom setting would help institutions promote student persistence (Tinto 1997).

During this time, more scholars became interested in documenting various factors that promote student retention, with Alexander Astin's (1997) large scale study of hundreds of institutions being well known. As part of a growing movement aimed at promoting student engagement in college that included work by George Kuh and others, Astin (1997) explored a variety of factors that helped facilitate this engagement such as living on campus, attending a teaching-oriented institution, and not working off campus. Kuh et al. has been a proponent of the notion that student engagement is synonymous with retention/persistence, noting later that "What students do during college counts more in terms of what they learn and whether they will persist in college than who they are or even where they go to college" (Kuh et al. 2005, 8).

While various scholars explored the efficacy of Tinto's model, some began to critique and refine it, explaining that it failed to fully consider a variety of external factors such as ability to pay the costs associated with college attendance (e.g., Cabrera, Stampen, and Hansen 1990). More problematic, the approach seemed to promote a deficit model of minoritized students by stating that home communities mismatched with an institution were responsible for minoritized students not succeeding at rates like their majority peers (Rendón, Jalomo, and Nora 2000; Yosso 2005). Tierney (2000) and Rendón, Jalomo, and Nora

(2000) have pointed out that the traditional models focused on integration placed the burden on minoritized students to conform to the institutions rather than expect "the total transformation of colleges and universities from monocultural to multi-cultural institutions" (Rendón, Jalomo, and Nora 2000, 138).

Hrabowski (2005) noted that minoritized students' success is affected by "motivational and performance vulnerability in the face of negative stereotypes and low expectations, academic and cultural isolation, peers who are not supportive of academic success, and perceived and actual discrimination" (126). Pointing to stagnant retention rates of Latina and Latino students and noting that institutions are failing to inquire about and adopt the successful retention efforts that Latina/o university students are already practicing, Sóloranzo, Villalpando, and Oseguera (2005) argued that "higher education needs to adopt more explicit race-conscious practices to truly enhance the success and achievement of Latina/o college students" (289). Nonetheless, much of the interest in retention comes from a different perspective and advocates a very different set of changes, changes grounded more in the economic interests of institutions and governments and not the ethical imperative to help students succeed.

RECENT INTEREST IN RETENTION AND PERSISTENCE: OPPORTUNITIES AND CHALLENGES

In the twenty-first century, federal and state governments have increasingly become interested in student retention, a trend that has emerged largely out of economic interest. One thread of this argument states that the US economy will need larger numbers of college-educated workers to compete in an increasingly globalized knowledge-based economy. Another area concerns the increasing cost of student loan debt along with increasing default rates, stemming in part from students who borrow money or use government grants (e.g., Pell Grants) and ultimately drop out of college without a job to pay for the accrued debts. Finally, states especially are increasingly concerned with reining in the costs of higher education and, in this perspective, one of the most wasteful areas of spending is educating students who never finish school.

It is not entirely clear where this government interest in student retention in higher education begins, but one likely responsible force has been the increasing costs of college tuition alongside the growth of large educational foundations such as Lumina, Achieve, and the Gates Foundation (Donhardt 2007). Lumina, for instance, has a $1.5 billion endowment and spends around $50 million in grants annually, which has helped make it tremendously visible and influential. Its primary focus, or Goal 2025, is aimed at "increasing the proportion of Americans with high-quality degrees, certificates and other credentials to 60 percent by 2025" (Lumina Foundation 2015). It intends to reach this goal by developing an "outcomes-based approach that focuses on helping to design and build an accessible, responsive and accountable higher education system while fostering a national sense of urgency for action to achieve Goal 2025" (Lumina Foundation 2015). Although focused primarily on increasing achievement in the K–12 system, Achieve has also directed some of its attention to higher education with similar aims to Lumina, asserting that "states must collect, coordinate, and use K–12 and postsecondary data to track and improve the readiness of graduates to succeed in college and the workplace" (Achieve 2015). As researchers interested in promoting student success through student learning outcome development and continual assessment of the work we do, we are on one hand interested in the possibilities that Lumina and Achieve promote. However, we share Adler-Kassner's (2012) concerns that organizations like these risk pushing a reductive, vocational-oriented form of higher education. We have been especially concerned with the rapid increase in high-stakes testing at the K–12 level and the associated push for machine scoring; consequently, increasing usage of words like "accountability" and "data" is troubling and we wonder how long it will be until a K–12-style testing regime comes to higher education. With the introduction of the Collegiate Learning Assessment as a measure of students' learning at college (a test that is partially based on written response but completely machine scored), this future may not be too far off.

A few trends have emerged at the state level that are shaping higher education, trends that were briefly mentioned in the introductory comments. First, presidents at major universities in states such as Arizona and Kentucky are receiving bonus packages for "sharply increasing student-retention rates," among other goals ("It's Bonus Time" 2013). In another area, state legislatures are increasingly pushing performance-based funding for higher education, which ties some amount of allocations toward metrics like student retention and graduation rates. According to the National Conference of State Legislatures ("Performance-Based Funding for Higher Education" 2015), this model is in place in thirty states with several others considering this move. In these states, annual state funding for public colleges and universities is linked to improvements in retention rates, and it's no secret why when in recent decades, many publicly funded state institutions have crossed a critical threshold:

student tuition accounts for more revenue than state appropriations. Therefore, institutions are desperate to find ways to keep students in classes. According to a Government Accountability Office's 2014 report, this milestone was reached on a national level in 2012. During the recession of the early 2000s, state funding decreased by 12 percent overall and by 24 percent per individual student ("State Funding Trends" 2014, 7). This reduction then brought a 55 percent parallel rise in student tuition (7). During this same time period, student enrollment increased by 20 percent, a "trend has been driven mostly by 4-year colleges, which experienced faster enrollment increases and steeper declines in median state funding per student than 2-year colleges" (8). As state funding becomes more scarce and at the same time dependent on meeting certain performance metrics, it is important for faculty to become more aware of these policy shifts and join the conversation in order to shape it in a productive way. As the title of Adler-Kassner's (2012) article alluded, these are "challenging times"; however, writing professionals have much to contribute to these conversations.

When we engage in work on student retention, it is important to think about the consequences of the higher stakes discussed above tied to student success rates, especially at institutions that serve high numbers of minoritized, first-generation, and returning students who have not traditionally been as successful in postsecondary education. Because the stakes are so high, clever administrators might look to initiatives that encourage certain student populations to enroll at a two-year institution in order to "prove themselves" before transferring to a university. While appearing to be more efficient on the surface, this kind of initiative would quietly move some student populations out of the four-year and into the two-year school in order to boost retention rates. As we work on this chapter, the news is filled with controversy over the president of Mount St. Mary's goal to identify early students who might struggle to succeed, encouraging them to start elsewhere, such as the "Army" or a "community college" (Mangan 2016). When faculty raised ethical concerns with this approach, which they felt boosted institutional retention numbers at the expense of students who might otherwise succeed, the administration tried to fire them. In these discussions, the notion of the four-year time to graduation, even though achieved by a minority of students nationwide, drives some of these discussions. For instance, the New Mexico lottery scholarship requirements were recently revised to increase students' minimum enrollment from twelve to fifteen credits per semester. If students fail to attain a sufficient GPA on these fifteen hours or drop a course, they stand to lose the scholarship permanently. Policies like these have the potential to harm students who stand the most to gain from retention efforts: first-generation, minoritized, language learners, economically disadvantaged students. Minoritized students, including Latinas/os, are already over-represented at community colleges. With only two out of twenty Latina/o students starting at community colleges transferring to four-year institutions (Sóloranzo, Villalpando, and Oseguera 2005, 279) we need to be alert for practices and policies that boost a particular institution's numbers at the expense of student opportunities. It is important to consider who is involved in defining student success: administrators, faculty, or students? When this definition is driven by administration without faculty and student involvement, we risk encountering more situations like Mount St. Mary's. Thus, we join the authors in this collection in arguing that it is vital for faculty, including writing program administrators, to be involved in discussions of retention and keep the focus on student success and not simply on boosting institutional numbers.

WHERE COMPOSITION HAS BEEN AND WHERE IT NEEDS TO GO

We are concerned that too often faculty are not involved in these conversations. Retention-related workshops and focus groups are often held on our campuses, but faculty are rarely, or perhaps sparsely, represented; the vast majority of participants work in student affairs, are assigned to student success initiatives, or collect and analyze data in institutional assessment offices. Alternatively, faculty might be involved—but through efforts to recruit potential English majors and not with any real attention to first-year introductory writing courses. Whether the division between faculty and "the rest of the university" is accurate, the implication in these contexts is that faculty are not responsible for contributing to student retention. From this perspective, it is as if curriculum and teaching have been black boxed and student success, retention, and persistence depend on what the rest of the university can do to assist students outside of that box.

So, why aren't faculty more directly involved in these retention and persistence conversations at the institutional level? As ample research has shown, student persistence is affected by a variety of factors, many of which are beyond the scope of any one individual course or two-course sequence: financial concerns; high school preparation; academic placement and progress; out-of-school responsibilities, whether the student lives and/or works on campus; if the student's parents went to college and whether *they* graduated; what the student's first language is; if the student feels as though she belongs on campus, can be successful, and is motivated to complete the degree; and so on. It is justifiable, then, for faculty to express concern over being held accountable for student persistence. Perhaps what faculty do is one small (albeit significant) piece of this puzzle, and perhaps the reason this retention conversation is dominated by university staff and administrators rather than faculty is that they are in the position to address the whole student (or at least more parts of that whole student). They can gather data on these demographics, implement far-reaching programs, and improve the processes that most affect students outside of the classroom. Justifiably so, many faculty resist being held responsible for student retention because of the perceptions that those conversations threaten academic integrity (think grade inflation), position faculty against an unfair metric (think evaluations based on number of students passing the course), and move our focus from the goal of educating and toward institutional quantitative metrics based on the numbers of students enrolling and graduating (think passing versus learning).

Given these concerns, however, how can first-year composition become more involved in student persistence conversations? If we flip the retention conundrum from institutional focus on percentages, dollars, and degree-completion rates to instead center on student learning, scholarship in writing studies has much to inform our understandings of issues that affect retention. The question of how and why students are or aren't successful in first-year writing courses is one that all of us care about. As noted, composition scholars are often not as present in retention efforts as they might be—and their expertise is not necessarily recognized by on-campus administrators. Our field's focus has largely followed Pegeen Reichert Powell's (2014) conclusion in exploring the role of first-year writing in retention: "while there may be very little we can do to prevent our students from leaving, we have a lot more control over what we do when they're sitting in front of us in our classrooms" (28). The challenge, though, is that when we focus solely on the classroom level, we miss larger changes that can lend themselves to institutional retention efforts without compromising our values as writing faculty.

Within the field of basic writing, some program and classroom-level efforts have taken up retention questions. Tracey Baker and Peggy Jolly found that enrollment in a basic writing program supported the success of conditionally admitted students, a result that helped save their program in the face of budget cuts (Baker and Jolly 1999). Greg Glau's (2007) influential work on the stretch program at Arizona State advocates both for the improved student experience and for the positive impact on retention. His data-driven research indicated that students in the stretch program—those more at risk for dropping out—were retained at higher rates than their counterparts. As other campuses implemented versions of the program, research often indicated a correlation with increased retention (Estrem, Shepherd, and Duman 2014; McCurrie 2009; Peele 2010).

Others have engaged with these questions from the placement viewpoint, working to enhance the opportunity for students to be placed into the appropriate class. Directed Self-Placement (DSP) research, for example, seems to indicate that students at some schools with DSP are retained at higher rates than their counterparts. Dan Royer and Roger Gilles, who are widely credited with introducing DSP, argue "success often begins with a proper estimation of one's abilities" (Royer and Gilles 1998, 70). David Blakesley, Erin Harvey, and Erica Reynolds report that a Stretch program, in combination with DSP, led to a 9 percent higher success rate for stretch students (Blakesley, Harvey, and Reynolds 2003). While there are questions about the lack of validity inquiry into DSP and alternative placement models, writing scholars have worked in these kinds of student-centered ways to better support student learning and success.

A variety of other efforts within writing studies has been linked to enhanced student learning and success. For example, Rebecca Babcock and Therese Thonus report on the improved retention for students who have required Writing Center visits (Babcock and Thonus 2012). Others note how learning communities—of which first-year writing courses are usually a key component—seem to enhance retention (Shapiro and Levine 1999). Still others explore how class size—often linked to retention efforts more generally—is key within first-year writing courses as well (Glau 2007).

HOW FACULTY CAN INFLUENCE RETENTION DISCUSSIONS AND SUPPORT STUDENT PERSISTENCE: TWO EXAMPLES

We offer two brief examples from Boise State University that have allowed two of the editors to address students' needs, offer a challenging curriculum, and contribute to campus-wide retention initiatives. These examples begin to demonstrate the complexity of retention issues—and how they can serve as a fulcrum of competing interests and motivations from a variety of stakeholders. They also demonstrate how challenging it is to engage with issues related to writing courses and retention.

The first involves placement and the challenges and rewards of systems-level change. Despite substantive national and local data on how problematic the Compass writing placement test was (a report from our institutional research office indicated that students might as well flip a coin to determine their initial writing course), a number of administrators from across our campus were initially reluctant to consider changing the process. After all, even though the Compass exam wasn't valid for accurate placement, it was efficient, deeply embedded in campus data systems, and provided a clear matrix for students, parents, and advisors. However, we were eventually granted permission to pilot an alternative. For several years, we developed, revised, and piloted an online multiple measures course-matching process called The Write Class. With every iteration of our pilot program, our data indicated that students were more successful in their writing class—and therefore more likely to continue at the university—when they used The Write Class for placement. In the spring of 2013, state-level conversations about developing more flexible placement strategies and reducing remediation and meant that we could propose and implement The Write Class as our sole placement process for all incoming students.

In 2012, the incoming class only used the state test score (Compass, ACT, and SAT) charts for placement. In 2013, the incoming class only used The Write Class. Without other substantive changes to curriculum, staffing structure, or funding, student retention rates rose by 5 percent. In other words, approximately 120 additional students successfully completed their first-year writing course than in the previous year. In what will likely surprise no one reading this collection, when students are in the first-year writing course that is best suited for them, they're much more likely to be successful. When they're successful in their first-year writing course, they're able to proceed to 200-level and upper-division courses. Yet to affect this change took years of advocacy, conversations, and piloting.

The second example is about repeating students, a population that has intrigued the four editors of this collection for years. As we reviewed course completion rates at Boise State, we realized that students who are not successful in a first-year writing course are more than twice as likely as first-time students to be unsuccessful the second time. As educators invested in supporting all students—and who operate from the belief that all students have the capacity to be successful in our courses—this finding troubled us. It also prompted us to set up an initiative to support these students through a series of low-stakes, reflection-driven interventions. Among these is a survey that asks students to reflect on the situation surrounding their previous course attempt(s) and to consider how this time might be different. We assumed that students were largely unsuccessful as a result of non-cognitive factors unrelated to school, such as changing work expectations or new family obligations. What we found was more complex. Such variables did play a role, but students were more likely to indicate that school-related concerns (e.g., struggling to adjust to college or to course material, feeling overwhelmed) affected their ability to complete the course. Knowing this has allowed us to reflect on our own curricula and pedagogies as we make adjustments to support students' persistence at Boise State.

As policies and politics shift at the state levels, the first-year writing classroom continues to play an integral role in many students' first-year experiences and can be a gatekeeper for some students, especially those concerned about their English abilities. Consequently, it behooves those involved in writing programs to attend to these larger discussions and become involved in not only shaping our own classrooms to support students but also in working to advocate for broader changes that align with our disciplinary notions of what should be done to promote student success.

CONTENTS OF THIS COLLECTION

In response to our call for work on retention, we received a wide variety of proposals representing different institutional contexts and different approaches to student retention in writing programs. We noticed two primary trends in the proposals we received: (a) those that took a broader view of retention discourses in institutions and beyond and imagined ways that composition could be involved in these discussions and (b) those that explored curricular changes within our programs to promote student success. With this in mind, we separated the collection into two parts: Part 1: Writing, Retention, and Broader Policy Contexts and Part 2: Writing Program Initiatives that Matter.

Part 1 begins with a chapter by Rita Malenczyk focused on how Writing Program Administrators (WPAs) involved in institutional discussions of student success can and should use an understanding of students' development as writers and thinkers to help their institutions stay on the "assistance" side of the line. Other chapters in Part 1 explore possibilities for collaboration between different institutional agents (Ashley J. Holmes and Cristine Busser), how big data might shape writing program administration retention and assessment effort (Marc Scott), possibilities for professional development among faculty in two-year college English departments (Joanne Giordano, Holly Hassel, Jennifer Heinert, and Cassandra Phillips), how success in first-year composition connects with overall student success (Nathan Garrett, Matthew Bridgewater, and Bruce Feinstein), and finally how a variety of external factors such as broader social policies factor in to student success (Sara Webb-Sunderhaus).

Part 2 shifts to writing programs themselves and conceptualizing moves within programs to better support student retention and persistence. It opens with a chapter by Pegeen Reichert Powell, who has been one of the leading voices in the field calling for more attention to initiatives focused on student retention. She asks WPAs to embrace the kairotic moment and think of Derrida's concept of "absolute hospitality" as they work to redesign their programs for students success. Other chapters focus on describing various program models including Washington State University's Critical Literacies Achievement and Success Program (CLASP; Beth Buyserie, Anna Plemons, and Patricia Freitag Ericsson), University of North Carolina at Pembroke's studio *PlusOne* program (Polina Chemishanova and Robin Snead), Arizona State University's Stretch Program (Sarah Elizabeth Snyder), supplemental instruction on a regional commuter campus (Sarah E. Harris), developmental learning communities at a Hispanic-Serving Institution (Susan Wolff Murphy and Mark Hartlaub), and an undergraduate mentorship program at Northern Illinois University, one of the most linguistically diverse institutions in the Midwest (Michael Day, Tawanda Gipson, and Chris Parker). The collection closes with an afterword by Linda Adler-Kassner that engages with the chapters and the broader political contexts of student retention and persistence.

As seen through the perspectives, conversations, strategies, and solutions discussed in these chapters, seeking opportunities to participate in national, regional, institutional, and programmatic conversations about retention and persistence is important for all stakeholders. Even as first-year composition has long been employing some of the best practices validated by retention research, we would argue that as valuable as our work is, and as important as our research and teaching objectives are, we often fall short of connecting our work to the bigger picture of student success—and we have probably have little idea about what other parts of the university do to promote persistence outside of the classes we teach. While composition studies is working at an advantage in many ways (after all, we do participate in first-year programs on our campuses, we do take assessment seriously, we do professionally develop our instructors), there is still much to be done. We need to consider ways to use data as well as our experiences to spur conversations that matter to us—conversations about retention, persistence, and student learning. Engaging in retention efforts on campus requires us to ask questions at *both* a student level and a programmatic/systems level. We believe it is a good time for first-year writing programs to contribute to the larger conversation regarding retention and persistence and to bring attention to themselves as key places for advocacy, research, and curricular innovation.

References

Achieve. 2015. "P-20 Data Systems." Accessed April 1, 2015. http://www.achieve.org/P-20-data-systems.

Adler-Kassner, L. 2012. "The Companies We Keep *Or* The Companies We Would Like to Try to Keep: Strategies and Tactics in Challenging Times." *WPA. Writing Program Administration* 36 (1): 119–40.

Astin, Alexander W. 1997. *What Matters in College? Four Critical Years Revisited.* San Francisco: Jossey-Bass.

Babcock, Rebecca D., and Terese Thonus. 2012. *Researching the Writing Center.* New York: Peter Lang. http://dx.doi.org/10.3726/978-1-4539-0869-3.

Baker, Tracey, and Peggy Jolly. 1999. "The 'Hard Evidence': Documenting the Effectiveness of a Basic Writing Program." *Journal of Basic Writing* 18 (1): 27–39.

Blakesley, David, Erin J. Harvey, and Erica J. Reynolds. 2003. "Southern Illinois University Carbondale as an Institutional Model: The English 100/101 Stretch and Directed Self-Placement Program." In *Directed Self-Placement: Principles and Practices,* ed. Daniel Royer and Roger Gilles, 207–41. New York: Hampton Press.

Brunk-Chavez, Beth, and Elaine Fredericksen. 2008. "Predicting Success: Increasing Retention and Pass Rates in College Composition." *WPA: Writing Program Administration* (1): 76–96.

Cabrera, Alberto F., Jacob O. Stampen, and W. Lee Hansen. 1990. "Exploring the Effects of Ability to Pay on Persistence in College." *Review of Higher Education* 13 (3): 303–36.

Donhardt, Tracy. 2007. "Rising Tuition Fuels Lumina's Reform Agenda." *Indianapolis Business Journal,* September 24. http://www.ibj.com/articles/13350-rising-tuition-fuels-lumina-s-reform-agenda.

Estrem, Heidi, Dawn Shepherd, and Lloyd Duman. 2014. "Relentless Engagement with State Educational Reform: Collaborating to Change the Writing Placement Conversation." *WPA. Writing Program Administration* 38 (1): 88–128.

Glau, Gregory. 2007. "Stretch at 10: A Progress Report on Arizona State University's Stretch Program." *Journal of Basic Writing* 26 (2): 30–48.

Hagedorn, Linda. S. 2012. "How to Define Retention: A New Look at an Old Problem." In *College Student Retention: Formula for Student Success,* ed. Alan Seidman, 81–99. Lanham: Rowman & Littlefield Publishers.

Hrabowski, Freeman A. III. 2005. "Fostering First-Year Success of Underrepresented Minorities." In *Challenging and Supporting the First-Year Student: A Handbook for Improving the First Year of College,* ed. M. Lee Upcraft, John N. Gardner, and Betsy O. Barefoot, 125–40. San Francisco: Jossey-Bass.

"It's Bonus Time for Arizona's University Presidents" 2013. *AZcentral.com.* September 23, 2013. http://www.azcentral.com/news/arizona/articles/20130925its-bonus-time-for-university-presidents.html.

Kuh, George D., Jillian Kinzie, John H. Schuh, Elizabeth J. Whitt, and Associates., eds. 2005. *Student Success in College: Creating Conditions that Matter.* San Francisco: Jossey-Bass.

Lumina Foundation. 2015. "Goal 2025." Accessed April 10, 2015. https://www.lumina foundation.org/goal_2025.

Mangan, Katherine. 2016. "A President's Plan to Steer Out At-Risk Freshmen Incites a Campus Backlash." *Chronicle of Higher Education*, January 20. http://chronicle.com /article/A-President-s-Plan-to-%20Steer/234992?cid=at&utm_source=at&utm_mediu m=en&elq=3bec93738c0a47bf821e0215ec90%205bfb&elqCampaignId=2270&elqaid =7587&elqat=1&elqTrackId=ad146026c54547318111d796%207e86e64c.

McCurrie, Matthew K. 2009. "Measuring Success in Summer Bridge Programs: Retention Efforts and Basic Writing." *Journal of Basic Writing* 28 (2): 28–49.

Mulhere, Kaitlin. 2015. "Keep Students, Earn More." *Inside Higher Ed.* Accessed March 19, 2015. https://www.insidehighered.com/news/2015/03/19/university-ties-money -salary-decompression-successful-retention-growth.

Peele, Thomas. 2010. "Working Together: Student-Faculty Interaction and the Boise State Stretch Program." *Journal of Basic Writing* 29 (2): 50–73.

"Performance-Based Funding for Higher Education." 2015. *National Conference of State Legislatures.* Accessed April 15, 2015. http://www.ncsl.org/research/education/per formance-funding.aspx.

Reichert Powell, Pegeen. 2014. *Retention and Resistance: Writing Instruction and Students Who Leave.* Logan: Utah State University Press.

Reichert Powell, Pegeen. 2009. "Retention and Writing Instruction: Implications for Access and Pedagogy." *College Composition and Communication* 60 (4): 664–82.

Rendón, Laura I., Romero E. Jalomo, and Amaury Nora. 2000. "Theoretical Considerations in the Study of Minority Student Retention in Higher Education." In *Reworking the Student Departure Puzzle*, ed. John Braxton, 27–56. Nashville: Vanderbilt University Press.

Royer, Dan, and Roger Gilles. 1998. "Directed Self-Placement: An Attitude of Orientation." *College Composition and Communication* 50 (1): 54–70. http://dx.doi.org /10.2307/358352.

Ruecker, Todd. 2015. *Transiciones: Pathways of Latinas and Latinos Writing in High School and College.* Logan: Utah State University Press.

Seidman, Alan. 2012. "Taking Action: A Retention Formula and Model for Student Success." In *College Student Retention: Formula for Student Success*, ed. Alan Seidman, 267–84. Lanham, MD: Rowman & Littlefield Publishers.

Shapiro, Nancy S., and Jodi H. Levine. 1999. *Creating Learning Communities: A Practical Guide to Winning Support, Organizing for Change, and Implementing Programs.* San Francisco: Jossey-Bass.

Sóloranzo, Daniel G., Octavio Villalpando, and Leticia Oseguera. 2005. "Educational Inequities and Latina/o Undergraduate Students in the United States: A Critical Race Analysis of Their Educational Progress." *Journal of Hispanic Higher Education* 4 (3): 272–94. http://dx.doi.org/10.1177/1538192705276550.

"State Funding Trends and Policies on Affordability." 2014. Report to the Chairman, Committee on Health, Education, Labor, and Pensions, United States Senate. United States Government Accountability Office. Accessed December 15, 2014. http://www .gao.gov/assets/670/667557.pdf.

Tierney, William G. 2000. "Power, Identity and the Dilemma of College Student Departure." In *Reworking the Student Departure Puzzle*, ed. John Braxton, 213–34. Nashville: Vanderbilt University Press.

Tinto, Vincent. 1975. "Dropout from Higher Education: A Theoretical Synthesis of Recent Research." *Review of Educational Research* 45 (1): 89–125. http://dx.doi.org /10.3102/00346543045001089.

Tinto, Vincent. 1988. "Stages of Student Departure: Reflections on the Longitudinal Character of Student Leaving." *Journal of Higher Education* 59 (4): 438–55. http://dx .doi.org/10.2307/1981920.

Tinto, Vincent. 1993. *Leaving College: Rethinking the Causes and Cures of Student Attrition.* Chicago: University of Chicago Press.

Tinto, Vincent. 1997. "Classrooms as Communities: Exploring the Educational Character of Student Persistence." *Journal of Higher Education* 68 (6): 599–623. http://dx.doi.org /10.2307/2959965.

Webb-Sunderhaus, Sara. 2010. "When Access is Not Enough: Retaining Basic Writers at an Open-Admission University." *Journal of Basic Writing* 29 (2): 97–116.

Wolf-Wendel, Lisa, Kelly Ward, and Jillian Kinzie. 2009. "A Tangled Web of Terms: The Overlap and Unique Contribution of Involvement, Engagement, and Integration to Understanding College Student Success." *Journal of College Student Development* 50 (4): 407–428. http://dx.doi.org/10.1353/csd.0.0077.

Yosso, Tara J. 2005. "Whose Culture has Capital? A Critical Race Theory Discussion Community Cultural Wealth." *Race, Ethnicity and Education* 8 (1): 69–91. http://dx .doi.org/10.1080/1361332052000341006.

PART 1

Writing, Retention, and Broader Policy Contexts

2

RETENTION ≠ PANOPTICON
What WPAs Should Bring to the Table in Discussions of Student Success

Rita Malenczyk

It [the soul] has a reality, it is produced permanently on, around, within the body by the functioning of a power that is exercised on those punished—and, in a more general way, on those one supervises, trains and corrects, over madmen, children at home and at school . . . over those who are stuck at a machine and supervised for the rest of their lives.
—*Foucault,* Discipline and Punish

I begin this chapter with two stories. The first concerns my oldest son, Sam (and I have his permission to recount the following). In 2013, after graduating from high school, Sam entered the University of Vermont (UVM) as an engineering major, something he felt would allow him to develop his considerable mechanical aptitude. However, a couple of weeks into his first semester, Sam began writing emails to me saying what students often say when they first arrive at a college away from home (we live in Connecticut): I hate this, I can't make friends, everybody here already has friends from high school, I'm too busy to have any fun anyway, I want to come back home. Though Sam had been on the fence about whether to go to the University of Connecticut (UCONN) or UVM in the first place—he was accepted at both—my husband/his father and I had encouraged him to go outside Connecticut to experience life elsewhere. When I received these emails, then, we encouraged him to stay out the year, thinking this was temporary homesickness and would pass. (After all, Sam's an expert skier, and Jay Peak, the very difficult mountain on which he cut his teeth, is visible from downtown Burlington—how busy could he be?) Nevertheless, Sam successfully filed—and paid for—a transfer application to the University of Connecticut, intending to continue his pursuit of an engineering degree a bit closer to home.

DOI: 10.7330/9781607326021.c002

The story, however, does not end there. In his second semester at UCONN, Sam changed his major to biology after discussions with advisors. He also realized that all the courses he wanted to take were biology and chemistry courses and that, as he told me in one email, he hadn't enjoyed a math course since the eighth grade. To put it another way, he was realizing that succeeding at the math courses required for an engineering degree would take more effort than he was willing to expend, and that mechanical aptitude didn't necessarily mean he'd be successful as an engineering student—or as an engineer, for that matter. My husband is a molecular biologist, so this decision was fine with him; I'd certainly never had anything invested in Sam's becoming an engineer; and both of us, as college professors, feel that the first couple of years of college should be exploratory. And Sam's always been good at science. These changes all occurred within the last year and a half; Sam remains unsure of what he will do with his biology degree, but he's comfortable with that uncertainty for now, and that too is fine with us. He's happy, then, with his decision to switch majors. He's living on campus, so he's enjoying what we consider the complete college experience despite not being that far from home. As far as his mechanical aptitude goes, he scored a good job as a bike mechanic at UCONN's outdoors center, maintaining their rental fleet of road and trail bikes and giving lessons on bike maintenance.

Story number two is about me, Sam's mother in one life and a WPA in another. In this story, those two identities converge. I direct the writing program and writing center at Eastern Connecticut State University, a regional comprehensive institution several miles down the road from the aforementioned UCONN. The Writing Center, which opened in 2008, is part of Eastern's Academic Services Center (ASC), which includes a math tutoring center, an area for subject tutoring, the Advising Center, and the office of our summer bridge program. While the last three areas had existed for quite some time, they had been separate units. Around 2007 Eastern decided, along with many non-elite colleges and universities in the country, that it needed to take major steps to improve student retention. (Like many regional comprehensives, our retention rate hovers at around 70%.) At the university president's insistence, the dean of Arts and Sciences applied for and obtained a four-year grant through Project Compass, a Nellie Mae Foundation initiative designed to increase retention of first-generation and low-income students as well as students of color. Because more than 50 percent of our students are first-generation and a significant number are low-income and students of color, this grant applied to most of our student body. Establishing the

ASC was a major, if not *the* major, use to which the grant funding was put, and since I and other faculty had been agitating for a writing center for quite some time, I had few complaints about having suddenly been presented with startup funds.

Of course, where there are tutoring and advising centers there is also the need for students to make appointments to visit those centers, and this need presented me with something of a conundrum. For the first several years, the Writing Center used WCOnline, a popular scheduling/recordkeeping program that fit our needs well. Unfortunately, WCOnline didn't work for the other Academic Services Center units, which had more complicated scheduling issues, and other scheduling programs such as TutorTrac appeared too cluttered and difficult for students to use when compared to WCOnline. So after several years all unit heads, including me, were invited to a presentation showcasing GradesFirst, which a Google search identifies as "a web-based student performance monitoring system." According to its website (http:// gradesfirst.com/), GradesFirst reduces paperwork and improves communication between advisors and faculty—all of whom have access to online notes taken about students. GradesFirst allows institutions to "maximize tutoring investment—reinforcing academic discipline and increasing student success." Their promotional materials explain that "making sure that students are utilizing the resources available to them ensures greater student success. GradesFirst tracks missed appointments, time spent in tutoring, and notes taken by tutors." It can also "reduce wasted appointment blocks caused by student no-shows. GradesFirst . . . sends personalized text and email reminders to students prior to scheduled appointments—increasing student accountability." Furthermore, "Tutor centers" can "receive detailed notices from advisors" and "notices of students marked at-risk."

As the GradesFirst representative proceeded through the presentation, showing us all how to use the program and what it might do, I noted that it could, in fact, do everything WCOnline was doing, and somewhat better (a reasonable expectation, given that it costs about fifty times more per year than WCOnline). Nevertheless, the enthusiasm with which some of the advising staff greeted the program's ability to keep track of all student movements made me uneasy. So I raised my hand and said, you know? As a parent of college and high school students—and as a former student myself—I'm not sure I want everyone on campus knowing when I screw up, or when I make a bad decision; it just seems creepy to me, like Big Brother is watching. There were a couple of nods, including one from the ASC director, a smart and ethical person who acknowledged, and continues to acknowledge, the importance of privacy issues. Be that as it may, after conversation with our Information Technology department about security, Eastern purchased GradesFirst for use beginning the following academic year.

One could place any number of interpretations on these stories, particularly within the discourse of retention so prevalent in many colleges and universities today. (Following Pegeen Reichert Powell, I distinguish in this chapter between "retention," which refers to an individual institution's keeping students at that institution until graduation, and "persistence," which refers to an individual student's efforts and success at achieving his or her educational goals.) A retention expert might, for example, argue that Sam would have stayed at the University of Vermont if he'd been monitored more closely, met regularly with advisors, and joined some clubs. The fact that Sam—like all three of my kids—hates being monitored, seemed to have had a perfectly good advisor, and has never joined a club in his life (I don't count sports teams here) suggests that such an argument begs the question. Nevertheless, Sam could be considered someone who, as retention experts might put it, "fell through the cracks," rather than someone who simply didn't like where he was and went somewhere else. Similarly, a retention expert might argue that Sam would have succeeded in UCONN's engineering program if he'd sought math tutoring, something he did not do and was not encouraged, for whatever reason, to do. However, because Sam just doesn't like math and therefore had no desire to complete four or more semesters of college calculus, I doubt tutoring would have been helpful to him. Nevertheless, a retention expert could *still* argue that he might have benefited from a carefully-designed first-year program that allowed him to explore all his options (see, e.g., Tinto 2012) rather than going through the messy business of trying and failing.

Regarding story number two—my story about GradesFirst—one could argue that *of course* it's a good idea to keep close track of students. We all have good intentions, right? We're not spying, really, even if you and others felt uncomfortable with the language of surveillance deployed in that GradesFirst meeting. And even if we are, it's for their own good. We want students to stay in school. So instead of letting them fall through the cracks, we ensure that there are as few cracks as possible to fall through. What's wrong with that?

In this chapter I address that question—the answer to which is, on some level, "nothing." Certainly, retention efforts may help some students whose parents are not, say, upper-middle-class college professors navigate the difficult early years of college and stay on to obtain degrees.

I argue, however, that implemented uncritically, retention efforts can turn a university into a panopticon, a Foucauldian[1] instrument of power and control that reflects a fear of the disorder that often accompanies human agency and human development, particularly the development that occurs in the adolescence of traditional-aged college students. The creation and marketing of programs such as GradesFirst, which enable unlimited access to student data, feed into this fear even as they perform useful services that help students navigate their college experience. Such a shift in the role of the university can pose an ethical conundrum for writing program administrators (WPAs), who are often involved in conversations about retention.

Perhaps most problematic for WPAs is the fact that this role shift is taking place primarily in public universities like Eastern, which have historically provided access to lower- and middle-income as well as first-generation students. Because retention efforts may indeed fill a need for those students, WPAs have an ethical obligation to participate in such efforts insofar as they help students reach their educational goals. However, institutional retention efforts can also create what some have called a two-tiered educational system in which wealthier students have a more wide-ranging intellectual experience, more choice, and therefore more freedom to set the course of their own lives within the social and political structures they inhabit. How, then, can WPAs assist in their institutions' retention efforts while acknowledging the scholarship in writing studies that has prioritized *all* students' own goals, voices, and intellectual development? Ultimately, I argue that writing studies and WPA scholarship might be brought to the table in administrative conversations about helping students stay in school and help shift institutional discourse from one about surveillance to one about making room for exploration and choice.

* * *

Perhaps unsurprisingly, my own interpretation of what I'll call "The Story of Sam, Still Unfinished" is one of discovery and growth. It is a truth universally acknowledged in the work of psychoanalysts, particularly Erik Erikson, that adolescence is when people begin to construct their identities in relation to society. Traditional psychoanalytic approaches hold that while younger children's maturation process is about developing a sense of self, adolescents try to figure out where that self belongs; most importantly, they need leeway to do so. Unfortunately for the adults around them, the experimentation that characterizes this process is by nature disorderly, unpredictable, and can be emotionally violent, as any parent of teenagers can attest; however, it is indispensible for the individual. Erikson connects this stage of development very specifically to career and lifestyle choice:

> the adolescent . . . looks for an opportunity to decide *with free assent* on one of the available or unavoidable avenues of duty and service, and at the same time is mortally afraid of being forced into activities in which he [*sic*] would feel exposed to ridicule or self-doubt . . .
> [H]e objects violently to all "pedantic" limitations on his self-images . . .
> [T]he choice of an occupation assumes a significance beyond the question of remuneration and status. It is for this reason that some adolescents prefer not to work at all for a while rather than be forced into an otherwise promising career which would offer success without the satisfaction of functioning with unique excellence. (Erikson 1968, 129, italics mine)

Adolescent experimentation can also have wide-ranging social consequences depending on who the experimenter is. The way such experimentation occurs for different people at the college level is illustrated fictionally yet realistically in novelist Jane Smiley's 1995 academic satire *Moo,* in which four female roommates, Keri, Sherri, Mary, and Diane, spend their first semester in the process of trying to reinvent themselves.[2] All four young women find, through the capacity for experimentation and critique that characterizes their new lives, that while there are some ways in which they can change, there are yet others in which they need to live with the burdens of their history. The student who experiences her history most keenly is Mary, the sole African American in the group and the only one from an urban area, who through her encounters with other students comes to more fully understand her isolation as a black student in a predominantly white environment. Though at the end of the novel Mary receives an assistantship and thus chooses to stay at the rural Midwestern state university at which *Moo* is set, rather than going back home to Chicago to save money and be in a more diverse environment as she'd originally planned, the novel leads us to understand that Mary will, through her choice of career and throughout her life, continue her process of defining herself within and against the white power structure she lives in.

One might argue, in fact, that the discovery/identification/experimentation process described by Erikson and illustrated in Smiley's novel, as well as in a range of nonfiction works such as Victor Villanueva Jr.'s *Bootstraps,* can serve students outside the dominant power structure (low-income and working-class students as well as students of color) even better than it serves those within it: it is one way they learn to critique and ultimately resist that structure (Villanueva 1993). Unfortunately, the ability to experiment and, therefore, develop one's critical capacity has become increasingly inflected with class privilege as the retention movement continues to pick up steam. While quality education has, of course, always been bound up with access, university administrations that have adopted the philosophy of such initiatives as Complete College America are now making clear the distinction between what rich and less-rich students can expect from the college experience, and are doing so in troubling ways; the media reporting on their efforts seem also to have embraced this distinction.

For example, in a 2014 *New York Times* piece called "Blowing Off Class? We Know," *Chronicle of Higher Education* staff writer Goldie Blumenstyk describes the uses to which "big data" is being put at some universities to improve retention rates (Blumenstyk 2014). At Ball State University in Indiana, for instance, students' card-swipe patterns are analyzed to see if they are engaging in activities that correlate with staying in school: visiting the career center, going to social events. However, if a student's card-swiping patterns show that his or her activity level has dropped, "a retention specialist will follow up with a call or an email to see how she's doing." While Blumenstyk acknowledges that such a level of monitoring is "Big Brother-esque" and may be "tinged with a little paternalism," she gives the last word to the foundations and pundits who embrace intense monitoring as an effective means of keeping low-income students in school. When confronted with the observation that elite institutions don't seem to oversee their students this way, said pundits note that "elite institutions can ensure that their students succeed simply by being very selective in the first place" but that, as a director at the Kresge Foundation points out, "the rest 'get the students they get . . .'" Casting what some might see as excessive interference in students' lives as an ethical imperative, Blumenstyk cites a vice provost at Georgia State: if students "run out of financial aid, 'they're dropping out and they're dropping out with debt and no college degree . . . We're giving them at least a fighting chance.'" Non-elite institutions, in the Kresge Foundation director's words, "have a moral obligation to help these students succeed." Blumenstyk further claims that efforts such as Ball State's "stem from a growing realization that students, especially low-income ones, don't have the luxury of making mistakes in the name of exploration."

It's difficult to argue with the Georgia State provost's statement about the financial cost of college, or with the Kresge Foundation director's claim about the moral obligation of colleges and universities to the success of their students (though the latter fails to factor in the degree to which students should also claim responsibility for, and pride in, their own accomplishments). However, as Pegeen Reichert Powell (2014) argues in her study *Retention and Resistance*, there is very little, if any, evidence that intrusive retention efforts such as those being employed at Ball State are as effective as administrators might hope, simply because nobody can ever really know why any given student might leave school. While there seem to be correlations between certain behaviors—for example, being involved in clubs, declaring a major early—and student retention, and while some schools have increased their graduation rates by being more proactive in the support they offer students (Blumenstyk cites Arizona State University as an example), ultimately retention rates may be moving targets. Reichert Powell (2014) observes that "The issue of retention reminds us of the forces in our students' lives that we simply have no control over: their emotional and physical health, their financial situation, their family obligations, their changing desires and goals" (13). Furthermore, in the case of several students Reichert Powell knew well and interviewed for *Retention and Resistance*, "there was no single, defining moment upon which their decision to leave college turned that could then be correlated to a program, faculty or staff member, or event that could have prevented them from leaving" (21).

Most problematic about intrusive retention efforts, however, is the fact such efforts are typically more about the institution than they are about the student, as Reichert Powell makes clear. She notes that retention programs based on widely read books such as Vincent Tinto's (1994) *Leaving College* "only attempt to align the individual student more thoroughly with preexisting intellectual and social values of the institution. These services do nothing to change the nature of the institution itself." (95). (As I noted earlier in this chapter, she emphasizes the distinction between two commonly-used terms, *retention*—which refers to a particular institution's keeping students enrolled there—and *persistence*, which refers to "an individual student's decision and effort to graduate, regardless of the institution" [Reichert Powell 2014, 6]) Institutional needs to keep students' "butts in seats" (4), as Reichert Powell puts it, are typically driven by financial concerns, *U.S. News and World Report* rankings, and the like—not by what might be the best choice for any given student struggling to find his or her way, and place, in society. This re-centering of the work of educational institutions on the preservation of the institutions themselves, rather than on the learning and growth of students they purport to serve, has a particularly "insidious role in perpetuating the dominant and oppressive structures of higher education today" (25).

One can see this role reflected in Tinto's (2012) most recent book, *Completing College,* in which the author frames retention as crucial to keeping the United States competitive in the world economy:

> A college-educated workforce is critical to our nation's ability to remain competitive; but where once we were world leaders in the proportion of our population between the ages of twenty-four and thirty-five holding a college certificate or degree, this is no longer the case. By most estimates we now are rapidly falling behind many other nations in our ability to produce college graduates . . . Given current demographic trends, there are danger signs aplenty that unless we do a better job in graduating more of our students from college, we will slip even farther behind. (chapter 1)

In other words, retention serves America, by providing it not necessarily with an educated, critical population that might be a danger to certain elements of its status quo—for example, racism, economic inequality—but, instead, with a workforce, cogs in an economic machine.[3] And while more privileged students can critique this system fairly comfortably, not-so-privileged students may struggle with such critique, I would argue, because they often have neither the money nor the time money can buy to engage in the disorderly process of intellectual and social development—a fact that perspectives such as Blumenstyk's (2014) suggest those students just need to live with.

This complex scenario I have presented recalls, as I have suggested, Foucault's description of panopticism in *Discipline and Punish.* Representative of the larger body of his work, which strove "to create a history of the different modes by which human beings are made subjects" (quoted in Rabinow 1984), Foucault deploys the figure of Bentham's panopticon, with which web-based programs such as GradesFirst and institutional "big data" programs such as the one at Ball State can be compared: they function as surveillance mechanisms that attempt to eliminate deviance and thereby preserve the social order (in this case, the educational institution using such mechanisms). They accomplish their goals by, as Foucault would argue, objectivizing the subject. The language that disturbed me in that initial meeting about GradesFirst—"maximize[ing] tutoring investment," "reinforcing academic discipline," tracking "students marked at-risk"—reduces complex individuals to financial categories, strips the discipline from the person being disciplined, categorizes people as simply "at-risk." In the end, however, what is at stake in retention-effort-as-panopticon is the elimination of disorder (or, the possibility that students' processes of experimentation might lead them to drop out or transfer) in favor of efficiency and control (or, the certainty that they will stay and keep the institution in business). For Foucault, the body is emblematic of desire, which defies regulation and is by nature disorderly (as is the process of adolescent experimentation and discovery). The body, uncontrolled, threatens the status quo. Discipline, however, "produces subjected and practiced bodies, 'docile' bodies. Discipline increases the forces of the body (in economic terms of utility) and diminishes these same forces (in political terms of obedience). In short, it dissociates power from the body; on the one hand, it turns it into an 'aptitude,' a 'capacity' which it seeks to increase; on the other hand, it reverses the course of the energy, the power that might result from it, and turns it into a relation of strict subjection" (Foucault 1975, 138).

Retention efforts which stress prescribed courses of action—early commitment to a major, attending study skills sessions, being involved in campus activities—might enable students to succeed in one sense but might also do so at the expense of the capacity—or, in Foucauldian terms, "the energy, the power"—to determine the course of their own lives. A student without such capacity may come to think, absent knowledge of alternatives, that the best course of study is one that gets him or her a job in industry (rather than, say, a graduate fellowship) immediately upon graduation. In institutions in which 50 percent of undergrads have parents who did not go to college, such a scenario is hardly unlikely. In *Unequal Childhoods*, sociologist Annette Lareau (2003) cites parental knowledge of how educational systems work as a defining factor in how well people from a range of economic backgrounds are able to navigate those systems and, therefore, critique certain aspects of them—as, for example, what courses or tracks their children are channeled into. Lareau's study suggests that working-class families, or families headed by parents who did not go to college, are more likely to defer to those with authority within those systems—principals, teachers—to decide what should be good for their children. For college students from such families, the university can become not a place for free thought but what Foucault would term yet another "disciplinary space," from which "one must eliminate the effects of imprecise distributions, the uncontrolled disappearance of individuals, their diffuse circulation" (143) to the benefit of the State; or, in this case, of the university, which in its obsession with numbers and rankings seems to have forgotten where its concerns ought to lie.

* * *

So here is where—as is perhaps traditional—I honor expected objections to what some might consider an unreasonable critique of retention efforts. For example, it could be argued that Reichert Powell's book *Retention and Resistance* is limited in scope: she followed only a few students she knew well. Where Reichert Powell's work usefully complicates the discourse of retention, however, is in its close attention to the details of students' particular lives and the complexities of those lives; in that sense, it's reminiscent of Mike Rose's (1989) *Lives on the Boundary* (1989), a canonical work in writing studies insofar as writing studies has a canon. Both Rose's and Reichert Powell's books put a human face on institutional policy, or (to phrase it another way) remind us that the facts and figures and percentages reported on retention are in fact embodied. Panopticism, via which human beings can be reduced to objects, thrives where embodiment is ignored or forgotten.

Having said that, I also don't disagree with those who might argue that some students can benefit from aggressive retention efforts. If, for example, you are a student who gets high a lot and/or sleeps in and misses classes, well, perhaps someone being in touch with you about that is the kind of wakeup call you need. Ironically, however (in this country of what some might call excessive individualism), too often efforts to help students succeed are cast in language, like Tinto's, that privileges the interests of the institution and the state, rather than the intellectual and personal growth of the student, "at-risk" or not.

Writing studies, of course, has historically emphasized that intellectual growth is the right of *all* students, and furthermore that such growth is essential to a critical and engaged populace (see, i.e., Reichert Powell 2014, 118). What, then, might WPAs do if and when they find themselves enmeshed in the (panoptic) discourse of retention? In general, as Reichert Powell reminds us, student choice and persistence—along with the messiness that often accompanies it—is what WPAs should prioritize above the interests of their institutions. Reichert Powell notes that while *retention* initiatives can have the interest of the wrong party in mind, *persistence* is more closely aligned with what writing studies has always been about: helping students to have more self-efficacy, to know how to respond to rhetorical situations, to be better writers regardless of where they write. Furthermore, and perhaps ironically, efforts to encourage persistence can also result in higher retention rates even if that is not their primary goal. Developing programmatic elements such as directed self-placement (DSP) that respect students' own goals for taking certain courses can increase student self-efficacy and perhaps, as Reichert Powell suggests, persistence (see, e.g., Inoue 2009). As Dan Royer and Roger Gilles, who first pioneered DSP at Grand Valley State University, observe, we shouldn't tell students what their goals for taking any course ought to be but, rather, respect the students' own goals:

"students are academic free agents with purposes we may never imagine. For one student, 'an easy A' is the appropriate course; for another student, 'after much effort, I just need a C' is the appropriate course. These are personal matters that WPAs should not condescend to answer for the student (Royer and Gilles 2013, 32)."

What should be taught in the courses students choose is a complicated matter. Reichert Powell appropriately cautions against designing writing programs, particularly first-year writing programs, structured on the assumption that students will continue in college, as such programs may not be helpful to those who do drop out or go elsewhere; rather, she advocates what she terms a *kairotic* pedagogy, or "educating the students in front of us" (2014, 6) who may wind up anywhere once they complete our courses. A first-year curriculum focused on writing as subject is, to me, the best way to give students a writing education they can take with them wherever they go. While Reichert Powell critiques such pedagogies as the Writing about Writing (WAW) approach advocated by Doug Downs and Elizabeth Wardle in their 2007 College Composition and Communication (CCC) article "Teaching about Writing, Righting Misconceptions," finding WAW too focused on academic writing (Downs and Wardle 2007, 113–15), to my mind she neglects the range of situations and approaches to writing presented to students in Wardle and Downs's (2014) *Writing about Writing* textbook, now in its second edition. While focused on disciplinary knowledge—the discipline being, in this case, writing studies—recent research has suggested that such a focus is as necessary to a writing course as biological principles are to a biology course if students are to be empowered as writers in a range of situations (see, i.e., Adler-Kassner, Estrem, Robertson, and Wardle 2013; Yancey, Robertson, and Taczak 2014). In *Writing about Writing*, students are asked to reflect in writing about themselves as writers, with models drawn from novelists and poets as well as academic writers; to write about their personal experiences with writing and the situations in which they write; and to analyze the discourse of workplaces, sports teams, and other organizations to which they belong—not just the discourse of academic disciplines. It is, I suggest, a book about writing that takes an academic *approach* but functions to enable writers in all situations, helping them make informed choices about style, stance, and audience and allowing them to reflect critically upon their lives.

Classes are not, of course, the only arena in which teaching occurs, and WPAs who direct writing centers (WCDs) can be particularly, and perhaps uncomfortably, aware of how retention efforts can appear to intrude on their work. To return to one of the stories I told at the beginning of this chapter: I'm certainly conscious of the fact that a grant intended to encourage retention provided the startup funds for the Writing Center. And as the person who files the Center's annual report on, among other things, usage rates, I know that the administration uses GradesFirst to analyze those rates, hoping to find that Center use increases retention among students marked "at-risk." However, data collection is a part of writing center life, and centers (and their directors) have more important things to focus on (i.e., one-on-one tutoring, online tutoring, tutor education, running group tutorials and workshops) than how someone in Institutional Research (IR) is reading their data. This isn't a flippant claim, but rather (I like to think) a realistic one: I have no control over what IR does. What I do have, however, is the fact that Writing Center use keeps increasing; that more than one tutor has told me how tutoring was the key to their staying at Eastern rather than go to (say) UCONN, because it made them feel challenged and valued; that tutor alumni have agreed to make a documentary with students in the Communication Department about how being a tutor contributed to their lives and work. To me, this is evidence of how the Writing Center contributes to student persistence of many different kinds.[4]

Finally, though assessment may not touch directly upon individual students, encouraging a more complex approach to course and program assessment is also important for continued engagement with retention efforts, as too often assessment efforts neglect the many factors that influence student development. Studies by Broad (2003) and, more recently, Dryer and Peckham (2014) have encouraged WPAs to look more closely at the complex negotiations that take place among faculty readers involved in assessment efforts; Elizabeth Wardle and Kevin Roozen have outlined an assessment plan that attempts to more fully describe the ecologies within which students develop as writers. Wardle and Roozen (2012) note that *all* of students' literate practices, not just their school literacies, come to bear on how they learn: "What a person writes privately out of school may, in fact, be deeply relevant to his or her efforts to take up a particular school genre" (108). They offer, then, a model that will "offer students, teachers, departments, institutions and other stakeholders a fuller, richer account of the kinds of experiences with writing that are informing students' growth as writers throughout the undergraduate years" (107). While focused on assessing writing and the learning of writing in academic settings, nevertheless this recent work in assessment has contributed to a deeper understanding of the wide-ranging human factors that influence any kind of student activity. A WPA could perhaps use this kind of rich placement, curriculum, and assessment data to help administrators in general think in a more complex, less institutionally-driven way about their students.

* * *

There isn't much interesting or new to say these days about my son Sam, whose interest in biology became focused on coursework in natural resource management; he's decided, finally, to pursue *that* degree, while continuing to work at the outdoors center. He now co-leads wilderness excursions, has been trained in wilderness first aid (which he initially referred to as "wildlife first aid," leading me to briefly envision him doing CPR on bears), and having what appears to be a focused and productive good time.

There are, however, new and interesting things going on with one of my writing center tutors, Kelly.[5] I met Kelly when she was a first-year student enrolled in my English-majors-only Introduction to English Studies class; she was quiet, paying close attention in class but hardly ever raising her hand. Yet I was blown away by the quality of her writing: it reached out and embraced the reader, connecting her reading for the class with her Latina background in evocative and heartfelt ways. She had entered the university through our summer bridge program, and that—coupled with what I saw in her writing—led me to ask her if she wanted to become a writing tutor and help, among others, those who could benefit from talking with someone who'd gotten to college through the same route. She agreed, yet after completing the required tutor education course the following semester, she disappeared from view for the rest of the academic year. I figured she'd lost interest in tutoring, but I also figured a Hail Mary pass never hurts, so at the beginning of this semester I emailed her and offered her, again, the opportunity to work in the Writing Center.

This time she took it. Kelly began tutoring at the beginning of this semester, but her path and mine didn't cross for about a month—at which time she emailed me and asked for a meeting to talk about perhaps changing her major (her regular academic advisor was ill). When she arrived for the meeting, I observed how happy and well-grounded she looked (it's hard to describe what it means to look well-grounded, but she did). She told me that while she'd initially declared a double major in secondary education along with English, she hadn't actually applied to the education program on schedule because her GPA wasn't high enough—there had been, she said without going into detail, a lot of things going on in her life. But now she was ready to re-focus on academics, and had spoken with an Education faculty member, who had told her she had the option of finishing her BA in English and then getting an MA in Education—a route a number of our students take. She was drawn to that option because it would let her achieve one milestone and complete another, the MA, in the same amount of time. What she wanted to know from me was what requirements she still needed to finish to get her BA in four years.

So I ran a degree audit, and together Kelly and I found that dropping the Education major would enable her to take, as she put it, "things I'm really interested in." She had also declared a history minor but didn't think she was interested in that any more, yet she did want to do a minor. We talked about the possibility of her declaring a writing minor, something I'd always meant to talk with her about but never had the chance to, and I recommended a number of courses that would allow her to explore her interest in and develop her talent for writing, fulfill the requirements for the English major, and give her enough upper-level credits to graduate on time. She's going to try, then, to register for Introduction to Creative Writing, Creative Nonfiction, Indigenous Studies in English, and/or African American Literature. Because her advisor's illness is long and serious, we agreed that I'd step up to fulfill that role for her, and that she'd contact me if she had questions and/or concerns between official advising periods. As she left, she smiled, shrugged, and said, "Who knows? I may decide not to do Education after all."

I don't claim that the conversation I had with Kelly was responsible for her seeming now to feel her life has opened up, that she has the space to explore, that new paths might have been cleared for her with the dropping of her second major. Quite the contrary: my sense is that something in her life outside the university has shifted, whether personal, financial, or both. I don't need, or for that matter want, to know. I'm just glad she seems to have found "the energy, the power" to chart her own course through a nation in which education at all levels has been too often reduced to testing, numbers, and data points. Ways of working toward changing *that* system are suggested elsewhere (e.g., Linda Adler-Kassner's 2008 *The Activist WPA*). Now might also be the time for many of us to revisit Rose's *Lives on the Boundary*. Like Reichert Powell, Rose chronicles in great and sympathetic detail the stories of individual students he met—not dehumanizing them, not reducing them to numbers, but honoring their lives and the choices that resulted from those students negotiating, in whatever way, the systems within which they were (and remain) enmeshed. Understanding the complexity of students' current lives can help all of us work more humanely and respectfully with them to plot their future lives, regardless of the context or institution in which those lives unfold.

Notes

1. In *Retention and Resistance*, Pegeen Reichert Powell (2014) employs Norman Fairclough's approach to critical discourse analysis (CDA) to analyze the discourse of retention, a methodology she acknowledges is indebted to Foucault (53–55); however, her approach is different from mine, which focuses on the figure of the panopticon.

2. I thank Shirley Rose for calling this aspect of the novel to my attention during a listserv conversation a long time ago.

3. Wisconsin Governor Scott Walker's botched attempt to rewrite the University of Wisconsin system's mission as workforce development rather than liberal education (Rivard 2015) is also emblematic of this line of thought.

4. See also Hughes, Gillespie, and Kail (2010), who conducted a national study about the value of tutoring for peer writing tutor alumni—a study one might show to one's dean.

5. Not her real name, though I do have her permission to tell her story.

References

Adler-Kassner, Linda. 2008. *The Activist WPA: Changing Stories About Writing and Writers.* Logan: Utah State University Press.

Adler-Kassner, Linda, Heidi Estrem, Liane Robertson, and Elizabeth Wardle. 2013. "Threshold Concepts of Writing and WPA Work." Panel presentation, Council of Writing Program Administrators annual conference, Savannah, July 19.

Blumenstyk, Goldie. 2014. "Blowing Off Class? We Know." 2014. *New York Times,* December 3. Accessed February 18, 2015. http://www.nytimes.com/2014/12/03 /opinion/blowing-off-class-we-know.html?_r=0.

Broad, Bob. 2003. *What We Really Value: Beyond Rubrics in Teaching and Assessing Writing.* Logan: Utah State University Press.

Downs, Douglas, and Elizabeth Wardle. 2007. "Teaching about Writing, Righting Misconceptions: (Re) Envisioning 'First-Year Composition' as 'Introduction to Writing Studies.'." *College Composition and Communication* 58 (4): 552–84.

Dryer, Dylan B., and Irvin Peckham. 2014. "Social Contexts of Writing Assessment: Toward an Ecological Construct of the Rater." WPA. *Writing Program Administration* 38 (1): 12–41.

Erikson, Erik H. 1968. *Identity, Youth and Crisis.* New York: W. W. Norton.

Foucault, Michel. 1975. *Discipline and Punish: The Birth of the Prison.* Trans. Alan Sheridan. New York: Random House.

Hughes, Bradley, Paula Gillespie, and Harvey Kail. 2010. "What They Take with Them: Findings from the Peer Writing Tutor Alumni Research Project." *Writing Center Journal* 30 (2): 12–46.

Inoue, Asao B. 2009. "Self-Assessment as Programmatic Center: The First-Year Writing Program and Its Assessment at California State University, Fresno." *Composition Forum* 20 (Summer). Accessed March 22, 2016. http://compositionforum.com/issue/20 /calstate-fresno.php.

Lareau, Annette. 2003. *Unequal Childhoods: Class, Race, and Family Life.* Berkeley: University of California Press.

Rabinow, Paul, ed. 1984. *The Foucault Reader.* New York: Pantheon Books.

Reichert Powell, Pegeen. 2014. *Retention and Resistance: Writing Instruction and Students Who Leave.* Logan: Utah State University Press.

Rivard, Ry. 2015. "Power of the Wisconsin Idea." *Inside Higher Ed,* February 5. Accessed February 18, 2015. https://www.insidehighered.com/news/2015/02/05/drafting -error-or-gubernatorial-assault-expansive-view-higher-ed-wisconsin.

Rose, Mike. 1989. *Lives on the Boundary*. New York: Free Press.

Royer, Dan, and Roger Gilles. 2013. "What Is Placement?" In *A Rhetoric for Writing Program Administrators*, ed. Rita Malenczyk, 23–34. Anderson: Parlor Press.

Smiley, Jane. 1995. *Moo.* New York: Knopf.

Tinto, Vincent. 1994. *Leaving College: Rethinking the Causes and Cures of Student Attrition.* Chicago: University of Chicago Press. http://dx.doi.org/10.7208/chicago/9780 226922461.001.0001.

Tinto, Vincent. 2012. *Completing College: Rethinking Institutional Action.* Chicago: University of Chicago Press. http://dx.doi.org/10.7208/chicago/9780226804545.001.0001.

Villanueva, Victor Jr. 1993. *Bootstraps: From an American Academic of Color.* Urbana: National Council of Teachers of English.

Wardle, Elizabeth, and Doug Downs. 2014. *Writing about Writing: A College Reader.* 2nd ed. Boston: Bedford/St. Martin's.

Wardle, Elizabeth, and Kevin Roozen. 2012. "Assessing the Complexity of Writing Development: Toward an Ecological Model of Assessment." *Assessing Writing* 17 (2): 106–19. http://dx.doi.org/10.1016/j.asw.2012.01.001.

Yancey, Katheen Blake, Liane Robertson, and Kara Taczak. 2014. *Writing across Contexts: Transfer, Composition, and Sites of Writing.* Logan: Utah State University Press.

3

BEYOND COORDINATION
Building Collaborative Partnerships to Support Institutional-Level Retention Initiatives in Writing Programs

Ashley J. Holmes and Cristine Busser

National conversations surrounding student retention rates place increasing pressures on university administrators to fix "problems" with students dropping out or not finishing at an institutionally defined, preferred rate. However, in *Retention and Resistance*, Pegeen Reichert Powell (2014) challenged composition scholars to think critically about how retention trends in higher education affect practices in our composition classrooms. Reichert Powell argues that writing teachers are often required to accept new programs or responsibilities, without concern for how their own philosophies may be compromised (126). As our institution's retention efforts have grown and received national attention, Reichert Powell's work prompted us to examine how top-down, institutional retention efforts are affecting composition teaching and administration at Georgia State University (GSU).

Within retention scholarship, a number of studies have pointed to the importance of collaborative partnerships, but few studies have looked closely and critically at collaboration between writing programs and institutional-level retention programs. In his chapter "Collaborative Partnerships between Academic and Student Affairs," Charles Schroeder (2005) argues that "collaboration is the principal strategy" for bridging what he and many other scholars in higher education administration identify as a "great divide" between academic and student affairs; moreover, Schroeder reminds administrators at all levels within institutional structures that "no one division or unit, acting autonomously can create an integrated, coherent, powerful, and seamless experience for first-year students" (206). Inevitably, the work of writing program administrators (WPAs) leading first-year writing programs and administrators leading

DOI: 10.7330/9781607326021.c003

first-year retention initiatives will overlap, and, ideally, by building alliances with effective communication and collaboration, these groups can help enhance students' first-year experiences and learning.

Our case study demonstrates how, even though there is coordination between the writing program and the Office of Student Success that administers retention programming at GSU, there are a number of missed opportunities for a collaborative and reciprocal partnership among key stakeholders in retention efforts. Our analysis focuses on the mix of logistical and pedagogical issues that have resulted from the implementation of institutional-level initiatives within first-year composition (FYC) courses. Ultimately, we conclude that writing teachers and administrators should be invited to meaningfully voice their concerns and ideas regarding, contribute to developing new materials and initiatives for, and assess institutional-level retention programs, especially because of the foundational role of FYC in retention initiatives and the sense of community that often arises out of small sections of FYC. While we identify a number of challenges to collaboration in our case study, we end on a hopeful note as we reflect on recently implemented initiatives that suggest a move from mere coordination to productive collaboration among administrators and instructors in the writing program and administrators who implement retention programming.

LITERATURE REVIEW

Much of the scholarship on student retention circulates within communities of higher education administration more broadly. In one of the foundational texts in this conversation, *Leaving College*, Vincent Tinto (1987) takes a stand against approaches to student retention that place blame solely on students' motivations and abilities. Implicating broader societal factors, Tinto describes the institution as yet another community students must be able to immerse themselves in and to navigate in order to persist until graduation. Nearly twenty years later, researchers have explored a number of ways institutions can improve their efforts to keep students in school, including: freshman learning communities (Tinto 1999), summer bridge programs (Ackermann 1991; Garcia 1991), minority student retention (Cabrera et al. 1999; Nora and Cabrera 1996; Seidman 2005), first-year seminar courses (Goodman and Pascarella 2006; Porter and Swing 2006), and the first-year "experience" (Ishler and Upcraft 2005). While studies of retention within Writing Program Administration scholarship are more limited, this area of research is growing as WPAs find writing programs, courses, and curricula being directly impacted by both the institution's retention objectives and the program's own goals for tracking student persistence.

One way WPAs have begun addressing retention within writing programs is by examining placement and assessment practices. For example, Beth Brunk-Chavez and Elaine Fredericksen argue that when the composition placement process "stems from the larger institution" or is assessed by standardized mechanisms such as Accuplacer, "it often fails students" (Brunk-Chavez and Fredericksen 2008, 91). Therefore, they advocate for writing programs to implement secondary placement measures that are "locally formulated," concluding that a combination of state-mandated and internal diagnostic measures would more successfully help identify students who may be at risk for failing the required first-year writing course (89–90). Their study is an excellent example of how WPAs can use their own research on retention to find ways of organizing and implementing retention programs from the bottom up.

Because many retention programs are initiated from the top down, WPAs are increasingly questioning ways that they can maintain some autonomy within that process. Brad Benz et al. (2013) examine the implications of three different institutions requiring students to read a common book their first year. They raise questions for WPAs about whether it is beneficial to "engage" or "resist" the common reading experience, and, if neither is a choice, how to respond to higher administration's imposing a common reading requirement (29). This study not only challenges top-down and mandated retention initiatives but also highlights many of the complexities involved when institutional-level retention programs intersect with the pedagogies and administration of first-year writing.

While some administrators and faculty are working to encourage students' success and boost retention rates, other scholars are questioning the initiatives employed to increase retention. Confronting retention initiatives from the perspective of basic writing, Matthew Kilian McCurrie (2009) calls for writing programs and faculty to consider that students' definitions of success might conflict drastically with what writing instructors and even higher administration consider success. Furthering McCurrie's study, Reichert Powell's (2014) *Retention and Resistance* is one of the first book-length considerations of retention and its impact on the teaching and learning of composition. Reichert Powell highlights the problematic trend of universities placing the responsibility to implement retention initiatives on FYC instructors, as they are likely the one teacher students will see before stopping out, dropping out, or transferring. Echoing McCurrie's argument and drawing on powerful student narratives Reichert Powell repeatedly questions what an FYC classroom should look like if instructors shift their approach to consider that some students will leave in spite of university retention efforts. Reichert Powell's work challenges WPAs and composition teachers to critically examine the discourses around retention within our institutions and to carefully consider the individualized needs and personally defined goals of students within our writing programs and classrooms.

Writing program administration and composition studies scholars are beginning to address some significant issues related to retention. Of particular importance for our study are the ways writing programs might retain some agency within retention initiatives that are promoted or mandated from the top down. While studies of retention and writing programs are clearly growing, we believe that this limited body of research would benefit from further expansion, especially because, as Brunk-Chavez and Fredericksen (2008) note, there are relatively "few studies [that] have examined retention and success in the composition classroom," and we would add within the writing program, "specifically" (76). We hope our study contributes to conversations around retention and writing by exploring the ways we might improve collaboration between institutional-level retention initiatives and their implementation within writing programs.

INSTITUTIONAL CONTEXT

GSU is an urban public research university centered in downtown Atlanta with approximately twenty-four thousand undergraduate and eight thousand graduate students.[1] GSU's student body is one of the most diverse in the nation, with approximately fifteen hundred international students and no racial or ethnic majority representing more than half of the population ("Quick Facts" 2015). GSU also has a number of first-generation college students and a majority of undergraduate students who have financial needs. For example, 58 percent of undergraduate students at GSU had Pell Grant funding in 2013, which rose from 31 percent in 2007 (Renick 2015). Considering these multiple factors that characterize the student body and affect retention efforts as a whole, a recent institution report estimated that GSU has "20,000 undergraduate[s] who are first-generation, Pell-eligible, non-white, and/ or have unmet financial need" ("Eliminating the Achievement Gap" 2013). Beginning as an evening school of commerce in 1913, GSU has historically been a commuter school; and, while GSU boasts five residence halls today, a number of students still commute from the greater Atlanta metro area and hold part- or full-time jobs.

Considering GSU's positioning as a public, urban research university is central to an analysis of its retention efforts. In their case study of improving persistence at the University of Texas El-Paso, Diana S. Natalicio and Maggy Smith argue that a university must make a commitment to knowing who their students are—to include defining "success" by taking into account the history and identity of the school itself. Natalicio and Smith contend that a successful first-year experience, "particularly critical at the public, urban university," involves a process of "transforming the individual lives of often highly vulnerable students" while also "promoting the socioeconomic development of the region" (Natalicio and Smith 2005, 157). This characterization of the public urban university rings true for GSU, especially as the institution seeks to maintain its commitment to underprivileged and underrepresented students while also enhancing its status as a research institution and investing in revitalizing downtown Atlanta.

GSU prides itself on serving the needs of a diverse student population, publicly framing the institution as "a national leader in graduating students from widely diverse backgrounds" ("About Georgia State University" 2015). Over the last five years, GSU has increased the number of degrees conferred by over 30 percent (5,857 in 2008 compared to 7,590 in 2013), despite not raising enrollments by the same percentage (Renick 2015). Indeed, GSU has garnered national attention for its innovative approaches to student retention, resulting in news articles highlighting increased graduation rates (Quinton 2013), educational policy studies such as "The Next Generation University" upholding GSU's efforts as a model (Selingo 2013; Selingo et al. 2013), and an invitation to the White House where President Obama praised GSU for "helping more college students find pathways to college" (Campus News 2014). Compared to peer institutions, GSU stands out as a leader in student retention rates. For example, a majority of urban research universities document a decline in graduation rates in relation to a rising percentage of students on Pell Grants; however, GSU's rates are "off the charts" because the graduation rate is relatively high (nearly 60%) compared to its equally high Pell rate (also nearly 60%) (Renick 2015).

The majority of retention programs at GSU are housed within the Office of Student Success, where a cohort of administrators work closely with academic and student affairs to ensure students receive academic help that also recognizes the social factors contributing to success. While GSU has a number of retention programs, we will briefly list the major institutional-level retention programs that connect with our study. First, Freshman Learning Communities (FLCs) entail students being assigned a block schedule of five to six shared classes during their first year; this schedule of classes includes a section of GSU 1010—an academic skills and resources course to promote success.[2] Second, the Success Academy is a learning community that targets first-year students who are the highest at risk for low retention rates[3] to begin taking classes (including specially-designated sections of English 1101) in the summer prior to their first year.[4] Third, the Panther Excellence Program is similar to the Success Academy, however students begin taking classes in the fall, rather than the summer; this set of fall classes includes a Panther Excellence Program designated section of English 1101. Fourth, the Early Alert program targets students within the first six weeks of courses in their first year, prompting professors to electronically submit names of students who may be "at-risk for failing."[5] Fifth, the First-Year Book program involves a book selected each year by a committee of faculty and staff that all incoming first-year students are given at Incept and expected to read before the start of their semester in August; the book is a required component of the content covered in English 1101 and the GSU 1010 course affiliated with students' FLCs. Sixth, GSU uses predictive analytics, combined with academic advising, to help students select courses for which they will be more likely to "succeed" (as defined by previous data); predictive analytics uses the previous ten years of GSU's retention, progression, and graduation data and 2.5 million grades from students in past GSU courses to predict "each student's [future] success in individual majors and courses" (Renick 2015).[6] As the coming analysis demonstrates, a number of these institutional-level programs intersect directly with the teaching and administration of first-year writing at GSU.

RESEARCH METHODOLOGY

We designed our study to qualitatively assess and begin to understand the way institutional-level retention programs intersect with and affect FYC teaching and administration at GSU. In 2015, we conducted interviews with three administrators affiliated with the Office of Student Success: Tim Renick, vice president for enrollment management and student success vice provost, who oversees GSU's retention initiatives more broadly and has often been the public voice of the institution on matters of retention; Nikolas Huot, assistant director of first-year programs, who oversees FLCs and the teaching of GSU 1010; and, Kate Kendall, administrative specialist of first-year programs, who primarily works with Early Alert and the First-Year Book program.

We also interviewed two administrators within Lower Division Studies and conducted focus groups with Graduate Teaching Assistants (GTAs). Lynée Gaillet, director of Lower Division Studies at the time of our interview, and Angela M. Christie, associate director of Lower Division Studies, met with us separately to answer interview questions about retention. Gaillet and Christie have both worked closely with the Office of Student Success in the past on issues ranging from scheduling specially designated sections of FYC to implementation of the First-Year Book program. The Lower Division Studies program at GSU administers required FYC courses, including the two-semester sequence of English 1101 and English 1102, as well as Honors sections of English 1103. Nearly all FYC courses (95% in Fall 2014 and 90% in Spring 2015) are taught and staffed by GTAs in the English Department who are in the process of earning PhDs in rhetoric and composition, literature, or creative writing.[7] We conducted two focus groups with a total of eleven GTAs who teach English 1101 and/or 1102 in Lower Division Studies; the GTAs' previous teaching experience ranged from one to four years, and many of the GTAs in the focus groups had experience teaching courses within the Success Academy, the Panther Excellence Program, and/or another Freshman Learning Community. All GTAs interviewed had experience teaching with the First-Year Book program because it is a required component of the English 1101 curriculum, and some had direct experience with the Early Alert system.

Our study was approved by GSU's Institutional Review Board, and, through informed consent, administrators gave us permission to use their names; GTAs selected or were assigned pseudonyms. Interviews and focus groups lasted between thirty minutes and one hour, were audio-recorded with permission, and were transcribed for coding and analysis. We analyzed the transcripts looking for common themes and organically developed categories (e.g., (mis)communication, pedagogy, top down, logistics—to name a few) based on these common themes. After creating our list of categories, we re-read the transcripts, more methodically marking for the organically developed categories. Our findings below represent what we deemed to be the most significant and relevant findings within our analysis of the data.

FINDINGS

In our interviews with administrators in both Lower Division Studies and the Office of Student Success, we found that both groups cannot help but work together because so many of the retention initiatives in Student Success involve the teaching of composition. While we found a few examples that demonstrate a workable relationship between the Office of Student Success and Lower Division Studies, the data we collected suggest that there are some underlying issues that may be preventing the groups from having a truly collaborative and reciprocal partnership that mutually benefits both units while also serving GSU students through retention programming. Both Nikolas Huot and Kate Kendall in Student Success expressed interest in improving communication between their office and Lower Division Studies, but each referred to time and resources as their biggest constraints from doing more. Moreover, director of Lower Division Studies Lynée Gaillet described the coordination between her office and Student Success as more reactive than proactive: "It is knee-jerk when there's a problem, often. We can problem solve, but it would be nice to not have the problems in the first place."

This study identified a range of logistical and pedagogical issues affecting the way retention initiatives are implemented within FYC at GSU. Our analysis leads us to conclude that building a more effective partnership among Student Success administrators, Lower Division Studies administrators, and GTAs teaching FYC would enhance GSU's overall approach to retention.

Logistical Issues

Course scheduling, as it relates to retention programming, emerged as a major logistical concern in our interviews with Lower Division Studies' administrators. Even though Huot in Student Success and Gaillet in Lower Division Studies both noted that they coordinate effectively to identify experienced instructors to teach summer sections of English 1101 for Success Academy students, Gaillet recounted the range of difficulties this poses for fall scheduling. In short, "because of financial reasons and enrollment," English 1102 seats originally designated for Success Academy students who took 1101 in the summer are opened to any student needing 1102 in the fall (Gaillet). The result, Gaillet explains, is that "many of the students who normally would take 1102 in the fall are doing so because they CLEP-ed out or have AP credit for 1101. And, so you have the two extremes—you have the Success

Academy students and then you have the high-achieving students who came in with credit in one classroom." In her experiences with this phenomenon, Gaillet said she has seen some of the best FYC teachers struggle to teach these two populations of students, sometimes requesting not to teach for Success Academy again. Another logistical consequence, told by GTA Hubert Walker, is that summer Success Academy classes are commonly placed in an 8:00 AM time slot for fall. Explaining that "[his students] could not adjust to a lifestyle that they . . . didn't expect to be a part of," Walker believes the time contributed to many students failing his class.

Issues regarding logistics do not end with Success Academy and the Panther Excellence Program; according to Lower Division Studies administrators, the timing of the selection of the first-year book has also proven inconvenient. Associate director of Lower Division Studies Angela M. Christie described how in past years her office, despite time crunches, has been able to find ways to integrate supporting pedagogical materials for the first-year book into its custom-published FYC textbook. However, the selection of the 2015–2016 book had not even begun at the time of our interview (January 2015). Therefore, she explains, "whatever the book happens to be, we now don't have an effective way—we'll think of one because we always do—but we don't have an effective way of integrating it in [the custom-published textbook]." By working on the Office of Student Success's timeline for the first-year book, Lower Division Studies is consistently positioned to retroactively insert this retention initiative into an already developed Lower Division Studies curriculum and textbook.

While these logistical problems would be difficult for the offices of Lower Division Studies or Student Success to anticipate, they suggest that improved communication and collaboration between the two offices would allow both units to begin addressing some of the scheduling and timing issues surrounding retention initiatives. In the next section, we identify some of the more troublesome concerns in how top-down mandated retention initiatives affect the specific classroom pedagogies of English 1101 and 1102 instructors and, at times, conflict with the pedagogical goals and objectives of Lower Division Studies.

Pedagogical Issues

One of the most apparent conflicts within our data is shown in Lower Division Studies administrators and GTAs wanting to meet their students' specific needs and Student Success administrators not wanting to overstep their role in students' education. This is an interesting and complicated finding because Student Success administrators believe that staying out of FYC pedagogy is appropriate for Lower Division Studies to maintain autonomy in its curriculum and area of expertise in teaching composition. For example, Huot explained that administrators in Student Success are "very conscious about not requesting to change the curriculum." Indeed, as we noted previously, collaboration between writing programs and institutional-level retention programs can lead to less autonomy; thus, the interest of Student Success administrators in steering clear of pedagogical meddling can be seen, on the one hand, as advantageous. On the other hand, our analysis below demonstrates how the impact of institutional-level initiatives on composition pedagogy is inevitable, and we believe that a hands-off approach to pedagogy by Student Success may actually be leading to more frustration for Lower Division Studies administrators and GTAs.

Conflicting Objectives

GSU's First-Year Book program is one of the most contentious retention initiatives addressed in our case study, primarily because of its pedagogical implications for English 1101. Both Lower Division Studies' administrators we interviewed expressed concerns about the First-Year Book program. According to Gaillet, the program is wrapped up in GSU's accreditation, making it a mandate. The selection of the book is organized by the Office of Student Success, but its pedagogical implementation is required in only English 1101 and GSU 1010 courses at GSU. In alignment with how Benz et al. (2013) describe common reading experiences, the First-Year Book program strives to establish community among new students and members of the university and facilitate interdisciplinary discussions. Even though a number of instructors and administrators we interviewed critiqued the First-Year Book program, as director of Lower Division Studies, Gaillet conceded the books have "come a long way to creating community."

In our focus group discussions, however, GTAs overwhelmingly agreed that they and their students did not like the first-year book selections. They explained that students in their English 1101 courses felt looked down upon for being assigned a graphic novel (*March* by John Lewis), could not relate to a book about September 11th (*Extremely Loud and Incredibly Close* by Jonathan Safran Foer), and/or felt that what might be perceived as an inspiring message was actually more condescending (*The Other Wes Moore* by Wes Moore). Overall, the GTAs felt that the top-down nature through which these books were assigned, and their accompanying messages, created more distance between the students and the university, as the books communicated the university's preconceived assumptions about incoming students.

More than just unpopular, though, the books selected by the university also "can go against the dictates of the course" (Gaillet). Corroborating this point, Christie explained "the first-year book, which is almost always a . . . novel is placed in a rhet/comp class that does not pay any attention to literature—that's not its goal." Of course, FYC has been historically plagued by others (often specialists outside of composition studies) trying to insert content into what is perceived as a content-less course. Indeed, such moves led Douglas Downs and Elizabeth Wardle to reconceive of FYC as an Introduction to Writing Studies (Downs and Wardle 2007). Concerns at GSU arise when GTAs are charged with introducing students to rhetoric and the writing process but are also asked to justify the teaching of a novel, which is often irrelevant to the rest of their curriculum. In our focus groups, GTAs described the first-year book as "counter-productive" and disruptive of a syllabus's "natural arc," and Lower Division Studies' administrators noted that, "from an observer's point of view, [it's clear that the] program was not created in conjunction with Lower Division Studies people." Among the scenarios common reading experiences can pose for WPAs is that university administrators, not representatives of English or Writing departments, are in control of students' first experience with college level reading and writing (Benz et al. 2013). Thus, GSU's First-Year Book program risks misrepresenting the values and objectives of the FYC sequence, which can prove disruptive to the classroom environment. However, knowing this program is tied to accreditation and central to retention efforts, we argue that this is one area where improved partnership and collaboration could enhance the pedagogical implementation of the book, while also increasing satisfaction of GTA instructors tasked with teaching the material.

Access to Information

Another major concern we noticed that has direct implications for the pedagogies in English 1101 and 1102 is that Lower Division Studies administrators and teachers do not always have access to the same kinds of information about students as the Office of Student Success. Having access to additional data can provide a more fully developed picture of the student population, and, as WPA Joe Moxley (2013) argued in relation to his program's use of analytics to examine instructors' assessment practices, data can be a powerful tool for WPAs and FYC instructors alike. Our data show that GTAs are frustrated by not having access to the FLC designations—and, at times, Success Academy or Panther Excellence Program designations—for their courses; additionally, Lower Division Studies' administrators do not always have access to data used to place students in retention-based initiatives such as Success Academy and the Panther Excellence Program.

In the case of FLCs at GSU, the program has expanded rapidly and without much pedagogical support for this expansion and its impact on FYC. The recent change from an "opt-in" to an "opt-out" model—meaning that students are now automatically placed in an FLC—has resulted in an increase in the number of FLCs to over one hundred and a rise in the number of students participating to approximately 70 percent of the incoming class (Huot). The rapid growth of FLCs means that GTAs teaching 1101 and 1102 are not as informed of the meta-majors affiliated with their particular sections; according to Huot, Student Success relies on the instructors teaching GSU 1010—the required academic skills course connected with each FLC—to reach out to the other instructors associated with the FLC to create cohesion. However, the GTAs we spoke with said this communication was not happening; in fact, when we asked participants in our focus groups if they knew whether their courses were affiliated with FLCs, the majority of them said no. A few zealous GTAs said they figured out they could look up the FLC designation in the catalog, whereas others asked the students enrolled in their course; however, there are a number of GTAs who simply do not take the time or do not know how to locate this information about the course they are teaching.

The combination of not knowing retention-based course designations in advance and Student Success administrators wanting to steer clear of pedagogical infringements prevents Lower Division Studies administrators and GTAs the opportunity to enhance their curricula. As Christie reflected on the change in the FLC structure, Lower Division Studies has been put in a position where "There isn't any effort . . . to try and make [the FLC themed] classes any different [from the] other classes [Lower Division Studies is] offering." The growth in FLCs also has led to less collaboration and interdisciplinary partnership that would likely enhance pedagogy. For example, Renick and Gaillet both explained how FLCs were supported nearly a decade ago at GSU through summer pay for faculty in a FLC to "collaborate and work on common syllabi and . . . share readings" (Renick 2015). However, Renick went on to explain that while this model is a "great idea pedagogically," it's "very difficult [and] expensive to sustain," in part because of the "large scale" on which GSU is trying to implement these programs.

Beyond FLCs, Christie also noted that Lower Division Studies administrators have little access to the information used to place students into Success Academy and the Panther Excellence Program: "the students who come into [Success Academy] have issues with learning that aren't made available to us. We're not sure why they're in the program." In sum, without the full context of understanding various student populations served by specific sections of English 1101, instructors and administrators in Lower Division Studies cannot as effectively address concerns that could possibly enhance not only students' retention but also their learning of course concepts. Even though Student Success administrators are trying to stay away from meddling with pedagogy, the impact of the retention programs they oversee on the English 1101 curriculum is unavoidable; thus, the need for more collaboration and better access to shared information would enhance both composition pedagogies and retention programming.

Growing Retention Programs and the Question of Resources

Something we see as both a strength and a potential drawback of GSU's retention programming is the high number and diverse range of programs being offered. As GSU continues to increase enrollments while maintaining its commitment to minority and underprivileged student populations, many of its retention programs are growing rapidly without the corresponding resources. Kendall in the Office of Student Success suggested that the reach of retention programs would be even stronger and would allow for more one-on-one relationships with students if their office had more staff. Huot also suggested that with the increased numbers of students served by a fairly small staff within Student Success, coordination with English 1101 and 1102 instructors "becomes a little bit complicated." Huot went on to say that one of the reasons Student Success is not able to "work as closely as we'd like to" with Lower Division Studies is "because of the number of FLCs that we're offering . . . we can't [collaborate] as well as we'd like between the instructor of GSU 1010 and the instructor of English 1101," for example—an issue we noted above in our interviews with GTAs.

However, we are concerned that an increase in resources may not necessarily improve the collaboration between Lower Division Studies and Student Success. For example, with more resources, Kendall imagines having staff members stop by students' classes and scheduling motivational speakers. These initiatives do not draw on the wealth of knowledge and experiences with first-year students and programming that already exist within the program structure of Lower Division Studies. Moreover, additional student surveillance by Student Success staff could be a harmful intervention for a group of students already marked by administrators as "at risk." While administrators in Student Success point to the need for more resources, we believe that better collaboration with existing units, particularly Lower Division Studies, would help alleviate some of the additional pressures faced by the growing number of students involved in retention programming. In fact, in our interview with Renick, he suggested that part of what he thinks makes GSU's model for retention programming such a success is that, "without great outlays of new funding," GSU has "been able to find innovative ways to use the staff we have more proactively to get students more personalized help." However, we believe using existing staff to try to reach more and more students in terms of retention will only be effective with a collaborative and reciprocal partnership between Student Success and Lower Division Studies that addresses the needs of all stakeholders.

CONCLUSION: A HOPEFUL FUTURE FOR COLLABORATION

Our case study demonstrates a number of logistical and pedagogical breakdowns resulting from a less than ideal model of collaboration between the Office of Student Success and Lower Division Studies at GSU. We argue that when retention initiatives are employed through a top-down model, administrators are missing an opportunity to gain feedback from WPAs and writing instructors on the effectiveness of their programs—this disconnect may be true on many campuses. As Reichert Powell (2014) argues, however, the small class sizes and curricular objectives of many FYC courses create an environment where students are more likely to make connections with other students and faculty members than other classes. While GSU administrators in Student Success noted the positive feedback they have received regarding their services on student exit surveys (Kendall; Renick 2015), GTAs observed students' confusion about placement into and the purpose of Success Academy and frustration with the GSU 1010 class as part of their FLC. Despite FYC instructors' unique position to collect valuable information on the effectiveness of the university's retention initiatives, they currently have no method for collaborating with the Office of Student Success to communicate this kind of information. There is no program—no time or place carved out—that invites GTAs to meaningfully discuss, develop, and/or evaluate retention programs with upper-level administrators. Based on our findings, we conclude that the perspectives of GTAs teaching FYC and administrators in Lower Division Studies need to be more meaningfully incorporated into retention programming—including ideas for new programs, feedback and assessment of current programs, and pedagogical support for incorporating retention-related materials into FYC.

Our study does give reason to be hopeful for an improved partnership in the near future, though. In our discussions with administrators in Student Success and Lower Division Studies, both groups identified strengths and weaknesses of current coordination efforts around retention, and both seemed interested in improving collaborative efforts to support a common goal around retention. In fact, we hypothesize that our study, by simply asking questions that drew attention to the relationship between Student Success and Lower Division Studies related to retention, has led to some changes; administrators in Student Success, even before we analyzed our data, were asking for our advice on how to improve collaborative efforts. Two initiatives that suggest a move in the right direction are (1) meetings for GTAs teaching in Success Academy or the Panther Excellence Program to voice their concerns and (2) involving graduate students in pedagogical planning related to the First-Year Book program. As for the former, Lower Division Studies originated the GTA meetings, but Student Success could easily tap into this resource to gather feedback on their retention programs that impact FYC. For the latter, we discovered that in the months since we conducted our interviews for this study, Student Success reached out to Lower Division Studies to begin addressing how to more effectively integrate the first-year book into the pedagogy of English 1101. We recently learned that Kendall, who we interviewed from Student Success, hired a GTA who teaches in Lower Division Studies to work with her over the summer to create supporting pedagogical materials for the first-year book to be implemented in the fall.

This new initiative to involve GTAs in meaningful development of program materials related to retention at GSU is perhaps the most promising and suggests a model that may be useful for writing programs at other institutions. To us, it indicates a shift from mere coordination between Lower Division Studies and Student Success, which has already been happening, to a more reciprocal approach to partnership through collaboratively building content and assessing programs in ways that will benefit students, teachers, and administrators across campus. Moreover, our case study demonstrates how WPAs can use research, in this case research into how institutional-level retention initiatives impact the teaching of first-year writing, to identify and assert their role in supporting student retention.

Notes

1. These enrollment numbers are from the 2014–2015 academic year and do not factor in the expected increase of enrollment when GSU consolidates with Georgia Perimeter College in 2016; most estimates suggest new, combined enrollment numbers of nearly 54,000 students (Badertscher 2015).

2. For Freshman Learning Communities (FLCs) at GSU, students are grouped by one of seven self-selected meta-majors: STEM (Science, Technology, Engineering, Mathematics), Business, Arts and Humanities, Health, Education, Policy and Social Science, or Exploratory. Ninety-five percent of non-Honors College first-year students participate in FLCs, and students who participate in FLCs have higher GPAs and higher retention rates (Renick 2015).

3. This is often defined by identifying students who have a lower freshman index (e.g., lower GPA, SAT, and/or ACT scores).

4. Success Academy spans from the summer prior through the end of spring in the first year and functions as a FLC. Students also participate in intensive advisement, academic skill building, financial literacy training, and team building practices (Kendall; Renick 2015). In 2014, the Success Academy served approximately 340 first-year students, and, over the past several years, has improved the retention rate of "at-risk" students from 50 percent in 2011 to 87 percent in 2014 (Renick 2015).

5. The Early Alert program usually defines "at-risk" for failing by excessive absences, lack of participation, low grades, and/or failure to turn in assignments.

6. GSU's usage of predictive analytics is a relatively new retention program, but perhaps one that is garnering quite a bit of national attention; it draws on existing data sets to make predictions for future trends to help with advising and establishing career pathways. GSU reports that the use of predictive analytics improves retention rates and results in reduced time-to-degree and cost for students (Renick 2015).

7. The Georgia Board of Regents requires that all GTAs take a graduate course in composition pedagogy prior to (or in tandem with) teaching English 1101. While the majority of funding goes to graduate students at the PhD level, advanced MA English students who have taken the required pedagogy course and are eligible for funding occasionally teach FYC courses. The remaining FYC courses not taught by GTAs are taught by English Department faculty or lecturers.

References

"About Georgia State University." 2015. Georgia State University. http://www.gsu.edu /about/.

Ackermann, Susan P. 1991. "The Benefits of Summer Bridge Programs for Underrepresented and Low-Income Transfer Students." *Community/Junior College Quarterly of Research and Practice* 15 (2): 211–24. http://dx.doi.org/10.1080 /0361697910150209.

Badertscher, Nancy. 2015. "Merger Will Produce One of Nation's Largest Universities." *AJC PolitiFact Georgia,* January 23. http://www.politifact.com/georgia/statements /2015/jan/23/gsu-alumni-association/merger-will-produce-one-nations-largest -universiti/.

Benz, Brad, Denise Comer, Erik Juergensmeyer, and Margaret Lowry. 2013. "WPAs, Writing Programs, and the Common Reading Experience." *WPA. Writing Program Administration* 37 (1): 11–32.

Brunk-Chavez, Beth, and Elaine Fredericksen. 2008. "Predicting Success: Increasing Retention and Pass Rates in College Composition." *WPA. Writing Program Administration* 32 (1): 76–96.

Cabrera, Alberto F., Amaury Nora, Patrick T. Terenzini, Ernest Pascarella, and Linda Serra Hagedorn. 1999. "Campus Racial Climate and the Adjustment of Students to College: A Comparison between White Students and African-American Students." *Journal of Higher Education* 70 (2): 134–60. http://dx.doi.org/10.2307/2649125.

Campus News. 2014. "Obama Cites Georgia State Retention Grants at White House College Opportunity Day of Action." Georgia State University. December 4. http://news.gsu.edu/2014/12/04/president-obama-cites-georgia-state-retention-grants-white-house-summit/.

Downs, Douglas, and Elizabeth Wardle. 2007. "Teaching about Writing, Righting Misconceptions: (Re)Envisioning 'First-Year Composition' as 'Introduction to Writing Studies.'" *College Composition and Communication* 58 (4): 552–84.

Garcia, Philip. 1991. "Summer Bridge: Improving Retention Rates for Underprepared Students." *Journal of the First-Year Experience & Students in Transition* 3 (2): 91–105.

Goodman, Kathleen, and Ernest Pascarella. 2006. "First-Year Seminars Increase Persistence and Retention." *Peer Review : Emerging Trends and Key Debates in Undergraduate Education* 8 (3): 26–8.

Ishler, J. L., and M. Lee Upcraft. 2005. "The Keys to First-Year Student Persistence." In *Challenging and Supporting the First-Year Student: A Handbook for Improving the First Year of College*, ed. M. Lee Upcraft, John N. Gardner, and Betsy O. Barefoot, 27–46. San Francisco: Jossey-Bass.

McCurrie, Matthew Kilian. 2009. "Measuring Success in Summer Bridge Programs: Retention Efforts and Basic Writing." *Journal of Basic Writing* 28 (2): 28–49.

Moxley, Joe. 2013. "Big Data, Learning Analytics, and Social Assessment." *Journal of Writing Assessment* 6:1–14.

Natalicio, Diana S., and Maggy Smith. 2005. "Building the Foundation for First-Year Student Success in Public, Urban Universities: A Case Study." In *Challenging and Supporting the First-Year Student: A Handbook for Improving the First Year of College*, ed. M. Lee Upcraft, John N. Gardner, and Betsy O. Barefoot, 155–75. San Francisco: Jossey-Bass.

Nora, Amaury, and Alberto F. Cabrera. 1996. "The Role of Perceptions of Prejudice and Discrimination on the Adjustment of Minority Students to College." *Journal of Higher Education* 67 (2): 119–48. http://dx.doi.org/10.2307/2943977.

Porter, Stephen R., and Randy L. Swing. 2006. "Understanding How First-Year Seminars Affect Persistence." *Research in Higher Education* 47 (1): 89–109. http://dx.doi.org/10.1007/s11162-005-8153-6.

"Quick Facts." 2015. Georgia State University. Accessed March 12. http://www.gsu.edu/about/quick-facts/.

Quinton, Sophie. 2013. "Georgia State Improved Its Graduation Rate by 22 points in 10 Years." *Atlantic (Boston, Mass.)*, September 23. http://www.theatlantic.com/education/archive/2013/09/georgia-state-improved-its-graduation-rate-by-22-points-in-10-years/279909/.

Reichert Powell, Pegeen. 2014. *Retention and Resistance: Writing Instruction and Students Who Leave*. Logan: Utah State University Press.

Renick, Tim. 2015. "Using Data and Predictive Analytics to Help At-risk Students Succeed." Presentation, Georgia State University.

Schroeder, Charles C. 2005. "Collaborative Partnerships between Academic and Student Affairs." In *Challenging and Supporting the First-Year Student: A Handbook for Improving the First Year of College*, ed. M. Lee Upcraft, John N. Gardner, and Betsy O. Barefoot, 204–20. San Francisco: Jossey-Bass.

Seidman, Alan. 2005. "Minority Student Retention: Resources for Practitioners." *New Directions for Institutional Research* 2005 (125): 7–24. http://dx.doi.org/10.1002/ir.136.

Selingo, Jeffrey. 2013. "How a Little Data Can Solve One of Higher Education's Biggest Problems." *Chronicle of Higher Education*, May 20. http://chronicle.com/article/How-a -Little-Data-Can-Solve/139347/.

Selingo, Jeffrey, Kevin Carey, Hilary Pennington, Rachel Fishman, and Iris Palmer. 2013. "The Next Generation University." New American Foundation. https://static.new america.org/attachments/2318-the-next-generation-university/Next_Generation_ University_FINAL_FOR_RELEASE.8897220087ff4bd6afe8f6682594e3b0.pdf.

Tinto, Vincent. 1987. *Leaving College: Rethinking the Causes and Cures of Student Attrition.* Chicago: University of Chicago Press.

Tinto, Vincent. 1999. "Taking Retention Seriously: Rethinking the First Year of College." *NACADA Journal* 19 (2): 5–9. http://dx.doi.org/10.12930/0271-9517-19.2.5.

4

BIG DATA AND WRITING PROGRAM RETENTION ASSESSMENT
What We Need to Know

Marc Scott

A student at a regional university in the Midwest wakes up in time to exercise before her second semester composition course.[1] On her walk to the gym, she glances at her phone, notices her unread emails, ignores them, and checks Twitter and Yik Yak before arriving at the gym where she swipes her student identification card and proceeds to an elliptical machine. She logs into the Wi-Fi, streams some music, and opens the Blackboard app on her tablet for her 10:00 AM composition course. Her plan is to skim the reading before class to refresh her memory and maybe find an idea to contribute to class discussion. However, before she arrives at the class's homepage, she notices a "course alert." She zooms in on the icon, taps it, and reads the brief message informing her that she has received a "green light" in her class. The green light, she learns after viewing a short tutorial on the university's YouTube channel, means that she's at "low risk" for failing her composition course. She returns to her reading for a while, then bundles up and walks back to her dorm to get dressed and ready for class.

This student provides an example of the increasing use of data in higher education. From an institutional standpoint, a student's life on campus is no longer quantified simply by enrollment, course completion, and graduation. Students produce vast amounts of data that universities increasingly collect, store, and analyze. For instance, swiping her identification card creates a data point that might be used by the university's director of athletics to track the number of students who are making use of the facilities. The student's time spent on her course management program and on each content page might also be collected, stored, and analyzed. Data also shape the student's education

DOI: 10.7330/9781607326021.c004

experience. Her course alert, similar to the "Course Signals" program implemented by Purdue University, notifies her that she's making satisfactory progress in the class, and the alert is a result of her instructor setting up "high," "medium," and "low" risk thresholds for failing the course that are based on grades, time spent in the course management software, whether or not she accessed the course's e-Reader, and if she visited the writing center or another campus resource. While the prevalence of data and technology in students' lives may seem futuristic to those of us who once clacked out essays on a typewriter, the fact is that universities and colleges are inundated with data that some institutions are attempting to leverage in order to improve retention and graduation rates. Whether a Writing Program Administrator (WPA) works with Big Data or not, the fact remains that such data have a significant impact on the landscape of higher education, and thus will affect their work. This chapter will help WPAs understand Big Data's opportunities and limitations with respect to graduation and retention assessment. In addition, I will argue that the most useful way for WPAs to consider Big Data in the context of graduation and retention rates is through the lens of current assessment scholarship.

DEFINING BIG DATA

Most definitions of Big Data differentiate between data, the methods of analyzing that data, and the resulting actions the data inform. A recent report on Big Data commissioned by the Executive Office of the president of the United States notes that "Most definitions [of Big Data] reflect the growing technological ability to capture, aggregate, and process an ever-greater volume, velocity, and variety of data, and the processing of data referred to in the report is typically referred to as either Data Analytics or Data Mining" (Podesta et al. 2014, 3). What makes Big Data, Data Analytics, and Data Mining a significant development is how data and their interpretations are being used, including informing decisions and even predicting behavior (Picciano 2012, 12; Seifert 2004). Scholars and analysts working with Big Data rarely separate the data and its analysis from the purposes that the information might serve. At the risk of reducing the important distinctions between the different terms, I'll refer to Big Data and its analysis simultaneously with the term "Big Data Analytics" (BDA).

In colleges and universities in the United States, administrative and regulatory stakeholders, such as legislators and state-wide and institutional administrators of various ranks, have recently begun to eye BDA as a tool for improving retention and graduation. Similar to discussions in industry and government, defining BDA in the context of higher education depends on contextual factors and potential uses of information gleaned from the data (Goff and Shaffer 2014, 95). Pointing to the need for accurate information in order to make decisions and the need for non-analyst stakeholders to make sense of complex data, Lane and Finsel (2014) add "veracity" and "visualization" to the "three Vs" typically aligned with Big Data: "velocity," "volume," and "variety" (8). Given the increased use of performance based funding in US higher education, administrators are marshaling BDA to understand retention and graduation trends and to measure interventions and policies that seek to improve student retention and graduation. For instance, Goff and Shaffer argue that discussions of retention and graduation require examinations of recruitment and admissions practices and that BDA can help institutions identify student profiles with the potential to succeed or "fit" at the institution, at least in terms of graduation and retention(Goff and Shaffer 2014, 93–120).[2] The definition of BDA with respect to retention and graduation might best be summarized as activities that seek to (1) use large data sets and analysis methods to measure the current factors leading to student loss, (2) identify attributes of students who succeed in or leave the institution, and (3) measure the impact of interventions or programs that seek to improve retention and graduation rates. Some interventions, like Purdue's Course Signals, Rio Salado Community College's Progress and Course Engagement (PACE) program, or Northern Arizona University's Grade Performance System (GPS), use BDA to measure retention factors (including performance and behavioral data); provide feedback to faculty, students, and advisors; and measure intervention effectiveness.

Whether WPAs work at an institution with a visible impact of BDA, the fact is that WPAs either are or will be affected by it. Schools with the resources to engage in BDA projects are able to target their recruitment and retention efforts and provide actionable data to stakeholders to enable interventions for struggling students and persuade potential students with a profile consistent with successful students at that institution to apply and enroll. Institutions lacking the capacity to generate or analyze data that can drive decision-making are therefore at a distinct disadvantage. For WPAs, having access to BDA could mean the ability to create more persuasive arguments that persuade stakeholders to consider increased funding or reduce the severity of proposed cuts. To provide colleagues in writing program administration with useful information regarding BDA, the balance of this chapter will accomplish three goals. First, I review important benefits of BDA, including its potential to improve retention and graduation rates. Then I survey BDA's limitations, especially in regard to retention assessment. Finally, I use examples from my experience directing a writing center and a developmental writing program to propose that WPAs consider writing assessment scholarship as the necessary framework for implementing BDA in writing program retention assessment efforts.

OPPORTUNITIES OF BIG DATA ANALYTICS

In journals, articles, reports, and book collections about Big Data and its potential to transform higher education, many scholars and writers outside composition studies critique colleges and universities for being behind the times in implementing BDA (Ferguson et al. 2014, 123). According to a survey project of BDA implementation in the United States, 70 percent of school officials at nearly four hundred institutions acknowledged its importance, but only a handful of institutions were making significant progress toward implementing BDA (Bichsel 2012, 21; Norris and Baer 2013, 11–13). Some authors cite resistance to change among university administrators and stakeholders (Macfadyen et al. 2014) and fear of cost and misuse of data (Bichsel 2012) as possible concerns about adopting BDA. However, the pressure to adopt BDA projects at universities and colleges continues to mount as it is increasingly looked to by lawmakers, higher education administrators, and scholars as a way to measure success and evaluate programs and institutions.

Non-profit organizations and governmental agencies urging the adoption of BDA cite the potential to predict student retention and graduation rates and tailor interventions to meet student needs. For example, in a Brookings Institute report, West (2012) argues that BDA can provide postsecondary educators with the ability to evaluate "a much wider range of student actions" so they might better understand student learning styles and provide instant feedback to students (1). West's optimism aligns in many ways with recent reports by the federal government suggesting that BDA can help educators and administrators identify differences in student learning, tailor curriculum to meet student needs (President's Council of Advisors on Science and Technology 2014, 14), and "make visible data that have heretofore gone unseen, unnoticed, and therefore unactionable" (Bienkowski, Feng, and Means 2012, ix). Another vocal and influential proponent of BDA, the non-profit organization Educause, argues in a 2013 brief that colleges and universities can leverage the predictive abilities of BDA to improve learning ("The Rise of Big Data in Higher Education" 2013). The report also argues for measures similar to those forwarded by Complete College America, such as reducing or eliminating "nonproductive credits" (particularly developmental education), and cites Arum and Roksa's (2011) *Academically Adrift* and its controversial, problematic critique of rigor in US higher education. The solution to what the report identifies as a lack of rigor and accountability is to implement BDA and other "IT resources to improve educational quality and guide students to higher rates of completion" (Griffin and Minter 2013, 2). The arguments in favor of adopting BDA often brush aside issues of privacy and profiling. For instance, in his Brookings Institute white paper, West argues that privacy concerns are "counter-productive" if BDA research can improve student success.

Researchers of retention and student success in higher education also tout some of the benefits claimed by the non-profit organizations and governmental agencies noted above. In a study of administrators at a large, Midwestern university that implemented a notification system based on BDA, respondents were largely optimistic about the system's potential to improve student success. One respondent noted that the notification system provides students "a better opportunity to figure out what they need to do in order to succeed. If students succeed academically they'll be retained" (Arnold, Tanes, and King 2010, 34). Other scholars have argued that BDA can help administrators predict impacts on retention (Ice et al. 2012, 64) and evaluate the effectiveness of BDA-prompted "nudges" (Wildavsky 2014). Several researchers underscore BDA's usefulness for faculty, such as its ability to provide formative assessment data (Greller and Drachsler 2012) and provide instant feedback to help faculty make appropriate pedagogical adjustments (Dietz-Uhler and Hurn 2013, 21; Lane and Finsel 2014, 12). As mentioned previously, some scholars and analysts advocating for BDA's implementation in higher education argue that universities may be able to target their recruitment efforts to students with profiles that might be a good fit at the institution (Goff and Shaffer 2014, 100). One important benefit suggested by those studying BDA's potential impact on higher education includes the possibility for institutions to "speak" to each other more through conversations about data. Through a grant from the Bill and Melinda Gates Foundation, researchers at public, for-profit, two-year, four-year, and research institutions shared data to identify trends affecting student retention and graduation. The researchers claim that the data they shared with other institutions had the potential to establish "benchmarking strategies that increase retention, progression, and completion" and in the context of developmental education specifically, they thought that sharing data across institutions could "provide opportunities to better inform policy oriented decision-making for at-risk populations" (Ice et al. 2012, 64). The data itself may prove useful to improving curriculum and identifying best practices. In addition, it can also have the important, ancillary benefit of bringing educators and administrators together across different institutions to collaborate and learn from one another.

The closer scholars are to classrooms, the more skepticism can be found in literature involving BDA, though the potential has not been ignored. Despite the dearth of scholarship specifically addressing BDA in composition studies, writing program administration scholars, particularly those investigating online or hybrid writing programs, such as Moxley (2013) at the University of South Florida, have noted some potential benefits of BDA, particularly with respect to assessment. The ability to compare data across different institutions has been explored by Pagano et al. (2008), and though their research emphasizes writing assessment using a common rubric across institutions and not BDA specifically, the benefits they identified include the increased communication and collaboration that came from discussion of large sets of assessment data. Such benefits are noted by scholars studying BDA and its impact on writing programs, such as Griffin and Minter's (2013) *College Composition and Communication* piece acknowledging both the "tremendous promise for writing program assessment" (153) and the important ethical issues regarding BDA, some of which will also be discussed below. Crow (2013), in a book chapter that provides a nuanced and careful look at privacy issues for BDA applications in writing programs, argues that the discipline should engage—carefully—in BDA assessment projects in order to "shape national conversations." WPAs and composition scholars studying BDA acknowledge its usefulness (Griffin and Minter 2013; Lang and Baehr 2012) and the rhetorical impact such data might have on important stakeholders.

LIMITATIONS OF BIG DATA ANALYTICS

A wealth of articles and books praise BDA and its potential to change business and commerce, including Mayer-Schonberger and Cukier's (2013) *Big Data: A Revision That Will Transform How We Live, Work, and Think* and *Wired* editor-in-chief Chris Anderson's (2008) statement about living in an age with enough data and the capacity to analyze it: reasoning through correlation is enough, he claims, because "[w]ith enough data, the numbers speak for themselves." However, several writers in the private sector doubt whether BDA can—or should—radically change society. For instance, Crawford (2013), a researcher with Microsoft, counters Anderson's claim and argues that "as we increasingly rely on Big Data's numbers to speak for themselves, we risk misunderstanding the results and in turn misallocating important public resources." Those misallocations have significant material and social consequences. The City of Boston, for example, released a smartphone app where individuals could report potholes, but failed to account for the fact that citizens in poorer parts of the city had at best uneven access to that technology. Or consider Chicago's "Heat List" that uses a complex algorithm to calculate which individuals might be at risk of becoming a victim of violent crime. Individuals can end up on the list for their criminal records, associating with suspected criminals or ex-convicts, disturbance calls and criminal activity in their neighborhood, and are subjected to increased scrutiny, including in-person warnings from the Chicago Police Department that "further criminal activity, even for the most petty offenses, will result in the full force of the law being brought down on them" (Gorner 2013). Summarizing a host of critiques leveled against BDA, boyd and Crawford (2012) criticize the "value neutral" assumptions many project upon BDA, the important issues of privacy and ethics, the complicated issue of "ownership" of personal data, and the very real threat of those conducting Big Data analysis to "[see] patterns where none actually exist" (668). Many of the reports on Big Data prepared by the Obama administration remain hopeful for its potential, and they also cite many of the concerns above, including the impact on civil liberties, privacy, security and law enforcement, and education. While some journalists, pundits, and lawmakers swoon at the potential of BDA, important and influential voices express concerns about the reality and costs of such potential.

A diverse group of academics, higher education administrators, and non-profit organizations support the idea of applying BDA to understand and improve learning, retention, and persistence to graduation. However, administrators and scholars closer to classrooms caution against overstating Big Data's potential. One important question in higher education circles regarding BDA, and one particularly relevant to WPAs, is simply, "Who can use it?" Typically, the individuals with the access and technical expertise to analyze large data sets on college campuses are in institutional research offices housed outside academic affairs. In a *Chronicle of Higher Education* piece, Conley et al. (2015) critique what they see as a "two-tiered system of research" in which scholars with the capacity to analyze Big Data and partnerships with social media such as Twitter and Facebook will have a significant advantage over researchers without such access. The same can be applied to BDA efforts to understand student retention and graduation. Macfadyen et al. (2014) argue that access to data "must be widespread and open" and shared with educators and education administrators, like WPAs, so they might ask meaningful, pedagogically related questions that can *improve* a program.

Aside from noting the limitation of access, recent publications regarding BDA's limitations in higher education follow two trends: critiquing *how* it is implemented and critiquing *why* it is implemented. Critiques about the design and implementation of BDA projects in higher education note poor faculty buy-in, privacy concerns, and technological and human limitations. Arnold, Tanes, and King (2010) surveyed administrators at Purdue University and found that administrators were concerned with faculty support of the Course Signals program. One participant in their study noted the need to get "faculty to buy into the fact that students are here to succeed, students are here to do well and that the faculty's job is not only to just impart information but also to ensure that the information is being understood" (34). The problematic assumption here, of course, is that faculty members lack the awareness the participant describes, but the administrator's frustration also hints at the anticipated resistance and lack of faculty buy-in. The methods for seeking buy-in for BDA at colleges and universities have also received attention, leading some scholars to suggest that implementing BDA will result in a paradigm shift necessitating across-the-board understanding of BDA (Ferguson et al. 2014, 126) and will require investment in time and resources for scholars and academic administrators (Lane and Finsel 2014, 14). The issue of buy-in also touches upon concerns about how Big Data might be used, a topic I'll return to shortly.

Critics of BDA (including those who advocate for BDA but critique wholesale, uncritical adoption) note important technical and human limitations to implementation. Arnold, Tanes, and King (2010) describe the difficulty of including data that might fail to mesh with analytic software, noting a significant issue in the Course Signals program is that it relies almost exclusively on data mined from a course management system. In a review of BDA and its emerging role in US higher education, Picciano (2012, 18) notes that "Traditional face-to-face courses that require significant data conversion time will likely render this approach problematic." Many WPAs oversee programs that integrate a course management system, but not all writing programs require usage of the system in all sections of first-year composition, so the data may not be representative. In addition to BDA's technical limitations, several writers note important human limitations. For instance, Stevens (2014), echoing a sentiment many WPAs will likely agree with, writes that "Educational measurement is political" (96) and notes the problematic assumption that BDA is value-neutral. BDA's limitations don't necessarily render it useless to colleges and universities, but as Uprichard (2014) notes in the *Chronicle of Higher Education*, blind allegiance to BDA has "unleashed a bizarre digitized version of the Enlightenment" that ignores important questions about why people conduct such inquiries. BDA is, and will likely continue to be, quite persuasive to higher-level administrators: it reduces *aspects* of learning—a messy and often inefficient process—to numbers that are then analyzed and interpreted and sometimes compared to other programs and institutions. The quality of those interpretations and comparisons will be hindered by technical and human limitations. Addressing the access issue mentioned above and integrating faculty and educational administrators into BDA projects might ensure the fairness and contextual appropriateness of interpretations and comparisons. However, faculty and those responsible for curricula and pedagogy (like WPAs, writing center administrators, and writing across the curriculum directors) should also be included in conversations about study design and methodology to ensure relevant and useful questions are asked.

Scholars and journalists discussing BDA's application to higher education also critique what is done with such data and the purposes for which they might be used. Some have suggested that BDA might be used to tailor recruitment efforts, and there have been important critiques suggesting that such practices might lead to student "profiling" or "tracking" and create self-fulfilling prophecies about student abilities (Arnold, Tanes, and King 2010, 30; Dietz-Uhler and Hurn 2013, 23–24). Lane and Finsel (2014, 18), writing in a collection largely supportive of BDA's application to higher education, caution that data will only "be useful if it can be extracted and refined to make decisions" and note the real problems of "data integrity, privacy, removing choice from students, and profiling students." They urge administrators and university officials to "pause and determine what data they want to use and how they want to use those data" (21). Several writers suggest making sure BDA projects provide actionable data that can improve learning and student services rather than what Macfadyen et al. (2014, 19) describe as "assessment-for-accountability" that values "tools for measuring performance or the status quo." WPAs may be comforted by the fact that most *scholarship* regarding applications of BDA in higher education reflects the concerns above and emphasizes the pedagogical use of BDA rather than marveling at its ability to monitor students and educators.

In composition and rhetoric, scholars discussing BDA note several of these same reservations about privacy issues (Crow 2013) and profiling students (Griffin and Minter 2013). Scholars in the discipline also critique the purposes of BDA projects, including the lack of attention to the design of Big Data inquiry and the problematic questions and assumptions asked of the data collected. Perhaps the most useful illustration of BDA's limitations in the context of our discipline is Lang and Baehr's (2012) "Data Mining: A Hybrid Methodology for Complex and Dynamic Research," which appeared in *College Composition and Communication* and reports on a useful example of BDA gone awry. The authors received notification from their university's institutional research office that several sections of first-year composition had a high failure rate (30% or more failed or withdrew) and the institutional research office assumed the issue rested with the lack of consistency among the instructors teaching those sections, and the letter suggested a number of measures (many of them already implemented by the writing program). The program amassed a database of records including student writing, instructor feedback, performance data, and attendance records, and using that data, they investigated the claims by the institutional research office. What they found is that the issue was not the instructors, but the students who often failed to submit work and in many instances had left the university or were on academic probation for poor performance in multiple courses. The assumption by the institutional research office should serve as an important reminder about the limitations of BDA: interpretations of data are laden with assumptions. The 30 percent failure and withdraw rate is, at face value, a figure which may lead administrators without contextual knowledge of the writing program to make problematic and inaccurate assumptions.

The gap in how individuals might interpret such data might be best explained by Moxley (2008), who argues that usage of data and their interpretations can be traced back to what he calls "Community of Control" or "Community of Learning" (186). Efforts to assess and collect data that serve the consolidation of power and exertion of control over others, like in Lang and Baehr's example, will often "reflect a lack of willing to listen, to be empathetic" (195) and typically lack the contextual knowledge needed to make accurate and ethical interpretations of data. Moxley advocates for a competing model, a "Community of Learning," emphasizing engagement and "the pursuit of truth and understanding"

(195) that places BDA initiatives more at the service of educators rather than solely devoted to the surveillance and control of programs. When BDA inquiries are conducted solely by those possessing technical expertise yet no understanding of the pedagogical context and/or the higher level administrators they might answer to, there exists little possibility that such data might be used to improve learning and retention in meaningful ways. WPAs are uniquely situated to ask writing program related questions that might require BDA and should be involved in the inquiry design and interpretation stages of a BDA project.

BIG DATA'S ROLE IN WRITING PROGRAM ADMINISTRATION WORK: ASSESSMENT AND CONTEXT

Given the concerns many within and outside the field of composition and rhetoric have voiced about BDA, it would make sense to become skeptical of its application to writing program assessment, especially regarding important issues such as retention and degree completion. After all, when WPAs design assessment projects to collect data rather than inform curricular decisions, the results rarely translate into improved learning and pedagogy. Neal's (2011) work in assessment and electronic portfolios poignantly highlights the problems of BDA and assessment design: when high-level university administrators eyed eportfolios as a way to mine data rather than a method for truly assessing the writing program Neal administered, the information collected was of little use to him and his colleagues and actually undermined the writing program's pedagogy (83–84). BDA does have a role to play in a writing program's assessment efforts, but only to the extent that it assists in the improvement of curriculum and understanding of context and if it adheres to the best assessment praxis informed by assessment scholarship. To align with current writing assessment scholarship, BDA inquiries should be contextually attentive and specific to a particular site as well as inclusive and sensitive to the needs and desires of faculty, students, and others affected by assessment findings (Broad 2003; Huot 2002; White, Elliot, and Peckham 2015). As Huot (2002) notes, assessment might be best viewed as a form of research and that metaphor appears particularly apt in considering BDA's usefulness as a tool in collecting and analyzing data. Good research and assessment projects, including those implementing BDA to understand retention and graduation rates, should pay careful attention to design, consider the project's ethical implications and impact on different groups, acknowledge its limitations, and support learning and growth.

To illustrate the role BDA *should* play in a WPA's efforts to assess retention and other crucial aspects of a writing program, I offer two examples of assessment projects at my institution that engage BDA as a source of data. My institution, a small, rural, open-access, public institution in Appalachian, Ohio, has significant obstacles with time to degree and student retention, obstacles made all the more glaring when the state recently announced a new performance funding model that has yet to be fully implemented but has already made its impact felt. The new model has initiated important conversations about how the university recruits students and the services it provides to the many underprepared students who enroll at our institution. We are one of only three public institutions in the state allowed to offer developmental coursework for underprepared students, and the ACT places a significant portion of our students into developmental courses.

When I arrived at my university, I directed our writing center, and BDA helped me generate an understanding of my program's context and the role my work played in retention and graduation rates. In addition to assessment projects such as focus groups of students and tutors, analysis of student texts, and survey projects, I also, like many writing center directors, collected data about the students visiting the writing center. I obtained information about the students who visited, the courses they were coming to the writing center for, the kinds of help they wished to receive, and what they ultimately worked on in their consultations. In my second year, I began collecting student identification numbers, and that opened up some potential BDA applications. At the end of each term, I emailed ID numbers to my university's institutional research office. With our university's data mining software, Tableau, the research office staff processed student IDs and identified trends and produced descriptive statistics about students visiting the writing center, including information about the percentage of commuters, ACT scores for students visiting the writing center, and even which high schools they attended.[3] In addition to identifying trends among visitors to the writing center, we also asked the office of institutional research to warehouse the student identification numbers for the purposes of assessing retention and graduation rates.

We continue to compile student IDs and will ask institutional research to process those numbers once a year so we might be able to compare student retention rates for students visiting the writing center to students who did not. Because we're in the early stages of this project, we have little information about what that impact might be, but because the project is self-initiated and not administration-mandated, we are able to "get ahead" of the data and supplement the findings with assessment projects that might help us understand why students visiting the writing center appear to have lower retention and graduation rates or to temper expectations that the writing center is a "silver bullet" that can "fix" an aspect of our institution's retention issues. One query we have forwarded to our institutional research office is a comparison of students visiting/not visiting the writing center within specific ACT score bands. This might provide us a more useful and realistic comparison, although relying on ACT scores remains problematic. In addition to longitudinal analysis of retention, the annual BDA "Check-ins" also provide useful demographic information about the writing center that can provide us with data that might assist in the allocation of resources or in the development of training materials for consultants. As one example of how the data provided us actionable information, the current WCD and I learned that we had a significant percentage of students living on-campus visiting the writing center, and we made adjustments to marketing and promotion with that information.

In the Spring 2014 semester I assumed the role as WPA of our developmental composition program, and BDA helped me assess my program's impact on student retention and success in that new position. In assessing my program's curriculum, I found BDA helpful in controlling for some factors and developing an informed interpretation of student pass/fail rates. In the Fall of 2014 my institution began enforcing a requirement that all students under the age of twenty-one must have an ACT score on file. Many administrators and faculty at the university assumed that students lacking a score would also be students who might lack preparation for college, decide to enroll in college at the last minute, and/or enroll only to receive a student loan check. Also in the Fall of 2014, the developmental composition program I direct implemented a new curriculum more aligned with the first-year composition courses and far removed from the grammar and mechanics approach that had been common for several years. After the curricular change and the ACT score rule implementation, there were significant improvements in the number of students passing our developmental composition courses, and we increased our course completion rate from 46 percent the Fall of 2013 to 53 percent in the Fall of 2014. However, the progress made in course completion was written off and attributed to the ACT score requirement, not the curricular changes.

Understanding the cause for the course completion rate increase was important. If the curricular changes could be tied to the increased completion rate, then that might persuade important stakeholders—including students, administrators, and even developmental composition instructors unsure about the efficacy of the new curriculum—that improving student retention and course completion can be addressed through resources spent on curriculum and pedagogy and not just through bureaucratic expedients. Through working with our office of institutional research, we found that students with similar ACT composite scores completed their developmental composition courses at a higher rate *after* the curricular changes. In other words, students with 17 as their ACT composite score, for example, passed developmental composition at a higher rate after the curriculum change than students with 17 in the year before the curricular change. A chi-square test to determine whether the changes were statistically significant informed us that the increase in students passing developmental composition was no fluke. Using ACT scores and pass/fail rates as a basis for comparison has its problems—as does a 53 percent course completion rate—but the data we were able to collect told us that although the ACT score requirement did have an impact, it didn't tell the whole story behind the data. The collaboration with institutional research allowed us, in one sense, to control for ACT scores, which permitted us to make the claim that the curricular changes have some role in the increased student passing rates. We also learned that students completing a developmental composition course in the Fall of 2014 passed their credit-bearing composition courses in the Spring of 2015 at a higher rate than students who had been placed directly into first-year composition. In fact, 71 percent of students who passed developmental composition in the Fall of 2014 passed first-year composition, compared to 65 percent of students who did not complete a developmental composition course.

CONCLUSION

While pleased with the data suggesting that our curricular changes have made a positive impact and that many developmental composition students are succeeding in first-year composition, I have certainly not lost sight of the fact that slightly less than half of students currently enrolled in the program I direct fail developmental composition. I need to know more about that. The data obtained from my university's institutional research office was essential to understanding—in the aggregate—the impact of my program on the students we teach. However, BDA doesn't replace the need for careful programmatic assessment and inquiry. Subsequent assessment projects will help us hone in on the curriculum's impact on student course completion and retention rates. For example, to develop a clearer picture of how and why students from the developmental composition program I direct are performing well in first-year composition, we're currently designing a portfolio assessment project that might help us understand what skills and abilities our program successfully teaches students and identify trends among portfolios of students who fail developmental composition. Another important inquiry project we're interested in pursuing is an assessment of how students from different racial formations perform in our program. Inspired by recent scholarship attending to assessment's intersections with race (Inoue and Poe 2012), my hope is that BDA may provide a method by which I can learn more about my program's policies, procedures, and curriculum and their impact on retention, course completion, and graduation rates of students from different races. Within the last four years, the African American students in my program have increased each year, but when compared against other students, we found that 36 percent of African American students pass a developmental composition course compared to 44 percent of their white peers. Researching, assessing, and learning more about how students from different racial formations perform in our program will help me initiate conversations with different stakeholders about the resources we provide students from underrepresented groups, many of whom are unprepared for college-level writing and who struggle to adjust to a university situated in an area very different from their home communities.

The larger point to be made regarding the above examples is that recent assessment scholarship and its emphasis on context, inquiry, and even social justice, should provide WPAs the guiding principles for how they implement BDA into the array of data they consult to administer and advocate for their programs. The values expressed by recent scholarship in the field of writing assessment can also provide WPAs with arguments that might counter uncritical assumptions about the role BDA should play in higher education and in the measurement of student retention and graduation rates. Showing an increase in students passing our developmental composition courses tells me a portion of my program's story. Following recent trends in assessment scholarship, subsequent inquiries will need to dig deeper and develop a better understanding of the impact of our curricular changes on student writing practices and the effect of this curriculum on students from different racial and ethnic formations. BDA can help me develop a partial understanding of that impact, but it does not and cannot replace careful and well-designed assessments that attend to context and that focus on learning and improving curriculum.

Notes

1. The author wishes to thank Christopher Shaffer for his contributions to this piece.
2. As we'll see later, using Big Data to assist recruitment of potentially successful students is problematic due to criticisms that such efforts might lead to "tracking" poorly performing students and creating self-fulfilling prophecies.
3. Knowing more about the high schools our students attended has prompted collaborative efforts between high school educators and administrators and our writing center.

References

Anderson, Chris. 2008. "The End of Theory: The Data Deluge Makes the Scientific Method Obsolete." *WIRED*. http://www.wired.com/2008/06/pb-theory/.

Arnold, Kimberly E., Zeynep Tanes, and Abigail Selzer King. 2010. "Administrative Perceptions of Data-Mining Software Signals: Promoting Student Success and Retention." *Journal of Academic Administration in Higher Education* 6 (2): 29–40.

Arum, Richard, and Josipa Roksa. 2011. *Academically Adrift: Limited Learning on College Campuses*. Chicago: University of Chicago Press.

Bichsel, Jacqueline. 2012. *Analytics in Higher Education: Benefits, Barriers, Progress, and Recommendations*. Louisville, CO: Educause Center for Applied Research; http://net.educause.edu/ir/library/pdf/ERS1207/ers1207.pdf.

Bienkowski, Marie, Mingyu Feng, and Barbara Means. 2012. *Enhancing Teaching and Learning Through Educational Data Mining and Learning Analytics: An Issue Brief*. Washington, DC: US Department of Education Office of Educational Technology.

boyd, danah, and Kate Crawford. 2012. "Critical Questions for Big Data: Provocations for a Cultural, Technological, and Scholarly Phenomenon." *Information Communication and Society* 15 (5): 662–79. http://dx.doi.org/10.1080/1369118X.2012.678878.

Broad, Bob. 2003. *What We Really Value: Beyond Rubrics in Teaching and Assessing Writing*. Logan: Utah State University Press.

Conley, Dalton, J. Lawrence Aber, Henry Brady, Susan Cutter, Catherine Eckel, Barbara Entwisle, Darrick Hamilton, Sandra Hofferth, Klaus Hubacek, Emilio Moran, et al. 2015. "Big Data. Big Obstacles." *Chronicle of Higher Education*, February 2. http://chronicle.com/article/Big-Data-Big-Obstacles/151421/.

Crawford, Kate. 2013. "The Hidden Biases in Big Data." *Harvard Business Review*, April. https://hbr.org/2013/04/the-hidden-biases-in-big-data.

Crow, Angela. 2013. "Managing Datacloud Decisions and 'Big Data': Understanding Privacy Choices in Terms of Surveillant Assemblages." In *Digital Writing: Assessment and Evaluation*, ed. Heidi McKee and Danielle DeVoss. Logan: Computers and Composition Digital Press/Utah State University Press; http://ccdigitalpress.org/dwae/02_crow.html.

Dietz-Uhler, Beth, and Janet E. Hurn. 2013. "Using Learning Analytics to Predict (and Improve) Student Success: A Faculty Perspective." *Journal of Interactive Online Learning* 12 (1): 17–26.

Ferguson, Rebecca, Leah Macfadyen, Doug Clow, Belinda Tynan, Shirley Alexander, and Shane Dawson. 2014. "Setting Learning Analytics in Context: Overcoming the Barriers to Large-Scale Adoption." *Journal of Learning Analytics* 1 (3): 120–44.

Goff, Jay W., and Christopher M. Shaffer. 2014. "Big Data's Impact on College Admission Practices and Recruitment Strategies." In *Building a Smarter University: Big Data, Innovation, and Analytics*, ed. Jason E. Lane, 93–120. Albany: State University of New York Press.

Gorner, Jeremy. 2013. "Chicago Police Use Heat List as Strategy to Prevent Violence." *Tribunedigital-Chicagotribune,* August 21. http://articles.chicagotribune.com/2013-08 -21/news/ct-met-heat-list-20130821_1_chicago-police-commander-andrew-papachris tos-heat-list.

Greller, Wolfgang, and Hendrik Drachsler. 2012. "Translating Learning into Numbers: A Generic Framework for Learning Analytics." *Journal of Educational Technology & Society* 15 (3): 42–57.

Griffin, June, and Deborah Minter. 2013. "The Rise of the Online Writing Classroom: Reflecting on the Material Conditions of College Composition Teaching." *College Composition and Communication* 65 (1): 140–63.

President's Council of Advisors on Science and Technology. 2014. *Big Data and Privacy: A Technological Perspective.* Washington, DC: Government Printing Office.

Huot, Brian. 2002. *(Re)Articulating Writing Assessment for Teaching and Learning.* Logan: Utah State University Press.

Ice, Phil, Sebastian Diaz, Karen Swan, Melissa Burgess, Mike Sharkey, Jonathan Sherrill, Dan Huston, and Hae Okimoto. 2012. "The PAR Framework Proof of Concept: Initial Findings from a Multi-Institutional Analysis of Federated Postsecondary Data." *Journal of Asynchronous Learning Networks* 16 (3): 63–86.

Inoue, Asao B., and Mya Poe, eds. 2012. *Race and Writing Assessment.* 7 vols. Studies in Composition and Rhetoric. New York: Peter Lang.

Lane, Jason E., and B. Alex Finsel. 2014. "Fostering Smarter Colleges and Universities: Data, Big Data, and Analytics." In *Building a Smarter University: Big Data, Innovation, and Analytics,* ed. Jason E. Lane, 3–27. SUNY Series, Critical Issues in Higher Education. Albany: State University of New York Press.

Lang, Susan, and Craig Baehr. 2012. "Data Mining: A Hybrid Methodology for Complex and Dynamic Research." *College Composition and Communication* 64 (1): 172–94.

Macfadyen, Leah, Shane Dawson, Abelardo Pardo, and Dragan Gasevic. 2014. "Embracing Big Data in Complex Educational Systems: The Learning Analytics Imperative and the Policy Challenge." *Research & Practice in Assessment* 9:17–28.

Mayer-Schonberger, Viktor, and Kenneth Cukier. 2013. *Big Data: A Revolution That Will Transform How We Live, Work, and Think.* London: John Murray Publishers.

Moxley, Joseph. 2008. "Datagogies, Writing Spaces, and the Age of Peer Production." *Computers and Composition* 25 (2): 182–202. http://dx.doi.org/10.1016/j.compcom .2007.12.003.

Moxley, Joe. 2013. "Big Data, Learning Analytics, and Social Assessment." *Journal of Writing Assessment* 6 (1). http://www.journalofwritingassessment.org/article.php ?article=68.

Neal, Michael R. 2011. *Writing Assessment and The Revolution in Digital Texts and Technologies.* New York: Teachers College Press.

Norris, Donald M., and Linda L. Baer. 2013. "Building Organizational Capacity for Analytics." Educause. https://net.educause.edu/ir/library/pdf/PUB9012.pdf.

Pagano, Neil, Stephen A. Bernhardt, Dudley Reynolds, Mark Williams, and Matthew Kilian McCurrie. 2008. "An Inter-Institutional Model for College Writing Assessment." *College Composition and Communication* 60 (2): 285–320.

Picciano, Anthony G. 2012. "The Evolution of Big Data and Learning Analytics in American Higher Education." *Journal of Asynchronous Learning Networks* 16 (3): 9–20.

Podesta, John, Penny Pritzker, Ernest J. Moniz, John Holdren, and Jeffrey Zients. 2014. *Big Data: Seizing Opportunities, Preserving Values.* Executive Office of the President.

"The Rise of Big Data in Higher Education." 2013. Educause. https://net.educause .edu/ir/library/pdf/LIVE1208s.pdf.

Seifert, Jeffrey W. 2004. "Data Mining: An Overview." CRS Report for Congress RL31798. Washington, DC: Library of Congress.

Stevens, Mitchell. 2014. "An Ethically Ambitious Higher Education Data Science." *Research and Practice in Assessment* 9: 96–97.

Uprichard, Emma. 2014. "Big Doubts About Big Data." *Chronicle of Higher Education* 61 (7).

West, Darrell M. 2012. *Big Data for Education: Data Mining, Data Analytics, and Web Dashboards."* Governance Studies at Brookings. Washington, DC: Brookings Institution.

White, Edward M., Norbert Elliot, and Irvin Peckham. 2015. *Very Like a Whale: The Assessment of Writing Programs.* Logan: Utah State University Press.

Wildavsky, Ben. 2014. "Nudge Nation: A New Way to Use Data to Prod Students into and through College." In *Building a Smarter University: Big Data, Innovation, and Analytics,* ed. Jason E. Lane, 143–58. Albany: State University of New York Press.

5

THE IMPERATIVE OF PEDAGOGICAL AND PROFESSIONAL DEVELOPMENT TO SUPPORT THE RETENTION OF UNDERPREPARED STUDENTS AT OPEN-ACCESS INSTITUTIONS

Joanne Giordano, Holly Hassel,
Jennifer Heinert, and Cassandra Phillips

In 2009, Pegeen Reichert Powell drew attention to the underdeveloped relationship between research on retention and scholarship in writing studies (Reichert Powell 2009), and Patrick Sullivan's (2008) work has critiqued the assumptions underpinning "success" in national conversations about student retention. Simultaneously, institutions of higher education are under pressure from local and national forces to increase student retention, with President Obama's "college completion agenda" (Department of Education 2011) and the philanthropic work of groups like the Lumina Foundation and Complete College America shaping policy and practice in higher education with the intention to expand the population of US citizens with postsecondary credentials. These national efforts have focused on increasing pathways toward degrees, decreasing time spent in reading and writing classrooms, and reconceptualizing the college experience. However, not enough attention has been paid to the role of instruction in the context of these initiatives and in retaining a shifting population of students at some institutions (including our own) that is increasingly underprepared for college reading and writing. National conversations have focused on students' preparation for college learning while omitting the importance of teaching preparation to reflect the changing realities of postsecondary writing instruction.

Our chapter reports on our efforts to address significant problems with student retention in writing courses at our statewide two-year access institution through intensive faculty development. We describe our work to create multifaceted and cohesive disciplinary professional development resources aimed at improving the academic success and retention

DOI: 10.7330/9781607326021.c005

of our students. We report on the challenges faced by participating composition instructors as they revised their approach to teaching academically at-risk students. We argue that sustainable, compensated professional development resources are critical for supporting student learning and retention—and faculty development must be supported if institutions are committed to retaining students. Writing programs at access institutions cannot address retention in a cohesive way without providing the faculty development to support instructors who teach students with significant and diverse learning needs.

COMPLEXITIES OF WRITING PROGRAM DEVELOPMENT AT ACCESS INSTITUTIONS

In the classrooms of access institutions, writing instructors can expect to encounter teaching and learning environments far different from the ones where they received their training (see Hassel and Giordano 2013). They can also expect to teach students with academic skills that are far different from the students they would have encountered as writing instructors during their graduate programs, especially if they were trained at a selective PhD-granting institutions. For example, we teach at the University of Wisconsin Colleges, a thirteen-campus, two-year institution of access with a rigorous liberal arts transfer curriculum. Despite being classified as a "High Transfer-High Traditional" Associate's College, our only admission requirement is high school completion or an equivalency degree, and 60.8 percent of students are first-generation; institutional data show that on any given year, 99–100 percent of applicants are admitted. In Fall 2014, 20.3 percent of ranked first-year students came from the bottom quartile of their high school graduating classes, and 54 percent came from the bottom half. In that same year, approximately 22.4 percent of newly admitted first-year students began college in a developmental writing course (see University of Wisconsin System 2015, 8–15). Despite our writing program efforts to accelerate students to credit-bearing composition through multiple measures placement with co-requisite studio support, the percentage of students needing developmental support has steadily climbed since 2007 when only 10 percent of first-year students enrolled in developmental writing.

This shift in our student population toward larger numbers of academically underprepared students has significant implications for student retention across our institution, especially for first-year writing. At our institution, both high school grades and placement data show a strong connection between college readiness and retention. During the 2011–2012 academic year, 94 percent of upper-quartile students were retained at the institution for a second semester, and 82 percent were retained to the University of Wisconsin System (either our institution or a four-year campus) for their second year. In contrast, only 75 percent of lower quartile students were retained to a second semester, and only half were enrolled anywhere in our state system for a second college year. An institutional study of success rates across five years of newly admitted students in developmental writing courses shows that 75 percent of students completed developmental writing on their first or second attempt, but only one-third eventually completed our core writing requirement within two years (Nettesheim 2014). Over five years, 20 percent of the 2838 students who started college in developmental writing did not complete the course and were not retained to our institution beyond their first or second attempt at taking the course, and an additional 9 percent completed the course but were not retained long enough to take a credit-bearing writing course. Further, only 25.5 percent of our students transfer and receive a four-year University of Wisconsin System degree within six years, compared to 65.5 percent of students in the state system (University of Wisconsin System 2014, 34). It is important to note that most of the developmental writers and lower quartile students in our institution (including those who are placed into credit-bearing writing courses) are ineligible to transfer to four-year institutions until they successfully complete our writing program or improve their grades. For the most part, when they are not retained at our access institution's two-year campuses, they are not retained to higher education.

Developing, assessing, and improving writing programs in the face of these changes in student readiness for college reading and writing is a complex process, and one that often relies on the contributions, experience, and expertise of many instructors. Indeed, at two-year campuses, having a designated writing program administrator (WPA) is rare. Carolyn Calhoon-Dillahunt (2011) observes in "Writing Programs without Administrators: Frameworks for Successful Writing Programs in the Two-Year College" that most two-year colleges do not follow the prevailing model of a single, compensated administrative authority dedicated to a writing program. Instead, such institutions have to develop other ways of maintaining the curriculum, instruction, and resource development that refreshes and supports a first-year writing (and oftentimes learning skills and reading) curriculum (Calhoon-Dillahunt 2011; see also Klausman 2008, 2010, and 2013 for additional discussions of writing program leadership in two-year colleges). Until

2013, our English Department used a committee model to address only some of the most pressing writing program issues. This committee relied largely upon the uncompensated service work of department instructors with a variety of backgrounds who had very little authority to effect change.

In addition to the relative rarity of WPA positions at two-year campuses, the vast majority of two-year college writing instructors teach off the tenure track. As David Laurence reports in the MLAs' "Demography of the Faculty," almost 80 percent of two-year college English instructors work off the tenure track compared to 60 percent at four-year institutions (Laurence 2008). Program development at such institutions thus necessarily involves addressing—as much as possible—the working conditions in which the vast majority of instructors are contingent.[1] For this reason, our attempts to redesign our curriculum had to involve a variety of instructional resources to support instructors' substantial pedagogical changes to their courses, regardless of their employment statuses (tenure-stream, full-time contingent, and part time). We also had to develop a variety of different types of resources to meet the needs of diverse instructors across the state, including online workshops, face-to-face training, and course material templates.

Two-year access institutions are rich and rewarding sites of teaching and learning even with perpetual challenges connected to curricular resources and program stability. For example, writing program development is complicated at two-year colleges for two reasons—first, there is a significant gap between instructors' graduate training and the demands of teaching the diverse range of students who enroll at open admissions campuses. And second, there is also a disconnect between the professional resources and relevant pedagogical research specifically designed to help two-year college instructors teach a student population with such diverse needs. As Paula Krebs recently wrote in *Inside Higher Ed:* "Most folks at doctoral institutions don't have a clue what goes on in community colleges. The departments don't, the individual faculty members don't, and it would be a rare graduate adviser indeed who had ever set foot on a community college campus" (Krebs 2014). In two-year colleges, English departments—or sometimes more broadly humanities or general education programs—offer transfer-level courses to students with a dizzying array of needs and do so with limited resources for professional development. This can make for enriching and energizing career path for instructors who teach in these spaces.

DESIGNING A WRITING PROGRAM TO
SUPPORT ACADEMIC SUCCESS

Over the past decade, a dramatic shift in our institution's student population resulted in instructors across the institution realizing that previous successful teaching strategies, assignments, and learning activities, whether imported from their graduate training or developed over many years with University of Wisconsin (UW) Colleges, were no longer effective for many of our students. Our department's shared understanding of this changing reality and desire to improve teaching and learning resulted in an intensive curricular redesign process with related faculty development opportunities. During the 2012–2013 academic year, we completely revised our writing program to create a cohesive set of courses that took students from the beginning of developmental writing through three semesters to the end of our core transfer research course. This work served as the starting point for designing professional development activities to support academic success for underprepared students. Our curriculum redesign work was part of a collaboration of instructors working both on and off the tenure track.

After many years of reading student work while assessing department and institutional outcomes, we had a very clear sense of how curriculum influences student learning. As such, we knew that a department curriculum revision would have to be undertaken with a great deal of primary and secondary research, detailed knowledge of our student population, experience and understanding of institutional policy, experience in the classroom, and disciplinary knowledge.

Before beginning our curricular redesign project, we systematically collected detailed placement data from several of our campuses to develop a clear picture of student readiness for college-level reading and writing, including standardized test scores, high school grades in relation to courses taken, a writing sample, and a student self-assessment questionnaire. Two of our project team members also conducted a series of research studies on students' transition to college-level critical reading and academic writing over a five-year period, including three studies that carefully examined data on student retention and student success rates in our first-year writing and learning support courses in relation to placement. Findings drawn from student success rates and close examinations of student writing subsequently informed the program revisions that led to departmental curricular and instructional shifts and subsequent grant funding to support our project. When combined with institutional data about student success outcomes, these departmental research and assessment activities helped us clearly identify that (a) a majority of students on our statewide writing program are underprepared for college-level reading, and (b) critical reading is a major barrier to successful completion of our institution's core writing requirement. Therefore, incorporating critical reading outcomes into writing courses became the starting point for redesigning all of the courses in our writing program and developing accompanying instructional resources and professional development activities. The redesign process responded to findings that suggested students were not only coming to first-year writing courses without robust and substantial critical reading skills and literacy foundations, but also they were struggling to connect readings to writing assignments in their first-year writing courses.

After using research and assessment data to identify student learning needs, we first articulated the student learning outcomes for the end of our degree-fulfilling composition course, English 102: Critical Writing, Reading, and Research, which fulfills our institution's core writing requirement. Drawing from an updated "WPA Outcomes Statement" (2014), we developed outcomes and competencies in five core areas: Critical Reading, Writing, and Thinking; Processes; Rhetorical Knowledge, Conventions of Academic Writing, and Composing in Electronic Environments. For example, for English 102, we have defined two learning outcomes for "Rhetorical Knowledge: Reading Texts": "Read and understand the rhetorical features of a variety of scholarly (research-based) texts to identify relevant source material appropriate to the writer's needs" and "Analyze and evaluate how disciplinary and generic conventions shape a text." These translate into the following competencies: "The writer produces source-based texts that demonstrate an understanding of scholarly genre conventions; identify how discipline-specific conventions shape the form and content of a text; and, select supporting sources appropriate to the writing situation."[2] Once the learning outcomes and competencies were defined, we used a backward design approach (see Wiggins and McTighe 2005) to develop a series of assessments, as well as learning activities and readings that would support student achievement of the learning outcomes for English 102. For the first time in the history of our institution, we had a clearly defined series of learning outcomes and competencies for our core writing requirement based on evidence of student needs and national standards. The backward design process allowed us to articulate a starting point for the core writing requirement course, which also became our end goal for the first credit-bearing course (English 101). We followed the same process for English 101 and our developmental writing course, and we subsequently updated the learning outcomes for our non-degree second language writing course. The end result was a cohesive series of courses that worked together to support student learning regardless of a student's starting point in the sequence. This curriculum development work served as the foundation for the faculty development program that ultimately emerged and was supported by the grant.

While the end result of this project was an award-winning program,[3] we already knew from previous years of experience that while a well-designed writing program looks good on paper, what makes a writing program successful is classroom teaching. While all instructors may use the curriculum if they so choose (assignments, suggested texts, and learning activities are available online), we also know from pedagogical research that using an example curriculum does not guarantee increased student learning. Instructors who do not understand the pedagogical approaches are ill prepared to independently adapt the curriculum, select appropriate reading materials, or design their own learning activities (see Artze-Vega et al. 2013).

Curricular redesign work without accompanying instructor development is ineffective. To address this gap between curricular redesign and necessary instructor development, in 2010, our department successfully advocated for a Developmental Reading and Writing Coordinator position and in 2013, after a strong appeal, our department was granted a quarter-time, budget-contingent WPA position. And while the workload is far more than the allocated reassigned time, our department had finally gained two compensated and dedicated positions to devote to program development. At the same time, we also had research on student learning at our institution. Both the research and the support of the positions allowed for time and opportunity to examine and advance our writing program effectiveness.

The challenge, then, was to enable these program staff to undertake projects that would support faculty development. Because we had no access to faculty development funding at an institutional or system level, the only source for external funding we could apply to was the University of Wisconsin System "Growth Agenda for Wisconsin" Grants Program, the goals of which were to increase the number of Wisconsin graduates, help create more well-paying jobs, and build stronger communities. While it was not an easy task to argue the relationship between instructional development and these priorities, we received funding for our project, "Professional Development for Core English Skills Instructors: Using Research-Based Teaching Strategies to Improve the Retention and Academic Success of Underprepared College Readers and Writers." Our grant funding application, based on the research we reported above about the challenges of retaining underprepared readers and writers, relied heavily on invoking the relationship between retention and instruction. That is, with pressure from external and internal decision-makers to raise rates of student retention, persistence, and graduation, it was imperative to demonstrate the link between effective instruction and student success—both in course grades and graduation rates and in learning and skills.

Faculty Development Work

One of the key principles for faculty development in term of curricular design was to help instructors view each course in the writing sequence as fulfilling an important role in students' development toward the skills required to complete degree-credit writing instead of as a free-standing set of assignments. The Two-Year College English Association's (2004) *Guidelines for the Academic Preparation of English Faculty at Two-Year Colleges* recommends graduate training that emphasizes composition pedagogy, reading pedagogy, and linguistics, along with additional coursework relevant to teaching the specific student populations at two-year colleges (including basic writers, multilingual students, and returning adult learners). The Two-Year College English Association guidelines also note that "Recent graduates of master's and doctoral programs are often applicants for these positions, yet many have not been appropriately prepared by traditional English graduate degree programs to confront and address effectively the needs of two-year college students" (7). This statement applies to the UW Colleges because, of the thirty-one faculty and approximately one hundred non-tenure track instructors (as at many institutions), almost all are literature or creative writing experts who have minimal or no formal training in teaching developmental English or working with underprepared students at an access institution. Even those instructors with ample graduate training in the teaching of writing are often ill prepared for meeting the pedagogical and curricular needs of academically at-risk students. The Two-Year College English Association (TYCA) guidelines also recommend ongoing training and professional development that is relevant to teaching in a two-year college, including that instructors "participate in an ongoing dialogue with other teacher-scholars and reflect in their classroom teaching their awareness of new theories and practices" (Two-Year College English Association 2004, 9). Both faculty and contingent instructors are in need of resources, training, and ongoing development related to teaching writing and developmental courses.

Because our institution is geographically dispersed across the entire state of Wisconsin, a key part of our faculty development work was providing instructors with a substantial set of online teaching resources. We created a new program website (University of Wisconsin Colleges English Department 2016) and developed web pages for each course that included curricular guidelines, assignment examples, learning activities, researched-based background readings, and professional development resources. We also developed a series of self-paced and self-directed online workshops designed to help instructors redesign each writing course. Later, additional workshops were created related to teaching reading as well as multiple measures placement, effective mentoring strategies for core skills instructors, teaching writing online, and studio writing pedagogy. Each workshop introduces instructors to key disciplinary background readings and research related to learner-centered pedagogies and teaching writing and reading at an access institution. Online workshop activities focus on helping instructors develop and receive feedback on their overall course design, assignments, learning activities, and other teaching materials. We also collected feedback and self-assessments from the grant participants throughout the series of pedagogical activities supported by the grant. Thus, we created a permanent repository of workshops and related instructional materials that could be used by new instructors in subsequent years and revised as needed in response to research on student learning and institutional changes. Having a robust set of materials available that were aligned with the program redesign made it possible to put together the subsequent pedagogical and training activities. We continue to use the website as a flexible resource for archiving face-to-face faculty development materials and creating new resources for ongoing program development work in response to regular assessment.

As part of the grant project, instructors received a professional development stipend to complete an online workshop and redesign one writing course. We also designed and facilitated two full-day workshops to supplement the online resources. Instructors from across the state came together to talk about working with academically at-risk students, receive and give feedback on revised or newly created teaching materials, and discuss strategies for assessing student learning.

Instructor Insights

We applied for and received Institutional Review Board (IRB) approval to collect multiple forms of feedback from instructor participants in order to assess the efficacy of the project, including instructor reflections, their assessment of students' progress in the course, and feedback on each of the face-to-face seminars. As a result, participating instructors offered a wide range of insights upon reflecting on their experiences with redesign project activities, often speaking to the value of organized professional development activities within departmental units. Overall, instructors valued the sense of community and support that the project offered them (including a validation of their new practices); however, common challenges emerged around balancing time for course revision work with other teaching, service, and non-work-related demands.

Respondents commented on the value of a sense of community that was created by organized professional development opportunities, with one participant noting,[4] "I did attend 2 of the 3 face-to-face meetings, and those are always helpful for checking one's own experience against that of others teaching the same class," a sentiment echoed by Lee Friederich, a UW Barron County instructor: "The in-person component of the workshop was especially helpful, I feel, because it modeled a 'learner-centered' approach in which participants created topics to focus on during the brief time we spent together." What these comments illustrate is how important the in-person meetings were to allowing instructors to participate in a community of learners and experience learner-centered pedagogy in action—particularly significant in a decentralized institution where face-to-face conversations among departmental peers are relatively limited.

In addition, this sense of community made it possible for the activities to be viewed as formative and part of regular professional conversations about shared work responsibilities rather than evaluative, as is the typical context for discussions about classroom teaching in our department and institution. For example, another instructor responded that the project "allowed me to revise without judgment & with lots of offers of help." A tenure-track instructor, Dr. Carrie Shipers, observed that "[students'] final research essays are much stronger than anything I saw in my previous classes because they're much more informed about their topics and they're more thoughtful in supporting their own points of view." A long-tenured senior faculty member participant, Elizabeth Zanichkowsky of University of Wisconsin-Waukesha appreciated the structured opportunity to rethink her courses:

> I have re-examined all of my assignments and used the example syllabus for ENG 102 several times now, and I have found my class better organized, easier to explain to students, and easier for them to follow because the assignments are coordinated and relevant to their final goal:

a well-argued and properly documented research paper. The most helpful parts of the project for me have been the online conversations with other instructors and reading their posts. In these discussions we had time to explore what worked, and why.

As the history of our institution revealed, prior to the creation of coordinator positions, our instructors (at all employment categories) relied on scanty resources and their own initiative to develop and revise course approaches. Teaching a four-course load every semester also leaves most instructors with little time to do deep pedagogical rethinking. Further, without resources or dedicated time to professional and pedagogical development, post-tenure instructors don't have access to the regular feedback that tenure-line and non-tenure track instructors have nor was there support for developing new teaching approaches to adapt to what has become almost a completely different student population in the last ten years.

This shift in student population, for example, as our departmental research findings showed, included an increasing need for students to have practice developing and using critical reading strategies. Projects like these offer a way for instructors to revise their courses to align with emerging student learning needs. Ann Mattis, of UW Sheboygan, for instance, observed that her participation in the project brought about curricular changes that incorporated reading-based learning outcomes more heavily into her first-semester course:

> Revising my English 101 course to foreground critical reading and the departmental learning outcomes has undoubtedly made the course more rigorous and enriching. Though my English 101 course had always emphasized the departmental learning outcomes, the course (post-grant workshop) has become more reading intensive, as it followed rather closely the recommended assignments for English 101.

This instructor's previous teaching position at a very selective private institution with a different student population, meant, necessarily, that she would need to adapt her instructional approach. Rather than the remedial or punitive act that curricular change might be perceived to be, this project instead provides resources to support instructors whose previous teaching experiences were at different institutional types with different missions, admissions standards, and curricular approaches. Without formal departmental opportunities (developed out of research *specific to that institution*) new instructors do not have the necessary resources to independently and individually adapt their approaches.

Departments have an obligation to provide such structured learning opportunities for new instructors and yet there are significant obstacles to creating and supporting such programs, both for program administrators and teaching staff. In "'Distinct and Significant': Professional Identities of Two-Year College English Faculty," Toth, Griffiths, and Thirolf observe "that one way to support part-time faculty and foster the enactment of their professional identities is by taking steps to ensure they have positive organizational socialization experiences," "especially when they first begin teaching" (Toth, Griffiths, and Thirolf 2013, 106). However, in our institution, as in many two-year college settings, instructors teach four (or more) courses per semester, with sometimes all four courses in the first-year writing program and course caps of twenty-two or twenty-four students. Prioritizing professional enrichment activities over the immediate "triage" of preparing multiple lessons and class periods every day can seem impractical or even impossible.

This tension between the immediate demands of teaching and the long-term investment in skill development was reflected in the experiences of one instructor working off the tenure track who, even though she chose not to complete the scheduled activities for compensation, appreciated the resources to support rethinking her courses. She wrote: "Although I did not complete the Grant Project, I thought my feedback might be useful as I did, actually, redesign ENG102 and am in the process of redesigning 101," elaborating that "In the end, I decided to use the resources to improve my class, but didn't choose to complete the project or seek compensation for it. I think this was largely due to my discomfort with the online format." This instructor's experience illustrated some of the challenges of these kinds of projects: the learning curve for instructors who aren't necessarily technologically oriented, the labor-intensive nature of simultaneously teaching exclusively first-year writing and working on curricular redesign—let alone balancing this work with service and research. Coupled with the other demands instructors have on their non-work time, it's no surprise that not all instructors were able to fully participate in the project. Nevertheless, she and others are able to make use of the resources in ways that fit with their needs and availability, which speaks to the importance of flexible and multiple forms of materials.

For example, participating instructors faced some material barriers to successfully completing the work on the timetable set by the academic and fiscal year. Timelines and the online format sometimes collided to make self-directed participation in online discussions and submission of materials challenging: "I found the online format quite confusing, and I felt continually unsure of what I was supposed to be doing and where I should be in the process. I didn't understand how what I was doing fit into the overall timeline, and I am afraid learned helplessness resulted," confessed one instructor who asked to remain anonymous. Other material barriers associated with working off the tenure track and thus having little control over her schedule described another instructor's barriers, as she noted: "Not having a class of 098 the following semester to validate program changes" prevented her from full implementation of the redesign. Scheduling and employment considerations were factors we hadn't necessarily considered when designing the project.

For those participants who faced time pressures, the requirement that instructors produce documents to contribute to an online "archive" of materials (that could subsequently be used to assess the project's effectiveness and add to a repository of materials) became unmanageable when combined with their other responsibilities. One tenure-track instructor noted this challenge of balancing the course revision with other obligations: "at the same time, sometimes I struggled to keep up with generating the assignment sheets, peer review guidelines, etc., even though a lot of that work was done for me 'and available on the website. I'm still in the process of revising some of the course materials so that they're more in my own words." Another non-tenure track instructor appreciated the opportunity to grow and to reexamine her curriculum, but like many writing instructors, finding time to fit in professional development and growth is difficult:

> For me, the main challenge was fitting a workshop (in which I was expected to produce thoughtful work) into my busy schedule, but I felt the facilitators were patient enough, supportive enough, and encouraging enough to help me succeed. I am always glad when I have the chance and challenge to look at the research on teaching in connection with course design, and the stipend, which I was able to apply to further Professional Development, was a great motivator for me.

For veteran instructors who had been teaching in the department for many years, like Dr. Elizabeth Zanichkowsky of UW-Waukesha, the opportunity to refresh her approach was welcome, but shifting emphasis in assessing student work was a stress point: "I found it difficult to adjust my reading expectations for student assignments, and to adjust my approach to grammar and mechanical difficulties, which almost all my students continue to present." For instructors across employment categories and length of instructional experience, developing in new ways as instructors presented a range of challenges including material, technological, logistical, and intellectual.

Nonetheless, participant feedback suggested that in substance, shifting to a new curricular focus that had been designed in response to research on student learning needs helped them better understand how and what students were learning in their writing courses. For example, Carrie Shipers, adjusting from a research-intensive institution with well-prepared students and multiple, unsequenced first-year writing courses, found her courses enriched by a new understanding of how students develop college-level reading, writing, and thinking skills, observing that "for the first time, I understood how to make assignments incremental in terms of the skills they required and how to help students progress in the course from assignment to assignment. Previously, I'd assigned multiple essays that did basically the same thing each time and hoped students would improve through repetition." UW-Barron County instructor Lee Friederich pointed to growth in her understanding of the value of self-assessment writing:

> On the macro level, I learned further appreciation of student reflection as an integral part of the writing and growth process. This metacognitive approach, I learned, helps students become more aware of the positive progress that they are making in their writing over the course of the semester while at the same time helps them to look ahead to the next step in their development as writers.

Ann Mattis, at UW-Sheboygan, highlighted the "takeaways" from assessing her students' end-of-semester work: "after reading my students' researched position essays, I am convinced that their reading skills and ability to identify what they were doing (e.g., synthesis and rhetorical analysis) had improved. In course evaluations, students mentioned 'reading' (as well as writing) as something they had improved upon over the course of the semester." What all these instructor comments reinforced for us was the value of continuing to reflect, talk, and develop as teachers at all stages of our careers—and the sometimes significant barriers to this necessary work.

They also illustrate and reinforce observations made in Christie Toth and Patrick Sullivan's (2016) article "Toward Local Teacher-Scholars Communities of Practice: Findings from a National TYCA Survey," which both comments on the material constraints of engaging in scholarly activity and offers practical suggestions for the field to make writing studies scholarship more accessible to and used by two-year college English faculty (Toth and Sullivan 2016). As they observe, teacher-scholar communities of practice, like the ones our faculty development project aimed to create, can make professional "engagement an authentic and collaborative component of teaching practice and, therefore, of professional identity" (263). Supporting the ongoing development of faculty in two-year college settings must be intentional and valued.

Implications and Conclusions

Ann Penrose's (2012) "Professional Identity in a Contingent-Labor Profession: Expertise, Autonomy, Community in Composition Teaching" resonated with us as we reflect on this project. As Penrose notes, professional development can have both enriching and coercive connotations:

> the concept of professional development can be corrupted under this power structure . . . under the conditions of contingent employment, "professional development" can easily be interpreted as a euphemism for brainwashing or remediation, deepening the skepticism with which such activities are often viewed in university culture. Under this interpretation, professional development activities are intended to regulate and regularize and thus present a clear challenge to an experienced faculty member's autonomy and professional identity. (Penrose 2012)

Our participants ranged from fairly new instructors who were adapting to the new setting and to the profession of teaching college writing generally along with tenured, senior faculty who had been teaching in the department for two decades. We agree with Artze-Vega et al. (2013), who note that "success in faculty development begins with admitting that we have more questions than answers and with accepting the challenge of continually revising our teaching and reassessing our learning" (177). But we are also left with questions about how to sustain development opportunities for instructors, how to manage intra-departmental disagreement about what department priorities for professional development should be, and how to continually refresh and support our development activities in a time of ever-receding resources.

We also want to highlight some of the continuing challenges we face in our own department—but that we think are shared by many institutions that are open-admissions and whose staff work primarily off the tenure track in part-time or full-time contingent positions. For example, some of our participants who revised a course planned to implement the curricular redesign the following semester or year—but working off the tenure track, they had little control over their course schedule, including which courses they were assigned and which were cancelled because of low enrollment.

Further, department change work is messy, difficult, and often recursive—with forward progress followed by regression, for various reasons. As Jeff Klausman (2010) reported on his survey of adjunct faculty at his campus, "I knew from experience that any changes to curriculum, any new assessment processes, any new professional development initiatives would be viewed with suspicion by our adjunct faculty, who have no job security and who have historically been institutionally marginalized," and "are somewhat to very resentful at teaching so much of a program's courses while receiving so little in terms of pay and benefits. Also, adjunct faculty are often invited to join full-time faculty in program work but have very little incentive to do that" (363). Though our project included both adjunct and tenure-line faculty, contingent instructors were the largest proportion, with twenty-two of the thirty participants who completed all the activities working off the tenure track, and just one of thirty participants a tenured member of the department. So while this curricular change work is valuable in providing instructors with resources to do their jobs better, the material conditions of their work (which may include little campus support for the efforts and employment instability subject to the fluctuations of enrollment) influences the overall impact of professional development. And with an English department staff hovering around 140 instructors, the actual number of participants and facilitators makes up just 25 percent of the total teaching staff.

With the increasing reliance on adjunct instruction in higher education, particularly in writing programs, we affirm the central importance of department-wide professional development resources for all instructors, particularly to support pedagogies, assessment methods, and course design that respond to the complex needs of students at open-access institutions. In *College English*, Ed Nagelhout and Julie Staggers commented on how departments can support faculty development, charging that many professional statements from CCCC (Conference on College Composition and Communication) and TYCA "focus primarily on miscast ideals of indoctrination and surveillance," arguing that though position statements do not consider "the reality of teaching as a contingent faculty member. They fail to consider lack of security; they fail to consider a standard workload; and, more important, they describe expectations in terms of 'characteristics' without considering the kinds of support necessary to develop skills for good teaching over time" (Arnold et al. 2011, 418). Recognizing these critiques, as a profession, we must consider that, as The Association of Departments of English (ADE) Ad Hoc Committee on Staffing notes, "[O]nly 32% of faculty members in English, across all institutions, hold tenured or tenure-track positions" (4). If we cannot develop sustainable opportunities for faculty professional development that supports all instructors regardless of employment status, then it will be next to impossible to improve overall quality of pedagogy, curriculum, and assessment, all crucial elements for student retention.

This project highlights several takeaways for our writing program and our instructors. The importance of permanence and flexibility of resources is paramount, as the changing nature of employment conditions for those who teach writing means there will always be ongoing needs for professional development and barriers to pursuing such activities, including relative instability of our WPA position and an increase in the percentage of department members working off the tenure track. However, the likelihood of sustainability of faculty development work beyond the project can be increased, we believe, through several strategies.

- First, build responsibilities for faculty development into position descriptions.

In our own institution, ongoing development was viewed largely as an individual responsibility, one that instructors managed independently and that catered to their specific interests. This is not a practical model for faculty development at access institutions, given the percentage of instructors who work at multiple campuses/institutions, earn low wages, and are ineligible in some departments for funding to attend conferences or pursue other external professional activities. Intradepartmental work is a critical strategy for onboarding new instructors, and increasing instructor effectiveness through mentoring.

- Second, use assessment of local student, instructor, and overall department needs to drive change and build the case for instructor development in relation to student retention.

Identifying—in a systematic way—the specific areas of growth in teaching and learning is key to creating benchmarks, building a baseline set of data, and supporting claims about faculty development that focuses on student success and retention. Our institutional research and the resources we were able to secure as a result of systematically collected evidence created both a foundation and leverage for additional opportunities, including helping institutional administrators understand the importance of faculty development, applying for program recognition through national organization awards, securing additional grant funding, and participating in conversations with philanthropic foundations and policy research groups.

- Third, value the work of ongoing course redesign and continual reflection.

For us, that means ongoing assessment of curricular and instructional resources in response to continuing shifts in our campus student populations and feedback from faculty development participants. Our department also revised our annual merit evaluation process using a more standard but still responsive and flexible rubric that more carefully defined the kinds of teaching and professional activities that were valued by the department. An emphasis on reflection can also mean securing or reallocating funds that support reflective and curricular revision work, acknowledging it as labor that is an expected, necessary, and vital part of effective teaching.

In these ways, we hope to sustain the positive changes in instructor development and evidence-based curricular programming that initiated at our access institution. Increasing retention of our diverse students cannot be separate from supporting our instructors' abilities to meet students' needs.

Notes

1. See Eagan and Jaeger 2009 for research demonstrating the inverse relationship between student transfer and exposure to contingent instructors.
2. The full set of learning outcomes for the first-year writing program are available at our program website: www.uwc.edu/literacy.
3. The University of Wisconsin Colleges received the Diana Hacker TYCA Outstanding Program Award in 2015: "Developing a Cohesive Academic Literacy Program for Underprepared Students in the University of Wisconsin's Writing Program" (University of Wisconsin Colleges English Department 2015). The UW Colleges use multiple measures placement and an integrated developmental and first-year writing program to address barriers to academic success for underprepared students. Multiple measures placement informs curriculum, learning outcomes, and faculty development activities that help academically underprepared students transition from developmental writing to credit-bearing composition and eventually complete a core transfer-level research course.
4. Participating instructors provided permission to quote their reflections and indicated whether to be named or quoted anonymously in this essay. This project received approval from the University of Wisconsin Colleges Institutional Review Board in 2013 and renewed approval for continuation in 2014.

References

Arnold, Lisa, Laura Brady, Maggie Christensen, Joanne Baird Giordano, Holly Hassel, Ed Nagelhout, Nathalie Singh-Corcoran, and Julie Staggers. 2011. "Forum on the Profession." *College English* 73 (March): 409–27.

Artze-Vega, Isis, Melody Bowdon, Kimberly Emmons, Michele Eodice, Susan K. Hess, Claire Coleman Lamonica, and Gerald Nelms. 2013. "Privileging Pedagogy: Composition, Rhetoric, and Faculty Development." *College Composition and Communication* 65 (Sept): 162–84.

Calhoon-Dillahunt, Carolyn. 2011. "Writing Programs without Administrators: Frameworks for Successful Writing Programs in the Two-Year College." *WPA: Journal of Council of Writing Program Administrators* 35:118–34.

Council of Writing Program Administrators. 2014. "WPA Outcomes Statement for First-Year Composition (3.0)." 17 July. http://wpacouncil.org/positions/outcomes.html. Accessed 23 September 2016.

Department of Education. 2011. "Meeting President Obama's 2020 College Completion Goal." July 11. http://www.ed.gov/news/speeches/meeting-president-obamas-2020 -college-completion-goal.

Eagan, M. Kevin, Jr., and A. J. Jaeger. 2009. "Effects of Exposure to Part-time Faculty on Community College Transfer." *Research in Higher Education* 50 (168).

Hassel, Holly, and Joanne Baird Giordano. 2013. "Occupy Writing Studies: Rethinking College Composition for the Needs of the Teaching Majority." *College Composition and Communication.* 65 (1): 117–39.

Klausman, Jeffrey. 2008. "Mapping the Terrain: The Two-Year College Writing Program Administrator." *Teaching English in the Two-Year College* 35:238–51.

Klausman, Jeffrey. 2010. "Not Just a Matter of Fairness: Adjunct Faculty and Writing Programs in Two-Year Colleges." *Teaching English in the Two-Year College* 37:363–71.

Klausman, Jeffrey. 2013. "Toward a Definition of a Writing Program at a Two-Year College: You Say You Want a Revolution?" *Teaching English in the Two-Year College* 40:257–73.

Krebs, Paula. 2014. "The Great Mismatch." *Inside Higher Ed,* October 15. http://app3 .insidehighered.com/views/2006/01/05/hall.

Laurence, David. 2008. "Demography of the Faculty: A Statistical Portrait of English and Foreign Languages." Modern Language Association. December 10. http://www.mla .org/pdf/demography_fac2.pdfhttp://www.mla.org/pdf/demography_fac2.pdf.

Nettesheim, Gregg. 2014. "New Freshman Retention by High School Rank by Course Load." Unpublished Institutional Report, University of Wisconsin Colleges.

Penrose, Ann. 2012. "Professional Identity in a Contingent-Labor Profession: Expertise, Autonomy, Community in Composition Teaching." *WPA. Writing Program Administration* 35 (Spring): 108–26.

Reichert Powell, Pegeen. 2009. "Retention and Writing Instruction: Implications for Access and Pedagogy." *College Composition and Communication* 60 (June): 664–82.

Sullivan, Patrick. 2008. "Measuring 'Success' at Open Admissions Institutions." *College English* 70 (July): 618–32.

Toth, Christina, Brett W. Griffiths, and Kathryn Thirolf. 2013. "'Distinct and Significant': Professional Identities of Two-Year College English Faculty." *College Composition and Communication* 65 (Sept): 90–116.

Toth, Christie, and Patrick Sullivan. 2016. "Toward Local Teacher-Scholar Communities of Practice: Findings from a National TYCA Survey." *Teaching English in the Two-Year College* 43 (3): 247–73.

Two-Year College English Association. 2004. "Guidelines for the Academic Preparation of English Faculty at Two-Year Colleges." National Council of Teachers of English. http://www.ncte.org/library/NCTEFiles/Groups/TYCA/TYCAGuidelines.pdf.

University of Wisconsin Colleges English Department. 2015. "University of Wisconsin Colleges Academic Literacy Resources." June 12. https://sites.google.com/a/gapps .uwc.edu/uw-colleges-academic-literacy-resources/.

University of Wisconsin Colleges English Department. 2016. "UW Colleges Academic Literacy Resources." http://uwc.edu/depts/english/resources. Accessed 23 September 2016.

University of Wisconsin System Office of Policy Analysis and Research. 2014. "Retention and Graduation: 2013–14." Informational Memorandum. https://www.wisconsin.edu /reports-statistics/download/educational_statistics/informational_memoranda/rg13 -14.pdf.

University of Wisconsin System Office of Policy Analysis and Research. 2015. Informational Memorandum. "The New Freshman Class: Fall 2014." https://www.wisconsin .edu/reports-statistics/download/educational_statistics/informational_memoranda /The-New-Freshman-Class,-Fall-2014.pdf.

Wiggins, Grant, and Jay McTighe. 2005. *Understanding by Design.* 2nd ed. Alexandria, VA: ASCD.

6

HOW STUDENT PERFORMANCE IN FIRST-YEAR COMPOSITION PREDICTS RETENTION AND OVERALL STUDENT SUCCESS

Nathan Garrett, Matthew Bridgewater, and Bruce Feinstein

WHY RETENTION MATTERS

Consider the following statistics from a video published by the Educational Testing Service (ETS) citing the Georgetown Public Policy Institute Center on Education and the Workforce:

- "By 2020, more than 2/3s of all jobs will require higher education.
- "Nearly 50% of community college students drop out by their second year.
- "Only 56% of four year degree seekers finish within 6 years.
- "Less than a third of full time 2-year degree seekers graduate within 3 years" (Educational Testing Service 2014).[1]

These findings show that a higher education degree is not only becoming more critical than ever, but that the road to that degree is surprisingly perilous and uncertain. While the research mentioned above brings a sense of urgency to retention issues, it's important to note that research on retention and improving student engagement and success has been going on for decades in various colleges and universities and by numerous educational organizations,[2] frequently focusing on socioeconomic, institutional, curricular, and student dispositional impacts on retention. Furthermore, students, their parents, and other stakeholders can now more easily assess universities via the United States Department of Education's College Scorecard website (College Scorecard 2015). The original goal of this website was to rank universities using several criteria, including the average annual cost of attending, the salary earned by graduates after attending, and the graduation rate of the university. The Obama administration, under pressure from universities and colleges, decided to drop the ranking aspect of this

DOI: 10.7330/9781607326021.c006

project, but it still easily allows prospective students and their parents to easily locate data, such as graduation rate, when looking into universities and colleges. This transparency is a good thing. And it is one factor that puts extra pressure on colleges and universities to devote time, resources, and money to improving graduation rates.

FIRST-YEAR WRITING'S PLACE IN THE RETENTION DISCUSSION

Writing studies has already contributed much to our understanding of what issues impact student learning in a writing classroom, for example, class size (Horning 2007; National Council of Teachers of English 2013), responding to student writing (Sommers, Rutz, and Tinberg 2006; White and Wright 2016), best practices for assessment (Broad 2003; Huot and O'Neill 2009), writing across the curriculum (Zawacki and Rogers 2012), and service learning components to writing courses (Deans 2000; Grabill 2007). Scholars in writing studies have studied these issues and practices (as well as many others) to help students achieve greater success as writers.

In addition, writing courses and writing classrooms are highly valued as pivotal sites in higher education. The National Survey of Student Engagement (NSSE) works with the Council of Writing Program Administrators (WPA) to "explore the relationships between writing and learning" and to use writing "to enhance students' mastery of course content and achievement of other important goals of higher education" (Anderson et al. 2015). Written communication is one of the pivotal VALUES Rubrics created by the Association of American Colleges and Universities. Most universities and colleges must assess writing in some way in order to remain accredited.

We also know that "first-year studies" courses and the student's first year at university or college are a critical time in engaging the student and laying the foundation for future success at the school. These first-year studies courses help students acclimate to university life, teach them how to use resources on campus, and assist students in developing study and other academic skills such as technology use and time management. It's not too surprising then that these first-year studies course have also been shown to improve student retention at university and college (Goodman and Pascarella 2006; Porter and Swing 2006). Similar to this positive curricular impact on retention is the success of summer bridge programs that help students—particularly students testing into basic writing—begin university and college on the right foot (McCurrie 2009).

To summarize, scholars in writing studies have diligently researched how to improve student success in writing classrooms, we know writing is valued in the greater context of higher education, and we know that the first-year (and preparing students to succeed in the first-year) is especially critical to long term success for a student in higher education.

But some in writing studies have called for greater attention when it comes to the specific relationship between first-year writing courses and the larger retention issues colleges and universities face as a whole. For example, in her *College Composition and Communication* (*CCC*) article "Retention and Writing Instruction: Implications for Access and Pedagogy," Pegeen Reichert Powell (2009) shows that first-year composition (FYC) has been somewhat absent from this conversation and argues that writing scholars should pay attention to the data and discourses surrounding postsecondary retention. And in their *Journal of Writing Program Administration* article "Predicting Success: Increasing Retention and Pass Rates in College Composition," Beth Brunk-Chavez and Elaine Fredericksen claim that while "Composition Studies has moved us forward in terms of placement and assessment," data on "retention and success in the composition classroom" has been lacking (Brunk-Chavez and Fredericksen 2008, 76).

Our project puts FYC at the forefront of retention, especially as it compares to other first-year courses and those courses which are in a student's major. While retention can be studied from a variety of viewpoints by considering socioeconomic,[3] institutional,[4] or attitudinal[5] impacts, our study is part of a larger segment of research that focuses on curricular impacts on retention rates. Curricular impacts can be quite varied, but the following research highlights how curricular policy affects retention and what some of these curricular variables are.

OUR STUDY: FIRST-YEAR COMPOSITION AND STUDENT RETENTION

While the scholarship indicates that FYC courses must play a critical role in student retention, few larger scale studies exist that explore this connection. We ask: is there anything unique about FYC compared with other first-year, second-year, or other general education (GE) curricular impacts? Our study examines FYC as a curricular variable just as other curricular variables (course costs, undecided options, and first-year studies courses) potentially impact retention. Because FYC touches the lives of nearly every student that comes through an institution of higher education, the relationship between student performance in FYC and their success at the university is one that can lead to further insights about the relationship between writing and student success in higher education.

We present quantitative data and analysis to highlight findings that demonstrate both the need to pay attention to the relationship between retention and FYC and to highlight unforeseen relationships between retention, FYC, and a student's other coursework. Specifically, our study analyzes institutional data to answer the question: does success and failure in FYC courses predict success and failure in individual majors? Our research produced four significant findings: (1) students who earn a C- or less in FYC (which at this university is considered failing) have only a 17 percent chance of graduation compared to a 53 percent chance for students who pass FYC; (2) the odds of a student passing an FYC course the second or third time retaking it fall dramatically; (3) contrary to impressions that a student's success is determined in the major courses, the researchers found that failing an FYC course has nearly the same impact for a student than failing a major-related class does; and (4) among all GE courses, we found a particularly important cluster consisting of first-year library science, first-year public speaking, and FYC that predicts retention stronger than any other GE cluster. And out of those three courses, FYC performance was the class most closely tied to impacting retention. Whether for reasons of motivation, language skills, first-generation status, work-life balance, or inadequate preparation, students struggling in FYC also struggle in their major. The FYC course, then, should have a privileged position in terms of paying attention to student success and retention.

In the first section of this chapter, we discuss the specific research questions, research methodology, and research site. Then, we analyze and interpret the data in our data analysis section. Next, our discussion section focuses in on the most important findings and discusses their implications more thoroughly. And, finally, this chapter concludes by presenting strategies for how writing programs can use this data to support student success and maximize a writing program's power, prestige, and position within a university in an era where support and resources can be limited.

RESEARCH METHODOLOGY

We worked with a small university's administrators and Institutional Review Board (IRB) to gain access to student course records. The university is located in a major metropolitan area, emphasizes design and professional degrees, and is a minority majority university that enrolls a large number of first-generation and transfer students.

Table 6.1. Student Information

Freshman Entering Cohorts

Year	Count	Graduated	Minority	Male	International
2004	131	55%	55%	27%	3%
2005	121	55%	52%	29%	5%
2006	135	63%	52%	44%	5%
2007	157	50%	53%	37%	10%
2008	145	43%	61%	48%	16%
Summary	689	53%	55%	37%	8%

Transfer Entering Cohorts

Year	Count	Graduated	Minority	Male	International
2004	237	70%	54%	49%	3%
2005	206	66%	47%	46%	4%
2006	177	64%	50%	45%	6%
2007	162	68%	51%	47%	2%
2008	198	59%	39%	45%	11%
2009	204	46%	39%	49%	11%
2010	195	46%	46%	47%	12%
Summary	1,379	60%	46%	47%	7%

Table 6.1 describes each cohort. There are some variances between cohorts, such as increased numbers of international students. Transfer student graduation rates also decrease over time, though that is partly a result of not limiting graduation to a six-year or four-year window. However, the composition of the cohorts does not dramatically change over time.

While data from Fall 2004 to Spring 2014 were provided, we excluded cohorts without sufficient time to graduate. The resulting data set included transfer students who entered between 2004 and 2010, and non-transfer (first-year) students who began between 2004 and 2008. In both cases, only fall entrants were included. Graduation status was not limited to a six-year or four-year window, meaning that students from older cohorts had more time to complete than students from newer groups.

After identifying students in these cohorts, we extracted all of their course grades. This resulted in a total of 52,142 rows of data. Each row contained the grade for a single course and the student's information (e.g., ethnicity, major, graduation status). Transfer courses from other universities were not included in the analysis.

All students are placed into writing and math classes. The FYC courses include three courses. Students may be placed in basic writing (WRIT 100), introduction to college writing (WRIT 111), or college writing (WRIT 112). Students must earn a C or above to progress through the WRIT courses. There are also two remedial math classes (MATH 049 and 149), which lead to college algebra (MATH 249).

The grade for each class was classified as *pass* or *fail*. Grades of C- or below were classified as a *fail*, since students must maintain a GPA greater than 2.0 to remain in good academic standing. While students can often continue in their major with a GPA under 2.0, earning a C- or below in FYC blocks them from all upper division GE classes, as well as some writing-based courses inside of their major. Students who earn a low GPA over two semesters are put on probation, and ultimately subject to dismissal.

DATA ANALYSIS METHODOLOGY

To understand the impact of course grades on retention, we used a simplified version of Association Rule Mining (see Agrawal, Imieliński, and Swami 1993; Ahmed, Paul, and Hoque 2014). In Association Rule Mining, a large number of individual events are examined to find interesting rules. For example, we could examine food in a supermarket cart. A potential discovery could be that people who purchase onions, beef, and chips also buy hamburger buns.

To prepare for the course grades for analysis, we generated a new field for each row. This field could have four possible states: pass and graduate, pass and drops out, fail and graduate, fail and drops out. These four states were then used to examine the predictive quality of a single course grade. These are shown in Figure 6.1. Note that we only used records from the *first* time a student attempts a course; a student can fail the course, but still graduate after taking the class again and passing it.

Setting our unit of analysis as the course is unusual. In our data set, a single student will show up multiple times, once for the *first* time *each* class is taken. Normal statistical approaches would organize the data by student, with a separate column (or attribute) for every class they take. However, there are hundreds of different classes in our data set. Organizing our data by student would result in hundreds of columns for each row. Most statistical approaches have difficulty dealing with this number of variables (especially since most would be empty). In contrast,

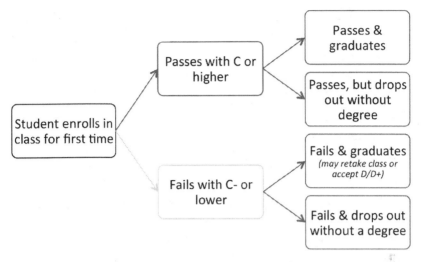

Figure 6.1. Course Grade Logic

Association Rule Mining allows us to analyze a virtually unlimited number of classes. The major problem with this type of approach is that students who take more classes are over-represented when compared to students who take few classes. However, since we are focusing on the impact of individual classes, this problem is avoided.

The most serious limitation of any project examining the historical impact of individual classes is a lack of causality. A correlation between two variables is relatively simple to show. However, it is impossible to know if the first variable influences the second, or if they are both explained by an underlying (possibly unmeasured) third variable. Correlational data is typically enhanced by including proxy variables for student preparation or demographics (such as SAT scores or minority status).

However, at this university, these variables are not equally distributed. For example, female students predominate in the fashion design program, and male students in architecture. A correlation analysis of the major demographics variables shows that while most are statistically significant, they are relatively small in magnitude. Table 6.2 shows first-year courses in the major and the three writing courses. It displays the correlation between these courses and demographic flags. Values not statistically significant are left blank.

While the table shows that demographics have a statistically significant relationship with success, the magnitude of this relationship is fairly small. The uneven distribution of these variables across programs also makes the results suspect.

Table 6.2. Achievement Correlation with Demographics

	Major & Writing Freshman Class Grades	GPA in Major (next term)	Overall GPA	Is Graduated
Is Domestic	0.02		0.03	0.01
Is Male	−0.10	−0.13	−0.17	−0.05
Is International	−0.02		−0.03	−0.01
Is Minority	−0.11	−0.14	−0.20	−0.10

Finally, the goal of this project was to generate information useful for curriculum design (as opposed to knowledge about the role of demographic variables). While the success is partially explained through underlying demographics, results developed by examining individual courses can be more useful for curriculum design and advising.

THE RELATIONSHIP BETWEEN COURSE GRADES AND LATER SUCCESS

Now that the methodology section has defined our approach, we can then begin to understand the relationship between pass rates and graduation. How does success or failure in a single class predict if a student will graduate?

The three classes in the writing sequence, and the remaining ten most common lower-division GE courses, are shown in Table 6.3. The courses are also grouped by year, as students taking sophomore classes have a higher likelihood of graduation than those taking first-year courses.

All of these courses prove to be useful predictors of graduation. For example, looking at COMM 120 (Public Speaking) shows that 17 percent of students failed the class on their first attempt. Of these sixty-seven students, only 35 percent successfully completed their degree. Students who passed the class graduated at much higher rates, with 66 percent completing their degree. The large difference between the two rates shows that COMM 120 is an important predictor of student success. While public speaking is not thought of as a high failure course, it rivals the rates in math and writing.

When evaluating the courses from an improvement standpoint, some are more important than others. For example, PPDV 100 is a one-unit introduction to college course. Students who fail this course the first time graduate at a rate of only 24 percent. However, only 4 percent of students fail the course. As a result, dedicating resources to

Table 6.3. Course Pass and Graduation Rates, First Attempt in Common GE Courses

Class	Students Taking Course	Students Failing Course	Fail Rate	Passed and Graduated	Failed and Graduated	Reduced?
FRESHMAN COURSES						
COMM 120: Public Speaking	619	67	17%	66%	35%	31%
LSCI 105: Info. Literacy	985	78	11%	63%	30%	33%
MATH 049: Algebra	584	76	20%	53%	35%	18%
MATH 149: Intermed. Algebra	632	73	17%	62%	33%	29%
PPDV 100: Intro to College	679	22	4%	54%	24%	30%
WRIT 100: Bridge to Writing	246	39	19%	46%	17%	29%
WRIT 111: Academic Writing	685	94	18%	59%	22%	38%
WRIT 112: Research Writing	952	76	11%	64%	26%	38%
SOPHOMORE COURSES						
ARTH 204: Modern Art	298	33	14%	66%	21%	45%
ARTH 205: Contemp. Art	951	85	14%	70%	37%	34%
ECON 203: Macro Econ.	287	36	23%	79%	45%	34%
MATH 249: College Algebra	472	52	20%	69%	46%	23%
PSYC 200: Intro Psychology	536	62	18%	75%	35%	40%

improving success in this class will have a small proportional impact on the institution.

It is also important to emphasize that a course may not necessarily have a causal relationship with graduation rates. For example, LSCI

105 (Information Literacy) introduces students to library research. This one-unit course has a failure rate of 11 percent, and failing students have a 33 percent lower graduation rate (reduced from 63% to 30%). But, failing a one-unit library course is not likely to have a direct effect upon graduation. Evaluating when a student took it (e.g., as a first-year, sophomore, junior, or senior) also showed little difference in graduation rates. Instead, failing this course signals an underlying problem. This problem could be a lack of student preparation, poor time management skills, or even a student's attitude toward GE courses. From an institutional improvement perspective, LSCI 105 serves as an important warning flag. While not *causing* failure, it signals advisors that a student falls into an "at risk" category.

As a campus with over half of the students in design and creative disciplines, the three math courses have often been viewed as the most significant GE hurdle. However, while failing these courses reduces student success, they are less of a problem than other classes. For example, students who fail MATH 049 (Elementary Algebra) have a reduced graduation rate of only 18 percent (from 53% to 35%). Of the first-year courses, this is the smallest "failure impact." MATH 149 (Intermediate Algebra) has a more significant predicted reduction (29%) but is still in line with other courses.

Of all of the first-year courses, students who fail the writing sequence have the lowest predicted graduation rate. Students who fail WRIT 100 (the most basic remedial writing course) have only a 17 percent predicted graduation rate. Failing WRIT 111 (Academic Writing) or WRIT 112 (Research Writing) reduces a student's chance of graduation by 38 percent, more than any other first-year class.

The sophomore courses are also valuable predictors of student success. With the exception of MATH 249 (College Algebra), they all result in a large failure impact. Even failing art history classes, which may not seem particularly critical, are associated with 34–45 percent lower graduation rates. Failing an art history course is unlikely to cause dropout, but it is a valid predictor of success.

THE NEGATIVE IMPACT OF REPEATING A COURSE

A picture of student success in a single course can be further enriched by examining second and third attempts at taking a course. In general, each time a student retakes a course, their success rate in the course goes down. Table 6.4 shows the success rates by attempt for core classes. Courses with fewer than five attempts on the nth attempt are left blank.

Table 6.4. Graduation Rates by Attempt

Class	*First Attempt*				*Second Attempt*				*Third Attempt*			
	n	*Fail Rate*	*Pass Grad Rate*	*Fail Grad Rate*	*n*	*Fail Rate*	*Pass Grad Rate*	*Fail Grad Rate*	*n*	*Fail Rate*	*Pass Grad Rate*	*Fail Grad Rate*
FIRST-YEAR COURSES												
COM 120	619	17%	66%	35%	42	33%	68%	21%				
LSCI 105	985	11%	63%	30%	75	19%	66%	36%	8	13%	57%	0%
MATH 049	584	20%	53%	35%	67	31%	61%	24%	9	11%	38%	100%
MATH 149	632	17%	62%	33%	68	29%	69%	35%	9	44%	80%	25%
PPDV 100	679	4%	54%	24%	23	0%	74%					
WRIT 100	246	19%	46%	17%	37	32%	40%	8%	6	50%	33%	0%
WRIT 111	685	18%	59%	22%	02	32%	55%	6%	23	57%	30%	0%
WRIT 112	952	11%	64%	26%	88	27%	53%	25%	19	42%	45%	13%
SECOND-YEAR COURSES												
ARTH 204	298	14%	66%	21%	11	36%	57%	0%				
ARTH 205	951	14%	70%	37%	48	13%	62%	0%				
ECON 203	287	23%	79%	45%	19	32%	77%	0%				
MATH 249	472	20%	69%	46%	40	30%	61%	17%	6	17%	20%	100%
PSYC 200	536	18%	75%	35%	39	31%	59%	25%				

A student who takes a class multiple times shows up more than once. For example, a student may fail the first attempt, and pass the second. Their first failing attempt will be used to calculate the columns under "First Attempt." Their second passing attempt will be used to calculate the columns under "Second Attempt."

The difference between passing and failing a course on the second attempt is dramatic. For example, students who fail COMM 120 (Public Speaking) on the second attempt have a 47 percent lower graduation rate than students who pass the course on the second attempt (from 68% to only 21%). Students who fail MATH 049 on the second attempt have a low rate of only 24 percent (from 61%).

The second time a writing course is taken is incredibly important. Students who fail WRIT 100 (Bridge to Academic Writing) on the second try have a graduation rate of only 8 percent, compared to 40 percent for those who pass on the second attempt. Failing WRIT 111 the second time reduces a student's graduation rate to only 6 percent, which is much lower than the 55 percent graduation rate of those who pass on the second attempt. Out of all of the core GE courses, failing a writing class reduces a student's graduation rate to the lowest number.

Interestingly, in non-FYC classes, students who successfully complete the course on the second attempt have a *higher* graduation rate than those who complete the course on the first attempt. However, writing courses are an exception to this pattern. Students who pass a writing course on the second attempt have a 4–9 percent reduced graduation rate over students who pass it the first time.

The writing courses are also extremely significant due to the large number of students retaking them. For example, 13 percent of enrollments in WRIT 111 represent a second attempt, and 3 percent a third attempt. As courses with high failure rates, and that predict extremely low graduation rates, these may serve as useful advising indicators.

The Positive Relationship between FYC and Major Courses

As shown in the previous section, writing courses are key predictors of success, even when compared to other first-year courses. However, the skills in writing courses are not closely linked to skills in design disciplines (e.g., fashion design, animation, or graphic design). Why then does failing writing classes predict lower graduation rates for animation students, for example?

In presenting early versions of this project to faculty from these design disciplines, one common response was to assert that major-based and GE courses require different student competencies. As a result, faculty asserted that failing GE courses did not suggest that students would do poorly in the major. They believed that students were doing well in major-based classes, but failing their GE classes. Faculty believed that their visually oriented students were being prevented from graduating by overly difficult GE classes that might not draw on their students' strengths.

Answering this assertion required some further data manipulation, and the creation of two distinct sets of course records. The first set included major classes taken by first-year students. While some universities prevent students from declaring a major until they enter their junior year, this university encourages students to declare a major in their first semester. While students primarily take GE classes during their first two years, they are required to take major-based classes as well. Almost all students take courses in their major classes during their first semester. The second set included course records from the three core writing courses. Each course falling in these two sets were then linked with the student's GPA in the major the following term. Only the first attempt at a course was included.

Several majors were excluded from this analysis. Some had very low numbers of students. Others programs were closed during the data collection period. Lastly, several majors offered the same classes both to majors and non-majors. For example, a communication student could have taken a COMM course as part of getting their communication degree, but alongside them may have been a business major taking the course as part of the GE requirements. Excluding the communication and psychology majors from analysis resolved this problem.

Essentially, this analysis attempts to ascertain the predictive quality of major courses and writing courses. If the writing course is not linked to success in the major, then there should be no relationship between a WRIT grade and GPA in the major (particularly for the next semester). If the two are related, then we would expect to see the writing and major courses both predict GPA in the major.

The simplest approach to answering this question uses SPSS to calculate the Pearson Correlation for both sets. A correlation is 1 when two variables are perfectly matched, and 0 when they are randomly related to each other. We calculated two correlation values. First, we calculated a 0.46 correlation between the grade earned in a **writing** course, and the average grades earned in the major the **following** term. Second, we calculated a 0.44 correlation between the grade earned in a **major** course, and the average grades earned in the major the **following** term. Each correlation is statistically significant at the 0.01 level, meaning that they are extremely unlikely to be the result of random chance. Because the two correlation values are almost identical, they support the belief that performance in FYC and performance in major classes are related.

Figure 6.2 demonstrates the relationship between the grade earned in a single course on the x-axis and student average GPA in the major on the y-axis. As an example, students who earned a B- in a writing course averaged 2.8 in their major the following term. Students who average a

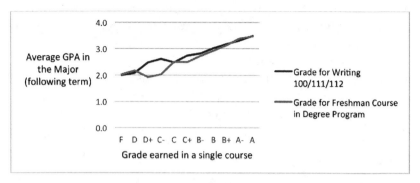

Figure 6.2. How Does a First-Year Course Predict GPA in the Major the Following Term?

B- in a first-year degree course averaged a 2.7 in the major the following term. The similarity of these results suggests that the writing courses are just as predictive of success in the major as degree courses.

Overall, Figure 6.2 shows that a single writing grade predicts the student's grade the following term *in the major*. The only major area of divergence is in the D+ and C- writing course grades. This may suggest that students struggling in the major tend to sacrifice their writing courses in order to pass their major classes. Otherwise, there is *virtually no difference* between earning a grade in a major course or a writing course. Both predict success in the major.

Most General Education Courses Grades Are Highly Correlated

Since writing courses are linked to success in the major, this leads to the question of how the other core GE course grades are related. Table 6.5 shows the Pearson Correlations between a student's grades in first-year GE courses, overall GPA, degree GPA, and graduation status (where 1 is graduated, and 0 is not graduated). All results are statistically significant. Cells are shaded to improve their visibility.

There are a number of interesting findings in these results. For example, COMM 120 (Public Speaking) continues to prove to be highly related to graduation and GPA. LSCI 105 (Information Literacy) is also a strong predictor of success. The writing courses are strongly related to both of these classes. This suggests the possibility that all of the classes share many characteristics related to overall student success.

The remedial math classes (MATH 049 and 149) are the weakest predictors of graduation and GPA among the set. While they are correlated

Table 6.5. GE Correlations

	Major GPA	Graduate	COMM 120	LSCI 105	MATH 049	MATH 149	PPDV 100	WRIT 100	WRIT 111	WRIT 112
Overall GPA	.91	.49	.67	.63	.48	.52	.45	.69	.71	.66
Major GPA		.46	.56	.54	.35	.38	.34	.53	.56	.51
Graduated?			.31	.28	.21	.20	.21	.28	.33	.33
COMM 120				.32	.33	.30	.32	.44	.49	.46
LSCI 105					.29	.34	.28	.43	.53	.42
MATH 049						.40	.19	.39	.24	.22
MATH 149							.15	.43	.30	.23
PPDV 100								.33	.32	.27
WRIT 100									.45	.22
WRIT 111										.49

with each other at a 0.4 level, this is not much different from their relationship with COMM 120 (0.33/0.30) or WRIT 100 (0.39/0.43). Their weakest course relationship is with WRIT 111 and 112.

These correlations suggest that there is some degree of clustering between related classes, but that, in general, most grades are related. Students who do well in core GE courses tend to do well in all classes. Overall, the strongest predictor of student success appears to not be math courses, but instead courses focusing on language and research skills (writing, public speaking, and information literacy).

DISCUSSION

Overall, first-year courses strongly predict student graduation and success in the degree.

First, performance in writing courses strongly predicts both graduation and success in the major. Among all first-year GE courses, failing a writing course is the best indicator of a student not graduating. Students who fail writing twice are particularly vulnerable. Even when looking at GPA in the major, we see that grades in writing classes are equally good predictors as degree courses.

Second, we see that performance in GE courses is strongly correlated. Within GE courses, there appears to be a cluster of courses focusing on language and research skills, including public speaking, writing, and information literacy, which is particularly strongly correlated with student retention.

Third, even small one-unit courses are valid predictors of success. While a one-unit "Introduction to College" course may not *cause* graduation, it is a valid predictor. It is possible that failing (or dropping) a small intro class signals that a student may be at more risk.

Overall, this study emphasizes the need for students and faculty to focus on writing courses. For institutions focused on improvement, dealing with high-dropout courses with highly predictive natures may be an ideal way to identify and resolve deficiencies. In particular, courses that focus on writing, communication, and critical thinking are related. Even when dealing with a largely domestic population, the increasing number of second language and first-generation students mean that colleges need to deal with language holistically and not through different discipline silos.

The results of this study are particular to a single campus, and may not be generalizable to all institutions. While the data is comprehensive, it is not broad enough to control for demographic variables. However, while demographic variables are important, in our data set, they had limited impact.

While demographics cannot be ignored, this study does show that writing courses can be significant predictors of success. While success in a FYC course may not *cause* success in the major, our findings show they are *related*. Whether it is for reasons of motivation, language skills, first-generation status, work-life balance, or inadequate preparation, students struggling in composition also struggle in their major.

CONCLUSION

The National Council of Teachers of English's (2013) policy research brief, "First-Year Writing: What Good Does It Do?," argues that FYC courses are unique because FYC "enhances rhetorical knowledge," "develops metacognition," and "increases student responsibility" (1–2). The brief also highlights that the "personal attention and low student/ student teacher ratios" (1) are key factors in retention and that these course characteristics are integral to the vast majority of FYC courses. Our study also highlights the uniqueness of FYC through using quantitative data and analysis to demonstrate that a student's performance in FYC, even when compared with a student's courses in the major and other GE courses, is a particularly strong predictor of whether she or he persists in her or his education.

Several curricular implications might be considered given our findings. What should be the policies of writing programs when it comes to allowing students to test out of writing classes (e.g., through AP classes or test scores, dual credit classes in high school, or placement exams) given their strong impact on academic success? At the same time, though, research has also shown that limiting students' ability to transfer in courses is negatively correlated with students finishing on time or finishing at all, and there is political pressure to increase transferability, not limit it (Monaghan and Attewell 2014; Raisman 2013). This tension between the importance of writing as a subject and set of strategies that takes time to develop and the importance of students being able to complete their degrees in a timely manner might be seen as in conflict. One potential solution would build on the strengths of writing across the curriculum programs so that students would continue to transfer in or test out of an FYC course and still have multiple, meaningful opportunities to engage with writing in a range of courses. The impact that writing ability has on students' success and persistence in their major might not be limited to just FYC writing courses but might also be impacted by writing intensive courses in their major or influenced by other elective writing courses. If this is the case, encouraging students to take writing elective courses or minor in writing could be another strategy to help promote success in the major and other GE courses while also preparing students for internships and work experience. Writing programs might reach out to university advisors and other departments to inform them of writing electives or minor options.

More research is needed on the extent to which FYC success and persistence can be impacted by other initiatives, values, and practices. As National Survey of Student Engagement founding director George Kuh notes, "institutions should aspire for all students to participate in at least two HIPs [high impact practices] over the course of their undergraduate experience—one during the first year and one in the context of their major" (NSSE 2007, 8). While writing classes have a long history as being a site for service learning, encouraging other HIPs such as undergraduate research with faculty and developing a learning community with/through writing courses might increase the effect writing courses have on an institution's overall student engagement, success, and retention. Since writing already is a high-impact practice, how might a course centered on writing incorporate some of these high impact practices? Might this have an even stronger impact on FYC's unique position in a student's academic preparation?

One limitation of our study is that while it tabulated ten years' worth of data, it was the data of just one school. We strongly recommend that our study be replicated elsewhere because empirical data should help guide writing program theory, policies, and practices. Although we began this study with the hope that our student population might give us generalizable findings, we caution that the findings may not be generalizable to institutions where entering students have different academic and demographic profiles. Like Richard Haswell (2005, 2012), we believe that empirical, data-driven studies are not replicated enough, so we hope that other schools adapt our methods to study their own populations to see whether they find similar results. Increasingly, the language of argument at universities is buttressed by empirical data. We hope that the data and analysis provided is useful to make arguments for the importance of writing and in particular FYC to colleagues in other disciplines and to college and university administrators.

Notes

1. For some specific reports that have compiled and ascertained these statistics, see Anthony P. Carnavale, Nicole Smith, and Jeff Strohl, the National Center for Education Statistics' and William C. Symonds, Robert Schwartz, and Ronald F. Ferguson (Carnavale, Smith, and Strohl 2013; Symonds, Schwartz, and Ferguson 2011).

2. For overviews of issues that affect retention, see Robert J. Sternberg's (2013) *Inside Higher Education* article "Research to Improve Retention" and Steven Mintz's (2014) *Insider Higher Education* article "Rethinking Retention."

3. Thomas G. Mortensen, Camille Stocker, and Nicole Brunt demonstrate how a student's personal or family financial situation is often a very good predictor of whether they will finish undergraduate work. Vickie Choitz and Patrick Reimherr's show that students who come from the second, third, and lowest income quarter are also more likely to be unable to come up with the money for higher education demonstrating a problem with students' access to and the availability of grants and scholarships to the students that need it most (Mortensen, Stocker, and Brunt 2012; Choitz and Reimherr 2013). And John Bound, Michael F. Lovenheim, and Sarah Turner confirm that students are taking longer to complete their bachelor degrees. They interestingly note that "they find no evidences that changes in the college preparedness or the demographic composition of degree recipients can account for the observed increases [in time it takes to finish]" but the "results suggest that declines in collegiate resources" and "increased hours of employment among students . . . likely increases time to degree by crowding out time spent on academic pursuits" (Bound, Lovenheim, and Turner 2012, 375).

4. David B. Monaghan and Paul Attewell show how institutions' transfer processes and policies can affect student graduation rates and progress to the degree (Monaghan and Attewell 2014). Neal Raisman's research argues that colleges and universities do not do enough to serve students, showing that the top four reasons students drop

out of a school are because "the college doesn't care," there's "poor service and treatment," it's "not worth it," and the course schedule is not accommodating to the student (Raisman 2013, 6–7). Fred W. Heldenfelds IV et al. argue for the importance of advising students in increasing student retention (Heldenfelds et al. 2011). And Christopher B. Nelson (2014) reports how improving numerous aspects of the university, including the aesthetics of buildings, health center resources, and student mentorship programs had the unforeseen benefit of improving student retention.

5. Daniel F. Chambliss and Christopher G. Takacs report that face-to-face contact is a significant factor in engaging and motivating students in higher education, and improves retention rates (Chambliss and Takacs 2014).

References

Agrawal, Rackesh, Tomasz Imieliński, and Arun Swami. 1993. "Mining Association Rules between Sets of Items in Large Databases." *Proceedings of the 1993 ACM SIGMOD International Conference on Management of Data*, 207–16. http://dx.doi.org/10.1145/170035.170072.

Ahmed, Shibbir, Rajshakhar Paul, and Abu Sayed Md. Latiful Hoque. 2014. "Knowledge Discovery from Academic Data Using Association Rule Mining." *Proceedings of the 17th International Conference on Computer and Information Technology (ICCIT)*, 314–19. http://dx.doi.org/10.1109/ICCITechn.2014.7073107.

Anderson, Paul, Chris M. Anson, Robert M. Gonyea, and Charles Paine. 2015. "The Contributions of Writing to Learning and Development: Results from a Large-Scale Multi-Institutional Study." *Research in the Teaching of English* 50 (2): 199–235.

Bound, John, Michael F. Lovenheim, and Sarah Turner. 2012. "Increasing Time to the Baccalaureate Degree in the United States." *Education Finance and Policy* 7 (4): 375–424. http://dx.doi.org/10.1162/EDFP_a_00074.

Broad, Bob. 2003. *What We Really Value: Beyond Rubrics in Teaching and Assessing Writing.* Logan: Utah State University Press.

Brunk-Chavez, Beth, and Elaine Fredericksen. 2008. "Predicting Success: Increasing Retention and Pass Rates in College Composition." *Journal of Writing Program Administration* 32 (1): 76–96.

Carnavale, Anthony P., Nicole Smith, and Jeff Strohl. 2013. "Recovery: Job Growth and Education Requirements Through 2020." *Georgetown Public Policy Institute: Center on Education and the Workforce* 14. https://cew.georgetown.edu/wp-content/uploads/2014/11/Recovery2020.FR_.Web_.pdf.

Chambliss, Daniel, and Christopher Takacs. 2014. *How College Works.* Cambridge, MA: Harvard University Press. http://dx.doi.org/10.4159/harvard.9780674726093.

Choitz, Vickie, and Patrick Reimherr. 2013. "Mind the Gap: High Unmet Financial Need Threatens Persistence and Completion for Low-Income Community College Students." *CLASP Center for Postsecondary and Economic Success.* http://www.clasp.org/resources-and-publications/files/CLASP-Unmet-Need-Brief-041213-final-ab-2.pdf.

College Scorecard. 2015. https://collegescorecard.ed.gov/.

Deans, Thomas. 2000. *Writing Partnerships: Service Learning in Composition.* Urbana, IL: National Council of Teachers of English.

Educational Testing Service. 2014. "ETS—Student Success and Non Cognitive Skills." *YouTube* video, 2:32. December 5. https://www.youtube.com/watch?v=4PE_-6bYV9Y.

Goodman, Kathleen, and Ernest T. Pascarella. 2006. "First-Year Seminars Increase Persistence and Retention: A Summary of the Evidence from How College Affects Students." *Peer Review : Emerging Trends and Key Debates in Undergraduate Education* 8 (3): 26–8.

Grabill, Jeff. 2007. *Writing Community Change: Designing Technologies for Citizen Action.* Cresskill, NJ: Hampton Press.

Haswell, Richard. 2005. "NCTE/CCCC's Recent War on Scholarship." *Written Communication* 22 (2): 198–223. http://dx.doi.org/10.1177/0741088305275367.

Haswell, Richard. 2012. "Quantitative Methods in Composition Studies: An Introduction to Their Functionality." In *Writing Studies Research in Practice: Methods and Methodologies,* ed. Lee Nickoson and Mary P. Sheridan, 185–96. Carbondale: Southern Illinois University Press.

Heldenfelds, W. Fred, IV, Harold W. Hahn, Joe Hinton, Durga D. Agrawal, Dennis D. Golden, Lyn Bracewell Phillips, A. W. "Whit" Riter III, Eric A. Rohne, and Raymund A. Paredes. 2011. "Institutional Strategies for Increasing Postsecondary Student Success." *Texas Higher Education Coordinating Board* 28. http://www.thecb.state.tx.us/.

Horning, Alice. 2007. "The Definitive Article on Class Size." *WPA: Writing Program Administration* 31 (1–2). http://www.wpacouncil.org/archives/31n1-2/31n1-2horning .pdf.

Huot, Brian, and Peggy O'Neill. 2009. *Assessing Writing: A Critical Sourcebook.* Boston, MA. Bedford: St. Martin's.

McCurrie, Matthew Kilian. 2009. "Measuring Success in Summer Bridge Programs: Retention Efforts in Basic Writing." *Journal of Basic Writing* 28 (2): 28–49.

Mintz, Steven. 2014. "Rethinking Retention." *InsideHigherEd,* December 9. https://www .insidehighered.com/blogs/higher-ed-beta/rethinking-retention.

Monaghan, David B., and Paul Attewell. 2014. "The Community College Route to the Bachelor's Degree." *Educational Evaluation and Policy Analysis* 31 (1): 70–91.

Mortensen, Thomas G., Camille Stocker, and Nicole Brunt. 2012. "The Inconvenient Truth . . . Family Income and Educational Attainment 1970–2010." *Postsecondary Education Opportunity* 235:1–16.

National Council of Teachers of English. 2013. "First-Year Writing: What Good Does It Do?" *Council Chronicle* 23 (2): 1–3.

National Survey of Student Engagement. 2007. "Experiences That Matter: Enhancing Student Learning and Success." *Center for Postsecondary Research School of Education* 59.

Nelson, Christopher B. 2014. "Reengineering Retention." *Inside Higher Ed,* August 25. http://www.insidehighered.com/views/2014/08/25/essay-how-improve-retention.

Porter, Stephen R., and Randy L. Swing. 2006. "Understanding How First-Year Seminars Affect Persistence." *Research in Higher Education* 47 (1): 89–109. http://dx.doi.org /10.1007/s11162-005-8153-6.

Powell, Pegeen Reichert. 2009. "Retention and Writing Instruction: Implications for Access and Pedagogy." *College Composition and Communication* 60 (4): 664–82.

Raisman, Neal. 2013. "The Cost of College Attrition at Four-Year Colleges and Universities." *Educational Policy Institute* 267.

Sommers, Nancy, Carol Rutz, and Howard Tinberg. 2006. "Re-Visions: Rethinking Nancy Sommers's 'Responding to Student Writing,' 1982." *College Composition and Communication* 58 (2): 246–66.

Sternberg, Robert J. 2013. "Research to Improve Retention." *Inside Higher Ed,* February 7. https://www.insidehighered.com/views/2013/02/07/essay-use-research-improve -student-retention.

Symonds, William C., Robert Schwartz, and Ronald F. Ferguson. 2011. "Pathways to Prosperity: Meeting the Challenge of Preparing Young Americans for the 21st Century." *Harvard Graduate School of Education: Pathways to Prosperity Project* 53. https://dash.harvard.edu/handle/1/4740480.

United States Department of Education. 2015. "The Condition of Education 2015." NCES 2015-144. National Center for Education Statistics: Institute of Education Sciences. Washington, DC: United States Government Printing Office.

White, Edward M., and Cassie A. Wright. 2016. *Assigning, Responding, Evaluating: A Writing Teacher's Guide.* Boston, MA. Bedford: St. Martin's.

Zawacki, Terry Myers, and Paul M. Rogers. 2012. *Writing across the Curriculum: A Critical Sourcebook.* Boston, MA. Bedford: St. Martin's.

7

"LIFE GETS IN THE WAY"
The Case of a Seventh-Year Senior

Sara Webb-Sunderhaus

In an April 2012 interview, Representative Virginia Foxx (R-NC), who chairs the US House Subcommittee on Higher Education and Workforce Training, was asked about her college experience and finances. Interest rates on student loans were set to double on July 1, 2012, and there was much discussion of the rate hike. A 1968 graduate of the University of North Carolina whose first-year tuition was $87.50 per semester, Representative Foxx wasn't opposed to the interest rate increase and offered her take on college students and debt: "I went through school, I worked my way through, it took me seven years, I never borrowed a dime of money. [. . .] I have very little tolerance for people who tell me that they graduate with $200,000 of debt or even $80,000 of debt because there's no reason for that" (Leonard 2012).

Consider these comments in light of Roxie,[1] a student at the public, regional comprehensive university at which I'm currently employed. An English major, she is a seventh year senior and should graduate at the end of her eighth year of college. She was required to take remedial math classes and has repeated several courses, or attempted multiple courses in order to meet one requirement, due to dropping or failing courses that became too difficult to manage with her life. Roxie works full time and commutes to campus, fluctuating between part- and full-time student status. She wakes between 7:00 and 7:30 each morning in order to ready her daughter for daycare and herself for work. By 8:45 she is at work, where she stays until 6:00, doing homework and the occasional errand during smoke breaks and lunch. Once home, Roxie is busy with childcare until her daughter's bedtime, at which point Roxie resumes homework before falling asleep between 1:00 and 2:00 AM. Although she receives financial aid, Roxie still has $50,000 in student loans as of this writing.

DOI: 10.7330/9781607326021.c007

Roxie's life is far more representative of the challenges today's students face than the student days of Representative Foxx. According to the most recent data available from the US Department of Education, "In 2012, there were about 13 million students under age 25 and 8 million students 25 years old and over." Most undergraduates work (43% part-time, 32% full-time), and 23 percent have children ("Center for Postsecondary and Economic Success Fast Facts" 2015). Of the 2015 graduating class, nearly 71 percent have student loan debt; the average debt per borrower is over $35,000 (Sparshott 2015). In short, these students bear little resemblance to students of yesteryear, yet all too often politicians and administrators—and even some college faculty—still envision today's students as financially stable and able to devote almost all of their attention to their studies, with no caretaking responsibilities. To return to Representative Foxx's comments, she concluded, "We live in an opportunity society and people are forgetting that. I remind folks all the time that the Declaration of Independence says 'life, liberty, and the pursuit of happiness.' You don't sit on your butt and have it dumped in your lap" (Leonard 2012). Like the 75 percent of her peers who work while going to school, Roxie is hardly sitting on her butt and expecting to have opportunities dumped in her lap, to use the representative's verbiage, yet that is the assumption Representative Foxx and those like her make.

Politicians, administrators, and even faculty must accept that Roxie and other college students today are not the type of students that many of us probably were—a fact that is too often used by some to scorn or shame students. They face challenges that are often far removed from the daily lives of their professors. Their lives are different, their needs are different, and as a result, the paths they must take to earn their degrees are different.

These differences mean that, if we as college administrators and faculty are serious about student retention and persistence, we will need to reconsider our curriculum, our course policies, and our relationships with our students. Malea Powell (2012) has written that our students and "their lives are denigrated as not quite good enough without the fix of Western literacy instruction . . . many of us believe they should be 'saved' from their lowly, savage lives" (401). If we hope to retain our students, we must heed Powell's words and meet students where they are, not where we think they should be; we must respect their histories and their futures, without imposing our own visions on them. In this chapter, I offer Roxie's story as a counternarrative to the stories that circulate about today's undergraduates: that they are entitled, ambivalent students who "sit on their butts" and wait for opportunities to be given to them. Roxie's case is indicative of many of the challenges she and her peers face, and it would behoove us as writing program administrators (WPAs) and faculty to listen to her story and heed her insights into what college students need from their professors and universities: knowledge-able, caring mentors; early professional development opportunities; and more flexible scheduling and course policies.

BACKGROUND ON THE STUDY AND PARTICIPANT

I first met Roxie in the Fall of 2009; she is my advisee and has taken multiple courses with me. I have gotten to know Roxie quite well, and when I started a new research project on how and why some students are retained, I knew I wanted her to participate. She consented, and we began interviews after receiving Institutional Review Board (IRB) exemption. I interviewed Roxie three times over the course of one semester; these semi-structured interviews ranged from sixty to ninety minutes in length, and planned and spontaneous follow-up questions focused on her early family life, K–12 and undergraduate education, and literacy beliefs. The interviews were transcribed by my undergradu-ate research assistant, and I analyzed the data by looking for emergent themes and patterns; I did multiple coding passes to ensure consistency and sufficiently limited categories. While Roxie's story is only one case study and cannot represent the totality of students' experiences, in many ways Roxie is typical of today's college student.

ROXIE'S STORY

When I first met Roxie, she was in some ways a "traditional" college stu-dent: she was young (eighteen), she was childless, and she was white. However, Roxie did not fit the old stereotypes in several ways: though clearly bright and talented, she was underprepared for the academic demands of college; she commuted; she was financially independent from her father; and she worked full time. These facts did not make Roxie unique at our institution. Most students commute and work, and many are financially independent. The challenges faced by students like Roxie are well known to many college faculty and administrators. We know many students are among the first generation in their family to attend college, we know almost all of them must work, and we know many are underprepared for the academic demands they will face. Yet we are often ignorant of other, less quantifiable problems, such as mental health issues, histories of abuse, and addiction, which can also impact their college careers.

These issues play an important role in Roxie's story. Roxie and her siblings were abused and neglected. As the oldest child, she took on basic caretaking for her siblings at a very young age; she also protected them at times from abuse, even going so far as to stop her mother from drowning one of her siblings in the bathtub. The abuse and neglect continued until her parents divorced and her father assumed full custody of the children, at which point the abuse ended. This childhood trauma later reverberated during Roxie's college career. Read et al. (2012) write that while starting college can be extremely exciting, "[i]t is also a time of instability and transition, hallmark features of which are an increase in autonomy, a decrease in adult supervision, a shift in both quantity and quality of peer relationships, and, for many, an increase in substance use" (427). This increase is particularly marked in students with trauma exposure and posttraumatic stress disorder (PTSD), as these two factors "heighten risk for alcohol and other drug consequences," particularly during the first few months of college (Read et al. 2012, 435). Although Roxie has never sought therapy and has no formal PTSD diagnosis, she was exposed to significant trauma in her formative years.

The transition from high school to college was very challenging for Roxie; echoing the violence of her childhood, she described it as "a slap in the face." Overwhelmed by being a full-time student, working full time, and doing homework, she cried frequently and questioned if she "was cut out for" college. Soon after beginning classes, she began having what she described as "anxiety attacks over homework and schedules," and like the students in Read et al.'s 2012 study, she turned to drugs and alcohol. An occasional marijuana user in high school, she "started using on a regular basis" during her first few weeks of college as a way to manage her anxiety: "I'd do my homework first, and then I would get high to calm down." She also engaged in frequent "partying," her term for drinking to the point of intoxication. The substance use Roxie described is what some psychologists and scholars call self-medication. Read et al. (2012) write self-medication is "prominent among theories posited to explain relations among trauma, PTSD, and substance involvement" (427). Further, negative coping strategies such as self-medication have been found to exacerbate the symptoms of PTSD, a reciprocal relationship that leads some students to further substance involvement (Read et al. 2014, 1058).

Roxie's substance use continued into her sophomore year, when she became involved in an emotionally abusive relationship. Abusive relationships are not uncommon for child abuse survivors, according to Fiorillo, Papa, and Follette (2013). In their study of 314 undergraduate women, the authors found "experiencing physical abuse in childhood is a distal risk factor for being victimized in dating relationships" (2013, 566). Such was the case for Roxie. In her words, her boyfriend "was one of those guys that just, he was abusive. Not physically, but he made everything feel like it was my fault . . . He's the one who introduced me to coke." He played a role in her dependency on other drugs as well: "It was coke first, and then I remember one night I was having so much trouble coming down. You grind your teeth, you writhe, you're in pain, anxious. You just cry because you don't know what to do. He gave me a Xanax, crushed it up, [and I] snorted it . . . I would snort Vicodin, Percocet, Klonopin, oxycodone." Her progression into more addictive substances is in keeping with the research of Arria et al. (2008), who found in their study of 1,253 undergraduates that during the period between new student orientation "to sophomore year, the largest increases [in substance use] were observed for prescription stimulants and cocaine, both of which more than quadrupled." Roxie's pattern of substance use is indicative of this finding.

During the seven to eight months Roxie was in this relationship and using drugs, she was still in school and managed to keep up with her studies to a degree. Yet Roxie was struggling greatly: "I had to be high to function in the morning when I would wake up. I would get up and even snort just a couple of lines to go to work." The following summer, Roxie came very close to overdosing and subsequently ended the relationship:

> I was sitting in a hotel room one night, because I had lost my apartment too, and I was just kind of bouncing around between cheap hotel rooms. I just remember looking in the mirror, [thinking] "what the fuck are you doing?" I had done so much that my heart was racing and I really thought I was going to die that night. I really, really did. The scariest part was, I didn't even really care at that point. I didn't. And he [her boyfriend] left me there. I was lucky I came to and I puked it up. I was really lucky. That's when I realized I was being used the whole time.

After this epiphany, Roxie moved in with her father. She credits him with helping her through the aftermath of the near-overdose, as well as Leo, her fiancé and the father of her daughter Evie. Roxie and Leo had been friends since childhood, and she describes his role in her recovery as essential: "[He] basically saved me, picked me up, and we've been together ever since . . . When I was around him, he didn't make me feel anxious. He made me feel like I was good." Roxie began weaning herself off drugs during the early months of her relationship with Leo;

given her poverty and lack of health insurance, any type of medical treatment or rehabilitation was out of the question, and quitting everything at once could have been dangerous and even fatal, given the types of substances and amounts she was using.

Her greatly reduced, occasional substance use continued throughout her third year at the university, until she learned she was pregnant. Roxie then immediately ceased all drug use: "The entire time I was pregnant, I was afraid she was going to come out and something was going to be wrong with her . . . I was so scared that I was gonna screw up her life, because of the mistakes I made. That's how I got off of it [drugs] completely once I got pregnant." When Roxie learned she was pregnant, she was enrolled in classes, but she decided to stop out that term: "I needed to take that semester off and focus on what I was going to do with my life. I have a kid now. I need to clean myself up. I need to get away from everything and everybody [from her addictive lifestyle], and I did." Roxie returned to school as a full-time student the following fall, her fourth year at the university, giving birth to Evie two weeks after the semester started. She has been continuously enrolled in classes ever since.

ROXIE AS TENACIOUS PERSISTER

Becoming a parent was a turning point in Roxie's life and her educational career, one that led her to become what Kinser and Deitchman (2007) call a "tenacious persister," their term for students "who have stopped out of college at least once without earning a degree or credential" (77).[2] In the years since Evie's birth, Roxie has approached her education with a newfound sense of determination and purpose. At our university, the birth of a child is the moment when students tend to drop out, yet for Roxie, her daughter's birth was her impetus for returning. According to Kinser and Deitchman (2007), this contrast is a hallmark of tenacious persisters, who "translate earlier obstacles into strengths." In their study of these students, the authors claim that "children seem to be an example" of potential obstacles that instead become an important part of the persisters' motivation to graduate (90).

During our interviews, I commented that Roxie came back to school at the moment when the university typically loses a student. Her response reveals her overwhelming desire to create a different kind of life for herself and Evie: "That's why I came back. I wasn't gonna be that [a mom who dropped out] . . . I was not gonna have Evie growing up with a mom working all hours of the night just to put her through school and buy her shoes . . . I wanted to, I still had dreams. Why was I giving them up? There was no reason to give them up."

Roxie frequently returned to this idea of wanting more for herself and her child. In our first interview, Roxie stated the reason why she wanted her degree so badly was "to be a good role model for her [Evie] because I never had one." She later added,

> I didn't want her [Evie] growing up and throwing it back in my face—"well, you quit." I wanted to be a better person, because at that point, even when I was pregnant with her, I was still struggling with, "Who am I?" I had lost all of that with [her abusive ex-boyfriend], and the drugs, and everything else. I didn't know what the hell was up or down. I just didn't want to be that anymore. When I got back to school, that gave me a hell of a lot more confidence. I feel better now that I'm in school.

She discussed how her father was absent for much of her childhood, as he worked multiple jobs and went to school full time, eventually continuing, "I just wanted to be around [for Evie]. I wanted to provide."

Kinser and Deitchman (2007) write that for tenacious persisters, their children "provid[e] a strong motivation for returning and doing well in school" (90), and Evie has certainly played a large role in Roxie's determination to graduate. However, Evie is not Roxie's only motivating factor. In all of our interviews, Roxie repeatedly expressed a desire to be a better person, for Evie's sake as well as her own, and contended that her education had improved her life in multiple ways, exemplifying Scribner's (1984) metaphor of literacy as a state of grace. Scribner argues that "the notion that participation in a literate—that is, bookish—tradition enlarges and develops a person's essential self is pervasive and still undergirds the concept of a liberal education" (13), and Roxie's responses illustrate this idea quite well.

At many points in our interviews, Roxie described how her education has changed her: "The beginning of college me . . . before I wasn't really so sure of myself or anything, whereas now, after I had Evie and came back, I'm a lot more confident and a lot more sure of myself. And I feel a lot better about myself. I actually do know who I am now and who I want to be." Scribner (1984) writes, "[T]he literate individual's life derives its meaning and significance from intellectual, aesthetic, and spiritual participation in the accumulated creations and knowledge of humankind" (14), and the role of Roxie's education in her identity formation indicates she has indeed gained "meaning and significance" from her intellectual pursuits. These gains have encouraged her to continue her education.

[handwritten marginal note: Motivation]

THE ROLE OF WRITING IN RETENTION AND PERSISTENCE

Roxie's professors—especially her writing professors—have played an important role in her persistence. Based on interviews with 1,600 students, Light (2001) argues that developing a meaningful relationship with at least one faculty member is a compelling factor in student retention. Similarly, the *Gallup-Purdue Index 2015 Report* (2015) contends, "Supportive and motivating relationships with professors and mentors are crucial to undergraduates' college experience" (Gallup 2015, 9), further noting that recent college graduates who strongly agree that their professors cared about them as a person, encouraged them to pursue their goals and dreams, and/or made them excited about learning are almost twice as likely to "strongly agree that [their] education was worth the cost" (8).

Supportive relationships with her professors have been critical in Roxie's continued progress to degree. She stated her professors' support has been "one of the biggest" motivating factors for staying in school, adding:

> I'll start doubting myself again, thinking I'm stupid. I'm not good enough to play with the big kids. Why am I even still here? I'm not smart enough to do this. I don't know. I've wasted how many years already, and what if I don't get a job after graduation? Those kinds of things start closing in on me a little bit, so receiving even just a little blurb or something from a professor helps immensely. They don't even understand how much.

Roxie particularly credited her writing professors for her success, stating, "Especially with my writing professors, when I turn in an assignment, what I really like is when they'll write a little blurb or something like that, praising me on something. We'll just get into a conversation with that, which leads to me asking questions and picking their brains to help me grow as a student."

Her professors' support has played a critical role in Roxie's intellectual development, and writing instruction can particularly contribute to these kinds of connections between faculty and students. Writing-intensive courses have been identified as a High-Impact Practice (HIP) by the Association of American College and Universities' Liberal Education and America's Promise (LEAP) initiative. LEAP defines High-Impact Practices as "techniques and designs for teaching and learning that have proven to be beneficial for student engagement and successful learning among students from many backgrounds" ("High-Impact Practices" 2016), and Finley and McNair (2013) note that these "practices have a profound effect on the experiences of underserved students," particularly with regard to retention (vi). Given the very nature of writing classes, compositionists are uniquely positioned to foster students' intellectual growth; as I have written elsewhere (Webb-Sunderhaus 2010), writing instructors "routinely—if not daily—read our students' writing and hear them speak in the classroom, acts which can give us insights into their thought processes and feelings and once again contribute to the connection between student and professor" (116). Further, in their collaborative research with the Council of Writing Program Administrators (CWPA) and the National Survey of Student Engagement (NSSE), Anderson et al. (2015) found that effective writing instruction "can also affect students' perceived development personally and socially opens a new category of the benefits of writing in college" (227). The impact Roxie ascribes to her writing professors' encouragement, as well as her earlier description of herself as a "better person all around" because of her education, are indicators of these potential benefits. Roxie's comments point to the positive role writing can play in students' perceptions of themselves and the value of their education.

Complementing her intellectual development, Roxie's professional development has been another factor in her tenacious persistence toward graduation. Roxie is an English major with a writing concentration, and she hopes to work as a copywriter after graduation. Much like her education, Roxie takes career development very seriously and has repeatedly and independently sought out professional and mentoring opportunities: "I wanted to start now, before I got my actual degree, so I had an idea of what is going to be expected of me." She began by assisting friends with cover letters and resumes; thanks to referrals over time, Roxie has built up a clientele and now earns a small income from this work. Roxie also reached out to a local online business that markets arts and entertainment events, and she has written multiple articles about the city's music scene for this company. She found a mentor in the owner of the company, whom she respects greatly and credits with teaching her a great deal about professional communication.

When I asked Roxie what motivated her to pursue these opportunities, she explained:

> I had this epiphany one day. I don't remember what class I was in exactly; I know it was an English class. I remember thinking to myself, how are they going to teach me everything I need to know before I get out of college? [I read an article about] how some college students don't do any internships or try to reach out and make connections before they graduate. Some of them graduate, but they can't find a job because they don't know any of those things . . . That's how I started it.

Roxie's epiphany led her to pursue a formal internship through the English department, which was underway during the semester of our interviews. She interned with a division of the university, writing four press releases as part of her work there.

Roxie's positive experience there made her more determined than ever to finish her degree and begin her career; in interviews, she repeatedly stated her internship and professional opportunities redoubled her commitment to her degree. "When I first started seeking out this information on my own," she said, "it just clicked for me really quick. This is what I want to do . . . It's definitely made me more committed [to school]." Later in the same interview, she summarized the importance of professional development for herself and other students thusly:

> It's made me more confident in myself. There have been times I'm sitting there looking at this pile of homework and I'm like, 'What is this even good for? What am I really learning? How am I going to apply this later, after graduation?' I didn't really understand what I was doing and why I was learning it [until her internship and other opportunities]. You take these skills and apply them to real-world practices, it's going to make the students more confident. It's going to make them work harder and make them learn better, of course. It's helped me in that way. It's made me a better person all around.

As Roxie's words illustrate, this early professional development has given her increased motivation and insights into the importance of her education. They have shown her that she can do this work, and she has grown in self-confidence as a result.

Although Roxie has had one internship, the professional experiences that came at the most critical juncture of her education—the first year after her daughter's birth—were ones she created on her own. While I will return to this point later, early professional development experiences sponsored by universities could do much to encourage students' persistence toward graduation.[3] Blau and Snell (2013) argue "greater PDE [Professional Development Engagement] will enhance the likelihood of a student graduating in a timely manner and having an appropriate job upon graduation" (690). In their study of 413 students, Luke, Diambra, and Gibbons (2014) found that students who displayed comfort in choosing a major and who connected their work in the classroom with their ability to find a job "were more likely to plan on returning to the institution the following semester" (215). Although further research is needed to understand more fully the role of early professional experiences, I will suggest for now that universities and writing programs must consider what part professional development can play in their student retention and persistence efforts. These experiences also need to become a much earlier part of the curriculum.

ROXIE'S CHALLENGES: INFLEXIBLE SCHEDULING, RIGID COURSE POLICIES, AND FRAYING RELATIONSHIPS

While Roxie is a tenacious persister, that does not mean her academic life is without complications. She identified her greatest challenge as attending class. She works from 9:00 AM–6:00 PM, but there are no evening courses that begin after 6:00 PM; upper-level online courses are also limited. The lack of night and online classes is especially true for foreign languages. At Roxie's university, English majors must take two years of foreign language instruction; the courses must be taken in a strict sequence (the first and third courses are only offered in the fall, the second and fourth are only offered in the spring), and none are offered online. One section of each language begins at 6:00 PM each semester, but given Roxie's work schedule, she would be at least fifteen minutes late to every class. Such tardiness is unacceptable to most professors, and her previous supervisor at work would not allow her to leave early. As a result, she had to take a year off from foreign language instruction, losing much of the progress she had made.

Given these realities, it's unsurprising that Roxie's grades have suffered. However, her academic performance has been diminished not only by missing class lectures and discussions, but also by attendance policies that institute a grade penalty when students miss more than the proscribed number of classes (typically two). Roxie has suffered this penalty multiple times due to caring for her daughter during illness; she has also withdrawn from math courses because additional absences would result in a final grade reduction of one full letter per absence, and as Roxie put it, "I needed all the help I could get to pass math."

As one who once used such an attendance policy, I can safely assert that some instructors' policies assume that students are simply ditching class. But that is a far cry from the life Roxie leads, and at times she has confronted professors on their assumptions. She recounted one such incidence with a foreign language professor: "When I came back after having my daughter, I remember he said something in class because I had missed the day before, the homework. He had said something [and was] calling those students out. And I went up to him after class, and I said, 'Hey, my daughter was sick yesterday and I wasn't able to get to a computer. She wouldn't let me put her down. That's why I wasn't able to email you.'" The professor subsequently apologized to Roxie.

When Roxie can't take necessary classes or drops them due to attendance, her degree progress slows:

> It's had a huge impact [on time to degree]. I gotta say most of the time it's discouraging. I'm just like, "Oh my God, another year? I still can't take this class?" . . . That's the stuff that sucks. It really does. You know, I think I've been about to graduate three times now, and then I figure out, "Oh, I need to take this. Oh, I still can't take that." Or I had to take a year off my language classes. It's very discouraging; it really is. It makes you feel like, the thing is, everybody thinks we're supposed to graduate in four years. It's not going to happen. It's just not. Life gets in the way. You have a shortage of teachers who can only teach certain classes . . . or you don't have the availability to be inside the classroom, and there's no online alternative, even though we're in the digital era. I don't understand how we don't have more online classes. I really don't. It's been discouraging.

These discouraging moments reinforce Roxie's doubts about her abilities to earn her degree, as seen in her earlier comments about not being "good enough to play with the big kids."

Compounding these feelings is Roxie's social isolation at school and in her neighborhood. She feels disconnected from her classmates, stating, "It really is hard, especially when you get into group work with other students, and we start talking . . . [T]hey just turned 21. They still want to go to the mall and things like that. They want to hang out, and I have to be in bed by 9:00." At twenty-four, Roxie is still young, but as she put it, with "everything that I've been through, I feel a lot older than most people I know." Unfortunately, Roxie no longer has much in common with her old friends, either. She grew up with a close-knit group of friends in the working-class neighborhood in which she still lives. Some of these friendships stretch back fifteen to twenty years; she has known her fiancé Leo since they were twelve. One of the commonalities in these relationships was a shared neighborhood and socioeconomic status; another was, as Roxie put it, "We've had a lot of the same personal background with our families." Leo grew up in a substance-abusing household, and the father of Roxie's closest female friend battered her mother. Because of these similar histories, Roxie said, "We all clicked."

These relationships are changing, however, and Roxie credits the changes to different educational attainment. Only Roxie has attended a four-year institution,[4] and she is very aware she is different: "I'm just now starting to realize, we are such different levels. I cannot hold a conversation with them anymore." She then told a story about playing a trivia game with her friends and drawing a card with Freud and a humorous caption. Roxie "laughed at the card—I laughed so hard . . . and they were just looking at me like I was stupid. 'What is so funny?' I was like,

'Did you read the card?'" It was at that point Roxie realized she was the only one who knew who Freud was.

These differences have crept into Roxie's two closest relationships as well. She related that she "can't talk very much anymore" to her best friend, because "she doesn't understand where I'm coming from." She later added, "It takes a toll sometimes with mine and Leo's relationship as well," and one of her greatest frustrations is that Leo didn't finish a community college welding program. Roxie explained, "That's what I'm trying to get him to do. His thinking is that he has a job in his industry, so why go ahead and finish it? I can keep talking until I'm blue in the face. It's about starting something and finishing it." While their relationship is still relatively strong, Roxie's comments reveal sharp differences in the way she sees the world compared to her home community: "I don't want to go to my job every day hating it for the rest of my life. And that's what they [her friends] do. What they think is that's just the way the world works. But it doesn't, and they don't get that. But you can only talk so much. And then sometimes it gets to the point where they think that I think I'm better than them, and that's not the case. And that's really frustrating."

As a result, Roxie feels torn between two worlds. She spoke at length about feeling as if she doesn't fit it anywhere, saying,

> I feel like I'm caught in the middle. I don't know why. Growing up with them [her friends], they know me. They know where I'm coming from and things like that. For some reason I feel like I'm still stuck in that mindset with them, even though I know I'm not. I've grown; I'm more educated. But I still feel dumber than everybody else here [at the university]. That makes me afraid to reach out and make new friends . . . It gets lonely.

What Roxie describes is a classic dilemma facing many working class, first-generation, and/or cultural minority college students (Delpit 1996; Gilyard 1991; Heath 1983; Sohn 2006; Villanueva 1993; M. Young 2004; V. Young 2007). This strain may increase with time for Roxie; I suspect that as she moves into her professional career, the distance she feels from her friends will only increase. But for now, she is managing these painful emotions and staying on track to graduate.

IMPLICATIONS: WHAT FACULTY AND WPAS CAN DO

Faculty members and writing program administrators have an important role to play in student retention and persistence. Faculty are the primary representatives of the university to students, and as Light (2001) argues, their mentorship can be critical to student success. As we have seen in this chapter, Roxie believes that some of her professors care and want to see her graduate, at times speaking glowingly of the support she has received. However, the difficulties she has encountered—dismissive faculty, a lack of online and evening courses, and harsh attendance policies—don't speak particularly well of some faculty and low-level administrators, such as department chairs and WPAs, who are in charge of scheduling. Roxie's story reveals ways we can help students like her fulfill their potential and earn their degrees, enumerated below.

1. Know our students.

During interviews, Roxie expressed a desire for professors to get to know their students—"*really* get to know them"—so they could more fully understand students' motivations and values, adding, "That makes me feel like you actually care about me. You want to help me get through this class and graduate." The importance of knowing our students seems readily apparent, but it is easier said than done in today's academic culture. Given the reliance on adjunct labor and growing demands on faculty, many have little time or incentive to get to know students in the ways Roxie describes. Our classes are larger, our service ever-increasing. We may be teaching at five or six different institutions in order to earn a (barely) living wage, or our tenure and promotion cases may rest on research. What is the incentive for getting to know our students and understand their lives, when research is what earns us jobs, tenure, and promotion? In addition, at my institution more and more staff responsibilities, such as running graduation audits on advisees, are now placed on faculty. These changes in faculty workload mean that we have less time to get to know our students. If we hope to improve retention and persistence, this must change.

2. Provide students with early professional development experiences.

If Roxie had not been a highly motivated student who independently sought out mentorship and professional development, she would have not had any professional experiences until her sixth year of college, when she was able to secure an internship through the English Department. Even students who graduate in four years do not typically have internships until senior year. This timing strikes me as too late, given the potential of early professional development to increase students' interest and commitment to their degrees (Blau and Snell 2013). Education majors are required to spend several weeks in a K–12 classroom during their first or second year of college, and other majors offer similarly early professional development. Why aren't English/writing programs doing the same? Such experiences could make a difference in universities' retention efforts.

3. Offer more online and hybrid courses, as well as evening and weekend classes.

The above statement is incredibly obvious, given ever-growing demand for online learning ("2013—Grade Change" 2015) and the demographics of today's college students. Yet there are still a significant number of faculty who are unable or unwilling to teach online, in the evenings, and on the weekends. In my department, the decision to teach in the evenings or on the weekends is up to faculty, and very few of our tenure-line faculty members want to teach at night; they never teach on weekends. Most of our evening and weekend courses are taught at the 100 and 200 level by adjuncts, who need money more than they need a convenient schedule. Similarly, the vast majority of the university's online options are at the 100 or 200 level, with few upper-level courses that meet major requirements; fewer than a fifth of my department's full-time faculty regularly teach online. In some programs, such as foreign language, there are no online options. Within my own writing program, no WPA has ever allowed an online basic writing course, due to fears students will be more likely to fail. While it is true online courses tend to have higher failure rates than face-to-face courses at the university due to some students' difficulty with using technology and working independently, online sections could also help many students who fail courses because of attendance.[5] In short, department chairs, WPAs, and faculty need to keep in mind the needs of professors *and* students when considering scheduling and online learning.

4. Reconsider attendance policies.

Many writing faculty at my institution have no-tolerance attendance policies that make no exception for legitimate difficulties. These punitive measures have arisen because class attendance is extremely poor; in my own 100 and 200 level classes, typically half of my students will no longer attend class by midterm. This pattern holds true across all disciplines and is a major incentive for strict attendance policies. I too once used such policies, but after working with students like Roxie, I realized I was inadvertently encouraging students to give up due to fear of failure—exactly what Roxie did in some classes. My syllabus now indicates that grade penalties are possible (not guaranteed) and includes wording that indicates exceptions can be made. Since I have moved to this gentler policy, attendance has not decreased, and students readily come to me when they face a difficult situation. These discussions have increased my understanding of students' lives and motivations.

FINAL THOUGHTS

During our last interview, I asked what, if anything, Roxie wished her professors knew about her life. Her answer attested to the difficulties she faces:

> [I wish they knew] everything. How I'm scraping by. How this [my education] is so important to me. [It] is so important to me that I stretch myself so thin. Some days I come in and I haven't slept in twenty-four hours. A professor will call on me to answer a question, and I have no idea what they just said *at all.* And that makes me feel stupid, even though I know that I know the answer. I'm just so tired I can't think straight. So yeah, that's something that I wish they would know.

As writing instructors and WPAs, we do not have the power to change the circumstances of Roxie's life outside the university; we cannot reduce the burdens she brings with her to the classroom. We can, however, change the burdens we place on her—and students like her—by our failure to understand her life, her motivations, and her needs. If we hope to improve the ability of students like Roxie to graduate, that is what we must do.

Notes

1. Roxie's name, like all others in this chapter, is a pseudonym of her choice.
2. Kinser and Deitchman (2007) also describe as tenacious persisters students who began college at least three years after they graduated from high school.
3. Here I define "early" as the first two years of higher education.
4. Her fiancé and her closest friend each attended two-year colleges but did not earn degrees.
5. In fairness, many universities (including my own) are reluctant to place students—particularly at-risk students or those with attendance problems—in online classes out of fear these students will not perform well.

References

"2013—Grade Change: Tracking Online Education in the United States." 2015. *Online Learning Consortium.* Accessed June 20, 2015. http://onlinelearningconsortium.org /survey_report/2013-survey-online-learning-report/.

Anderson, Paul, Chris M. Anson, Robert M. Gonyea, and Charles Paine. 2015. "The Contributions of Writing to Learning and Development: Results from a Large-Scale Multi-Institutional Study." *Research in the Teaching of English* 50 (2): 199–235.

Arria, Amelia M., Kimberly M. Caldeira, Kevin E. O'Grady, Kathryn B. Vincent, Dawn B. Fitzelle, Erin P. Johnson, and Eric D. Wish. 2008. "Drug Exposure Opportunities and Use Patterns among College Students: Results of a Longitudinal Prospective Cohort Study." *Substance Abuse* 29 (4): 19–38. http://dx.doi.org/10.1080/08897070802418451 http://www.ncbi.nlm.nih.gov/pmc/articles/PMC2614283/.

Blau, Gary, and Corrine M. Snell. 2013. "Understanding Undergraduate Professional Development Engagement and Its Impact." *College Student Journal* 47 (4): 689–702.

"Center for Postsecondary and Economic Success Fast Facts." 2015. *CLASP.* Accessed June 13, 2015. http://www.clasp.org/issues/postsecondary/fast-facts.

Delpit, Lisa. 1996. *Other People's Children: Cultural Conflict in the Classroom.* New York: New Press.

Finley, Ashley, and Tia McNair. 2013. *Assessing Underserved Students' Engagement in High-Impact Practices.* Washington, DC: Association of American Colleges and Universities.

Fiorillo, Devika, Anthony Papa, and Victoria M. Follette. 2013. "The Relationship between Child Physical Abuse and Victimization in Dating Relationships: The Role of Experiential Avoidance." *Psychological Trauma: Theory, Research, Practice, and Policy* 5 (6): 562–9. http://dx.doi.org/10.1037/a0030968.

Gallup, Inc. 2015. *Gallup-Purdue Index 2015 Report: Great Jobs, Great Lives: The Relationship between Student Debt, Experiences and Perceptions of College Worth.* Washington, DC: Gallup, Inc.

Gilyard, Keith. 1991. *Voices of the Self: A Study of Language Competence.* Detroit: Wayne State University Press.

Heath, Shirley Brice. 1983. *Ways with Words: Language, Life, and Work in Communities and Classrooms.* New York: Cambridge University Press.

"High-Impact Practices." 2016. *LEAP Campus Toolkit: Resources and Models for Innovation.* Accessed March 21, 2016. http://leap.aacu.org/toolkit/high-impact-practices.

Kinser, Kevin, and Jay Deitchman. 2007. "Tenacious Persisters: Returning Adult Students in Higher Education." *Journal of College Student Retention* 9 (1): 75–94. http://dx.doi.org/10.2190/W143-56H0-6181-7670.

Leonard, Andrew. 2012. "Sneering at Student Debt." *Salon,* April 19, 2012. http://www.salon.com/2012/04/19/sneering_at_student_debt/.

Light, Richard J. 2001. *Making the Most of College: Students Speak Their Minds.* Cambridge, MA: Harvard University Press.

Luke, Chad, Joel F. Diambra, and Melinda Gibbons. 2014. "An Exploration of Complimentary Factors in Career and Student Development in the Liberal Arts." *College Student Journal* 48 (2): 209–20.

Powell, Malea. 2012. "2012 CCCC Chair's Address: Stories Take Place: A Performance in One Act." *College Composition and Communication* 64 (2): 383–406.

Read, Jennifer P., Melissa J. Griffin, Jeffrey D. Wardell, and Paige Ouimette. 2014. "Coping, PTSD Symptoms, and Alcohol Involvement in Trauma-Exposed College Students in the First Three Years of College." *Psychology of Addictive Behaviors* 28 (4): 1052–64. http://dx.doi.org/10.1037/a0038348.

Read, Jennifer P., Craig R. Colder, Jennifer E. Merrill, Paige Ouimette, Jacquelyn White, and Ashlyn Swartout. 2012. "Trauma and Posttraumatic Stress Symptoms Predict Alcohol and Other Drug Consequence Trajectories in the First Year of College." *Journal of Consulting and Clinical Psychology* 80 (3): 426–39. http://dx.doi.org/10.1037/a0028210.

Scribner, Sylvia. 1984. "Literacy in Three Metaphors." *American Journal of Education* 93 (1): 6–21. http://dx.doi.org/10.1086/443783.

Sohn, Katherine. 2006. *Whistlin' and Crowin' Women of Appalachia: Literacy Practices Since College*. Carbondale: Southern Illinois University Press.

Sparshott, Jeffrey. 2015. "Congratulations, Class of 2015. You're the Most Indebted Ever (For Now)." *Real Time Economics* (blog). *The Wall Street Journal*, May 8, 2015. http://blogs.wsj.com/economics/2015/05/08/congratulations-class-of-2015-youre -the-most-indebted-ever-for-now/.

Villanueva, Victor. 1993. *Bootstraps: From an American Academic of Color*. Urbana, IL: National Council of Teachers of English.

Webb-Sunderhaus, Sara. 2010. "When Access Is Not Enough: Retaining Basic Writers at an Open-Admission University." *Journal of Basic Writing* 29 (2): 102–21.

Young, Morris. 2004. *Minor Re/Visions: Asian American Literacy Narratives as a Rhetoric of Citizenship*. Carbondale: Southern Illinois University Press.

Young, Vershawn A. 2007. *Your Average Nigga: Performing Race, Literacy, and Masculinity*. Detroit: Wayne State University Press.

PART 2

Writing Program Initiatives That Matter

8
ABSOLUTE HOSPITALITY IN THE WRITING PROGRAM

Pegeen Reichert Powell

I came to research retention as a teacher, wondering whether there was anything I could do, in the classroom, to prevent students from leaving college before graduation. The answer I arrived at after several years of research and writing is "no." As I argue elsewhere, some students should leave—it's better for them to attend to more pressing priorities in their lives and not spend money on courses they can't give their attention to—and it is not my business to prevent them from leaving. Moreover, when most students leave, the problems are so multifaceted, and multiplied by the number of students who are making this decision, so numerous, that there is really no way for an instructor or a college to develop a single approach or course that could prevent every student from leaving (Reichert Powell 2013).

However, while there is little we can do to prevent students from leaving, this does not mean that we should ignore the discourse of retention. In fact, I argue the opposite: writing program administrators and instructors should pay close attention to how that discourse functions at our institutions. First, we are in a position to bring our experience with students in and out of the classroom to bear on the conversation about retention, a conversation that is often dominated by budgets and enrollment concerns. Second, understanding attrition as a feature of the context in which we work, knowing that students may leave, no matter what we do, could help us design and teach better courses. We should not design courses purely in an effort to retain students. We should teach substantial, rigorous courses that situate writing and rhetoric in a context broader than four subsequent years at a single institution. The clarity that comes from recognizing the inevitability that some of our students will leave before graduation enables us to see our work as writing instructors and the purpose of our courses in a new light.

DOI: 10.7330/9781607326021.c008

This shift in focus is crucial: from a focus on trying to prevent students from leaving, to a focus on how and what we might teach when we know that some students will leave. We focus on preventing students from leaving when we are committed to a chronological pedagogy:

> A chronological pedagogy assumes a linear process, an exercise of skills development from one course to the next, as well as the curricular structures to support a predictable progression. Such a pedagogy requires that students move through the process in a certain way, but when students drop out or transfer, the process is interrupted. These interruptions are thought of as exceptions to the rule of progress. However, the issue of retention reminds us that these may not be exceptions, but the rule itself, in many institutions. (Reichert Powell 2013, 18)

Chronos, then, limits our understanding of the course and our students' educational lives. By contrast, kairos enables instructors and students to look for opportunities in the particular confluence of people and events in a given classroom. A kairotic pedagogy understands that the specific mix of students on our roster in any given semester and all of the factors influencing their work in our course, many of which are beyond their control or ours, provide a unique opportunity for doing productive rhetorical work. As such, a kairotic pedagogy does not focus on preventing students from leaving, but instead assumes that some may leave and, further, sees the potential for teaching and learning in the very reasons they might leave (family obligations, changes in priorities or goals, physical or mental illnesses, and so on).

In this chapter, I describe a course that embraces kairos. I do not offer it as a model, but as an example that demonstrates the nature and value of a kairotic pedagogy. Further, I explain that the course embeds in our pedagogy a critique of the dominant discourse of retention, and thus creates a pocket of resistance to the logic of the market-driven university, a logic that frequently relies on this discourse. As such, it offers a more humane, respectful approach to students in our first-year writing programs than the pragmatic philosophies of Writing Program Administrators (WPAs) who embrace what Marc Bousquet (2004) refers to as "the rhetoric of 'pleasing the prince'" (12). Finally, I explore Derrida's (2000) notion of absolute hospitality as an ongoing challenge for WPAs who seek to create a space in higher education that is truly open to students, regardless of their paths through higher education, and I argue that a kairotic pedagogy helps us do that.

KEY CONCEPTS: A KAIROTIC PEDAGOGY

When I assumed the role of WPA in the Program in Writing and Rhetoric at Columbia College Chicago, it was generally agreed that it was time to revise the first writing course in our two-semester sequence. Columbia College is a private college, situated in the South Loop of downtown Chicago; although almost all of the college's roughly ten thousand students graduate with majors in the arts and media, they are also required to take a core curriculum rooted in the liberal arts. Historically, the college has seen its mission as serving students who might not meet traditional measures of college preparation, such as ACT/SAT scores or high school GPA, but who have talent in their fields. This generous admissions policy is evolving slowly toward more rigorous admissions standards. The problem of retention remains a dominant feature of our institutional context: our most recently posted six-year graduation rate for new, full-time freshman is 41.7 percent ("Key Indicators" 2015). We lose students who decide they would prefer a more traditional major and so transfer; students who leave to pursue paying work as actors and musicians; students whose educational background did not prepare them for college-level work; and students who drop out or transfer for all the myriad reasons students do so at institutions across the country.

For the reasons I explain above, when we revised the first-year writing course, we did not set out to design a course whose purpose it was to raise the retention rate. Nevertheless, knowing that over half of our students may not remain enrolled in our institution affected how I understood the role of first-year writing in students' educational trajectories. I was less concerned with preparing students for future academic or professional writing than I was with inviting students to understand, in new ways, the varied rhetorical contexts in which they were already participating—including, but not limited to, the writing they were doing in the other courses they were taking that semester. Prioritizing participation over preparation is a principle of a kairotic pedagogy.

As we thought about the varied rhetorical contexts that our students participate in, what struck us most was the nature and pace of change in terms of how we compose and circulate writing. We are not in a stage of transition from an era of print to the digital era; rather we are entering an era when change itself is the dominant characteristic. Our program struggles, as most programs are struggling, with how to understand what "writing" means in this networked, digital environment, and how to understand the scope and responsibility of this course with respect to the technologies and modes available to our students as communicators. As Marvin Diogenes and Andrea A. Lunsford say, "writing is no longer a stable, black-and-white affair: writing is Technicolor, oral, and thoroughly integrated with visual and audio displays" (Diogenes and Lunsford 2006, 142). Especially at a college with majors in graphic design, film, audio arts, photography, and so on, what of these other modes do we include in the first-year writing course, and what do we leave to our colleagues in their respective fields?

It is not just the proliferation of available communication resources, but the pace of change that challenges anyone designing a first-year writing course. Platforms such as tumblr and Instagram come and go, as anyone trying to keep up with teenage children's social media activities can attest. How much time do we spend with students in class familiarizing them with a platform that may not even exist in a year? Technologies change day-to-day, and yet access to them remains uneven. In an institution that can't afford to provide or require all students to have a laptop, iPad, or other device, what one student could do with his phone would be impossible for another student. Even genres shift as they move online and incorporate digital elements: the genre of the "resume" is a case in point. An instructor ten years ago might have been able to review with students the typical features of the resume; now, however, as job searches are conducted almost entirely online, and as job-seekers not only reply to job ads but also market themselves via multimodal websites, there is little about the "resume" that is stable long enough to incorporate into a curriculum.

A kairotic pedagogy, open to opportunities as they arise, is responsive to the pace of change in the technologies and software that make composing and circulating writing a constantly shifting enterprise. The challenge, though, is to provide students an analytical and heuristic intellectual framework that enables them to approach any new writing task they are faced with in college or out. A committee of seven instructors in the Program in Writing and Rhetoric spent a semester reading relevant literature together and determined that, rather than build the course around specific genres, platforms, or media, we would build the course around key concepts in writing and rhetoric that could provide a stable structure that writers can work with to approach a variety of rhetorical contexts.[1] We brainstormed all of the possible concepts we thought would be productive as part of this framework, some of which we were already teaching (like ethos). From that larger list, after mini-presentations we gave each other about all the possible concepts, and after much deliberation and rounds of voting, we arrived at ten key concepts, from classical rhetoric as well as fields that study multimodal composition:

Affordances	Field
Alphabetic text	Genre
Arrangement	Image
Circulation	Kairos
Ethos	Remix

While we think that these ten concepts are particularly productive in the course so far, it is possible that our list may change, and other programs may certainly identify different concepts that work better. What matters for us is teaching "circulation" instead of Twitter, "genre" instead of the persuasive essay, "image" instead of Instagram, "affordances" instead of podcasting. These are not discrete vocabulary items for students to memorize, but complicated, interrelated concepts that inform both the production and the consumption of texts.

As part of the course revision, we wrote a textbook that introduces the concepts, including a chapter for each concept and a handful of readings about the nature of writing and rhetoric in the digital age (e.g., a chapter from Richard Lanham's *Economy of Attention* and an excerpt from Scott McCloud's *Understanding Comics* about the relationship between word and image). It is not quite a custom reader, because the majority of the content is written by us rather than a collection of previously published work. However, because the printing process is the same as a custom reader, we have the flexibility to revise whenever we want, which allows us to keep examples current and to include very recent student work. We intend to change the cover image each year, for instance, featuring student art or photographs submitted in a program-wide contest.

A typical fifteen-week section of this course is organized around clusters of key concepts. So, an instructor might introduce alphabetic text, image, and affordances in weeks one through four; genre, field, and ethos in weeks five through nine; remix, arrangement, circulation, and kairos in the final weeks of the semester. All in-class exercises and assignments are designed to teach students fluency in these concepts. The goal is for students to be able to talk about other people's texts—their classmates', online examples, published writing—as well as their own projects and rhetorical choices using the concepts. The concepts are also used as criteria when students read each other's work and when instructors evaluate their students' work. In the first four weeks, a student might produce a project that uses images alongside alphabetic text, and the success of that project lies in whether or not the student can describe, in writing, the choices she made considering the affordances and constraints of both image and alphabetic text. A photography major may be able to use a stunning original image, but this does not guarantee a better grade than the student who literally cuts and pastes an image from a magazine onto a poster board, as long as the latter student is able to describe with fluency the affordances of that particular image in light of her rhetorical goals. As the course proceeds through the remaining weeks of the semester, additional concepts are folded into the conversation so that our hypothetical student with the poster board may look back on that first project, and now through the lens of circulation and arrangement, would be able to talk about the strengths and weaknesses of the choices she made.

So what makes this course and the pedagogy associated with it kairotic? Why is this course suited to classrooms and institutions where attrition remains an issue, where some students will move through higher education in a predictable fashion, while others will not? First, these concepts provide a framework for approaching countless rhetorical situations, but there is no chronological progression through a set of skills and no pre-determined set of genres to master. Rather, each concept, alone but especially articulated with other concepts, allows readers and writers to approach new tasks with a rich understanding of what is being asked of them and what they can accomplish. While the concepts are perfectly suited to thinking through the challenges of academic writing (e.g., *ethos, genre, field*), the course does not assume that this is the only rhetorical situation in which students will find themselves during the semester or afterward. Rather, taken together, the key concepts teach students to think deliberately about the semiotic resources available to them as they navigate all their communication.

Moreover, a significant understanding of kairos is that it is the ability to respond to emerging situations dexterously. With the concepts, we are giving students and their instructors a language with which to explore the possibilities inherent in the crises that inevitably arise in individual students' lives and in classrooms. It's no accident that *kairos* itself is a key concept, but all of the concepts are meant to provide students with a way of approaching unpredictable and complicated situations. David M. Sheridan, Jim Ridolfo, and Anthony J. Michel explain that their understanding of kairos and agency "references the 'struggle' of the prepared rhetor within complex and multifaceted contexts that are simultaneously material, discursive, social, cultural, and historical." As such, according to these authors, "rhetorical success is contingent upon networks of human and nonhuman actors, including multiple semiotic modes and multiple media of production, reproduction, and distribution" (Sheridan,

Ridolfo, and Michel 2012, 11). The concepts are meant to help students situate themselves as informed agents within these networks—for example, to understand how their texts may *circulate*, to consider how to construct an effective *ethos*, to think about the *affordances* of the various modes available to them, including but not limited to *alphabetic text*.

We teach these concepts as shifting from one situation to the next: this is an acknowledgment, built into the course itself, that we do not—indeed cannot—predict the academic, personal, professional, or civic situations that our students will face. Sheridan, Ridolfo, and Michel (2012) refer to the "prepared rhetor." The invocation of a rhetor who is prepared may suggest a particular chronology, that one must practice a certain set of moves in order to achieve a level of preparation that guarantees success. There is no denying that the more practice one has, the better able one is to write effectively (or to play piano, kick a ball, treat sick patients, teach a class). However, a key difference between a kairotic pedagogy and a chronological pedagogy is the relationship between preparedness and participation. A chronological pedagogy assumes that one must prepare before he or she can participate in future courses, in one's field or profession, or in other significant rhetorical situations. A kairotic pedagogy like the one I describe here assumes that each rhetorical situation opens up opportunities for response that are unique to that situation. Our key concepts are meant to help students recognize those opportunities and approach each task thoughtfully and deliberately, even if they never practiced this particular communication task before. One might argue that our course conflates preparation and participation. Sheridan, Ridolfo, and Michel (2012) argue that kairos "refers precisely to the moment when theory becomes practice" (10). The key concepts as we teach them are taught at that moment, when theory becomes practice. The theoretical richness of a concept like *genre*, or *remix*, or *kairos* is appreciated and enacted by students when they are participating in exploring the concepts in the context of their own rhetorical goals.

Thus, participation becomes an important guiding principle. We see the principle of participation enacted in the nature of the writing some students are doing in the course. As Gunther Kress (2010) argues, "participatory affordances of current media technologies blur former distinctions of production and consumption, of writing and reading" (144). When students include photographs they find online into their own work as they study image and arrangement, or produce and publish fan fiction as they study remix, they blur those distinctions between production and consumption. Studying these kinds of writing events, in the context of our course, are moments when theory becomes practice. As such, participation is not put off until some future time. Because of our focus on participation, instead of preparation, the student who leaves college at the end of the course, or even half way through, does not miss out on the opportunity to participate thoughtfully in the production and circulation of cultural texts. And ideally, even the crises that lead to a decision to leave might be understood through the lens of these key concepts and responded to with rhetorical dexterity on both the part of the student and instructor.

Moreover, this shift changes the relationship between first-year writing and the rest of the college curriculum. When one removes a course from the burden of chronology, one relinquishes the learning objective that students attain skills or knowledge that they will transfer to other academic contexts. In our course, our emphasis is not on the transferability of the concepts to future courses but on the transience and contingency of these concepts. For example, we don't teach students how to create a positive ethos with the hope that this is a skill they might transfer to other writing tasks; instead, we teach students that ethos is a shifting construct that must be negotiated each time we sit down to write. Likewise, we don't teach students the genre features for the texts they are likely to encounter in other courses; instead, we teach students that genres are always in flux and that each situation requires learning anew what the expectations are of each particular group of readers.

In this respect, our course is akin to the approach first described by Elizabeth Wardle and Doug Downs as "writing about writing" and with those approaches that draw on threshold concepts. However, a significant difference between our course and these other approaches is that both writing about writing approaches and the literature on threshold concepts emphasize the importance of disciplinarity. As Elizabeth Wardle and Doug Downs argue, the dominant assumption underlying the writing about writing approach is that "our field has particular research- and theory-based views of writing" and that "some of that research and theory can and should be taught to undergraduates in gen-ed writing courses." In this 2013 reflection on their original article about writing about writing, Wardle and Downs align this assumption with Jan Meyer and Ray Land's notion of "disciplinary threshold concepts" (Wardle and Downs 2013). Others in composition studies who likewise have turned to the notion of threshold concepts also emphasize disciplinarity. For example, Linda Adler-Kassner, John Majewski, and Damian Koshnick explain that threshold concepts "serve as lenses for analysis *within the epistemological context of a discipline*" (Adler-Kassner, Majewski, and Koshnick 2012, emphasis added).

Some of our ten key concepts may be identified as threshold concepts by our colleagues in the field, and it is our own immersion in the fields of writing studies and rhetoric that drew us to these concepts. However, we do not teach these concepts in a disciplinary context. We do not teach them through the composition studies research and scholarship that dominates Wardle and Downs's first-year writing textbook (Wardle and Downs 2014). Nor do we teach the concepts as the threshold to a particular discipline. The very metaphor of a "threshold" assumes a particular chronology, that there is a before and after one crosses the threshold. Rather, our course relies on the kairotic encounters with textual examples that students and instructors come across in their daily lives as readers and writers, and on the work students produce in the course itself.

This distinction between the kairotic pedagogy that I describe and these other approaches is, in part, due to the fact that Columbia College doesn't even offer an English major, much less a writing studies or related major; there is no need to foreground writing studies or rhetoric as a discipline that one might pursue. But this emphasis on transience and contingency in the content and pedagogy of the course intentionally mirrors the transience and contingency experienced by many students, especially those who are most at risk for leaving before graduation. Our approach is mindful of the fact that if students leave college, the rhetorical situations they find themselves in will be shaped far less by disciplinary knowledge than by the myriad forces that circulate in a digital, networked environment.

ABSOLUTE HOSPITALITY: A CHALLENGE FOR WPAS

If we stop focusing on the problem of keeping students enrolled, and instead, we acknowledge the complexity of students' lives and their agency and capacity to make choices about when and where to go to college, then, I argue, we are developing a much more humane, respectful approach to the people who seek an education at our colleges and universities. Retention becomes a heuristic for considering what, how, and whom we teach, and a course like the one I describe can embed this approach to the issue of retention deep in our pedagogy. Embedded in our pedagogy, this approach is not up for debate in the same way it would be if we made these arguments in committee meetings and budget proposals. As such, it has the potential to create a pocket of resistance within the market-driven university. We effectively remove retention from the discourse of academic management and resituate it in our teaching.

What I'm arguing for here is counter-intuitive to anyone working in higher education today. In a landscape in which institutions are competing for students, and programs within institutions are forced to justify their worth on the sole basis of student enrollment, it may not be popular to accept as inevitable that some students may leave and that the first-year writing course is *not* designed with the sole purpose of preparing students for success in future academic courses.

Not only is it counter-intuitive, it is also intentionally not very pragmatic. In "Composition as Management Science," Marc Bousquet (2004) critiques the reliance on pragmatic philosophies in composition and rhetoric, especially among WPAs who embrace what Bousquet refers to as "the rhetoric of 'pleasing the prince'" (12). Bousquet is especially concerned with our discipline's approach to labor, specifically the over-reliance on part-time faculty, but I extend his critique to other problems that WPAs encounter and about which they must advocate, such as class size, budget issues surrounding faculty development, etc. The discourse of retention swirls throughout all of these problems facing WPAs.

One feature of the discourse of retention is its seductive nature. Retention as a topic is especially well suited to the ideological work of the market-driven university, because the discourse is amorphous enough to conflate sincere concerns about student success and the budget concerns about keeping butts in seats. A WPA is motivated for pedagogical reasons to argue for lower caps, and may do so by suggesting that lower caps will lead to improved retention. However, even if this causal relationship intuitively seems legitimate, not only is it very difficult to prove, but participating in the discourse of retention in this context is a capitulation to what Bousquet calls the "pragmatist-managerial version of materialism." Put simply, it is talking about students in the terms established by those concerned primarily with budgets, rather than in terms established by those concerned with teaching and learning. According to Bousquet, "for pragmatists, markets are real agents, and persons generally are not, except in their acquiescence to market dicta" (Bousquet 2004, 25). Quoting Richard Miller's "The Arts of Complicity: Pragmatism and the Culture of Schooling," Bousquet laments, "What most troubles me about the pragmatist movement is the way it seeks to curb the ambitions of our speech and rhetoric. In the pragmatist account, contemporary realities dictate that all nonmarket idealisms will be 'dismissed as the plaintive bleating of sheep' but corporate-friendly speech 'can be heard as reasoned arguments'" (26).

Therefore, when I argue that we might accept as inevitable that some students may leave and we should teach and design writing programs accordingly, I am resisting the pragmatist approach that dismisses such "nonmarket idealisms." Bousquet explains that part of the success of the pragmatist approach is that it conceals its own "market idealism"— the belief in the market as a force that transcends history and human agency—underneath "a rhetoric of exclusive purchase on reality" (24). Ironically, in the case of retention, it is far more real to acknowledge that students will leave and that there may be little we can do about it. According to one review of the relevant data at the national level, "College graduation rates for those who start college may be decreasing or increasing, depending on the data set used. Or, if one uses the longest data set (from the Census Bureau), college graduation rates may be unchanged over the last fifty years" (Mortenson 2005, 43). Attrition has always occurred, but the discourse of retention has turned it into a problem to be solved, rather than as a feature of the context in which we teach.

Counter-intuitive, and deliberately not very pragmatic, what I'm saying about retention and first-year writing has the potential to open up to a different way of thinking about our programs and our institutions. Here, I explore the metaphor of hospitality as a productive challenge for WPAs who want to pursue this opening. In particular, I argue that striving toward Derrida's (2000) notion of absolute hospitality, though impossible to achieve, compels us to take students on their own terms, and a kairotic pedagogy helps us do that.

Very little has been written about hospitality in the field of composition studies, or in fact, in all of English studies. Richard Haswell and Janis Haswell have written the only monograph-length study in all of English studies, and they identify only four articles about hospitality in composition studies (Haswell and Haswell 2015, 15). In an earlier article co-authored with Glenn Blalock, "Hospitality in College Composition Courses," the Haswells argue that authentic hospitality "as cultural narrative, social practice, and ethical goal, has the potential to enhance learning and perhaps radically alter the interchange between composition teacher and writing student" (Haswell, Haswell, and Blalock 2009, 708). They extend this argument to all of English studies in *Hospitality and Authoring: An Essay for the English Profession*, where they claim that "hospitality is the necessary companionable gesture to every genuine act of literacy" (Haswell and Haswell 2015, 3).

I share their interest in hospitality, but as a guiding metaphor for how we might envision a program and institution that recognizes that students may come and go in unpredictable ways. Hospitality seems a particularly apt notion to pursue for composition studies, for several reasons. First, I think our disciplinary history and identity is often constructed as open, hospitable even, to "outsiders." Second, if hospitality is about border crossing, we are situated in a liminal space, at the nexus of several borders—the literal borders of classrooms, the border between home and school and between high school and college, the border between disciplines. Finally, as Haswell, Haswell, and Blalock (2009) demonstrate, "in any act of traditional hospitality . . . all participants, materially or mentally, are on the move." They point out "Being stranger and transient is the fate, of course, of students and teachers everywhere" (721).

My underlying argument about retention is that students will leave: yes, many will leave with a diploma after completing four or five consecutive years at the same institution. However, at an institution like the one I teach at, where the majority of students will leave before graduation, the transient nature of the students makes hospitality a productive metaphor to pursue.

Specifically, I'd like to turn to Derrida for the way that he identifies a paradox within the idea of traditional hospitality. Derrida (2000) argues that in order to extend hospitality, one must first exert sovereignty over one's home, and "sovereignty can only be exercised by filtering, choosing, and thus by excluding and doing violence" (55). This violence occurs through language:

> The foreigner is first of all foreign to the legal language in which the duty of hospitality is formulated, the right to asylum, its limits, norms, policing, etc. He has to ask for hospitality in a language which by definition is not his own, the one imposed on him by the master of the house, the host, the king, the lord, the authorities, the nation, the State, the father, etc. [and we might add, the academy or the discipline] . . . If he was already speaking our language, with all that that implies, if we already shared everything that is shared with a language, would the foreigner still be a foreigner and could we speak of asylum or hospitality in regard to him? (15)

The terms on which traditional hospitality is extended are the terms of the host, who has the right to filter, choose, and exclude, and these terms include imposing the language of the home/institution on the foreigner, an imposition Derrida describes as violent. The paradox, then, is that in order to generously extend hospitality, the host exerts violence. When hospitality works—when host and foreigner are able to enter into a pact of hospitality—it is because the foreigner is not in fact a foreigner. He or she can already speak with the host in the host's language.

If higher education is hospitable, then I would argue it is in the traditional sense. Colleges and universities select and exclude, and insist on everyone sharing the same language. It is typically the job of the first-year writing program to impose this language, or at least to provide an additional gate our guests must pass through before they are truly invited in. The metaphor of the "threshold" in threshold concepts implies an entrance, which conceivably may be blocked if one does not master the relevant concepts.

In light of the paradox of traditional, or "conditional" hospitality, Derrida (2000) offers "absolute hospitality": "absolute hospitality requires that I open up my home and that I give not only to the foreigner . . . but to the absolute, unknown, anonymous other, and that I *give place* to them, that I let them come, that I let them arrive, and take place in the place I offer them, without asking of them either reciprocity or even their names" (25, emphasis in original). Unconditional or absolute hospitality exists on the terms of the guest, who confronts the host with the unknown, who does not speak the same language, and who necessarily changes the home/institution with his or her otherness.

Derrida's (2000) absolute hospitality is a useful metaphorical challenge for a WPA and other college administrators to think about international students and world Englishes, most obviously, but also students who are unprepared for college by traditional measures: veterans, students with disabilities, and all the populations that colleges and universities have typically admitted without considerations for how these populations must necessarily change our institution. Rather, when we have been open to these demographics, extending to them traditional hospitality, we have also exerted the sovereignty over our home: we have insisted that they speak our language, that they observe the house rules, and that they follow our strict schedule. Then when they leave before graduation, like a guest leaving before dinner is served, we consider it rude.

Claudia W. Ruitenberg (2011), arguing for an ethic of hospitality in education, distinguishes absolute hospitality from our typical sense of "inclusion," which "presupposes a whole into which something (or someone) can be incorporated" (Graham and Slee, quoted in Ruitenberg 2011); an ethic of hospitality, on the other hand, appreciates how "the arrival of the guest may change the space into which he or she is received" (32). She argues, "In an ethic of hospitality education must be constructed in such a way as to leave space for those students and those ideas that may arrive. This may seem like an absurd demand: if they may (or may not) arrive, how do we know who or what they are and *what kind* of space we should leave for them?" (33, emphasis in original) When we don't know who will arrive and who won't—and I would like to extend this to who may leave—then we must ask ourselves, "Does what I am about to do leave a possibility for my assumptions about knowledge and teaching and learning to be upset by a new arrival?" or by an unexpected departure? (33)

When a student leaves in the middle of his first semester of college for financial reasons, for example, the discourse of retention characterizes this as a disruption in the traditional educational trajectory of four consecutive years at the same institution. Such a departure upsets the institution because of the implications for budgets as well as published graduation and retention rates, compelling the institution to try to prevent such a departure. This is traditional hospitality, in which under the terms established by the host/institution, such a departure is aberrant, a problem.

However, a writing classroom that embraces a kairotic pedagogy, enacted in the course I describe in this chapter, not only leaves open the possibility for assumptions to be upset, but is designed to seize those opportunities when they happen. We teach the key concepts as contingent, shifting concepts that enable writers to participate *right now* in rich, interesting rhetorical situations. When the student approaches his writing teacher to inform her that he is leaving, this occasion is not characterized as a disruption to the fifteen-week syllabus, but as an opportunity for learning: ethos means something different now as the student attempts to communicate with family, banks, and the student financial services office, or the student's circumstances become an exigency for participating in the circulation of arguments about debt in higher education. The concepts themselves and the attitude engendered by embracing a kairotic pedagogy help the instructor work toward absolute hospitality, by teaching on the terms established by the guest/student who is leaving.

The course and kairotic pedagogy then become a small space for absolute hospitality. Even when students don't leave, the course assumes that all writing tasks, and all classrooms, have the potential to be upset— by arrivals and departures, by readers and other writers, by exigencies that shape the situations themselves, and by technologies that dominate our practices in the twenty-first century. Although Haswell and Haswell (2015) are more interested in traditional hospitality, they do explore Derrida's (2000) notion of absolute hospitality in the context of reading student writing, arguing for a complete surrender to a student's text, allowing ourselves as teacher-readers the experience of getting "lost" in student work like we do when reading for pleasure (91). They say, "Surrendering to a text is more than Coleridge's 'suspension of disbelief.' It is an act of reception that precedes belief and perhaps, as Derrida suggests, precedes any anticipation or determination" (91). Although they don't connect this experience to the concept of kairos, I argue that this approach to reading student writing is facilitated by a kairotic pedagogy. An instructor can approach each student text on its own terms, seeing it for what it is in that moment, what learning opportunities are available to the teacher-reader, rather than reading in anticipation for what happens next chronologically, the inevitable evaluation and grade.

To the extent that a WPA has authority over the curriculum and pedagogy in her program, this space for absolute hospitality is possible. There are other moments when the principles of absolute hospitality might inform a WPA's work, too. As we craft placement policies, for example, we might consider whether we are open to students whose educational backgrounds and levels of preparation could "change the space into which he or she is received" (Ruitenberg 2011, 32). The argument to mainstream basic writers might be an example of such an ethic of absolute hospitality (McNenny 2001). Getting rid of the first-year writing course as a pre-requisite for other courses removes the course from the constraints of chronology and explicitly challenges the myth that writing is a basic skill that should be learned before the student moves on. Moreover, it is a move toward absolute hospitality, as it says to the student "we'll take you in this writing class or program on your own terms, whenever you're ready." A kairotic pedagogy can do this.

Placement policies and prerequisites are rarely established by the WPA, acting alone, however. And these examples illustrate Ruitenberg's (2011) point that absolute hospitality is a "demand that is impossible to fulfill, but that confronts all of our decisions and actions." It is "the impossible challenge that should interrupt pedagogical and curricular decisions and the subject who makes such decisions. This ethic, at every turn, poses the question, 'Will you let the other take place?'" (33). Moreover, Ruitenberg argues that "the achievement of unconditional hospitality would be self-defeating"; if the host extends absolute hospitality, then she can no longer exert sovereignty over the home, which means she is no longer the host, which means she is not in a position to extend hospitality (33).

Ultimately, what I am arguing for here may indeed be impossible. While the course I describe is a course that assumes students may leave, nonetheless it's a course in an institution that specifies admission criteria, graduation requirements, and treats this course as a pre-requisite, assuming we are preparing students for future courses. Nevertheless, while impossible, striving toward the ethic of absolute hospitality in the program, the pedagogy, and the course not only answers the question "will you let the other take place?" but also, "will you let them leave on their own terms."

Note

1. I would like to acknowledge with gratitude the work of my colleagues who served
    on this committee: Jennifer Ailles, Matthew McCurrie, Nita Meola, Hilary Sarat-St.
    Peter, Jonn Salovaara, and Ryan Trauman. I am especially grateful to Hilary, who
    first articulated our goal as providing an analytical and heuristic framework, and
    who has continued to help me think about our course in relation to "writing about
    writing" and threshold concepts, approaches to writing instruction I discuss later in
    the chapter.

References

Adler-Kassner, Linda, John Majewski, and Damian Koshnick. 2012. "The Value of
Troublesome Knowledge: Transfer and Threshold Concepts in Writing and History."
Accessed April 15, 2015. *Composition Forum* 26. http://compositionforum.com/issue
/26/troublesome-knowledge-threshold.php.
Bousquet, Marc. 2004. "Composition as Management Science." In *Tenured Bosses and
Disposable Teachers: Writing Instruction in the Managed University*, ed. Marc Bousquet,
Tony Scott, and Leo Parascondola, 11–35. Carbondale: Southern Illinois University
Press.
Derrida, Jacques. 2000. *Of Hospitality: Anne Dufourmantelle Invites Jacques Derrida to
Respond.* Stanford: Stanford University Press.
Diogenes, Marvin, and Andrea A. Lunsford. 2006. "Toward Delivering New Definitions of
Writing." In *Delivering Composition: The Fifth Canon*, ed. Kathleen Blake Yancey, 141–54.
Portsmouth, NH: Boynton/Cook.
Haswell, Janis, Richard Haswell, and Glenn Blalock. 2009. "Hospitality in College
Composition Courses." *CCC* 60 (4): 707–26.
Haswell, Richard, and Janis Haswell. 2015. *Hospitality and Authoring: An Essay for the
English Profession.* Boulder: University Press of Colorado.
"Key Indicators: Fall 2015." 2015. Columbia College Chicago. Accessed March 9, 2016.
http://about.colum.edu/effectiveness/PDF_Folder/KeyIndicators_FA2015.xlsx.pdf.
Kress, Gunther. 2010. *Multimodality: A Social Semiotic Approach to Contemporary
Communication.* New York: Routledge.
McNenny, Gerri. 2001. *Mainstreaming Basic Writers: Politics and Pedagogies of Access.* New
York: Routledge.
Mortenson, Thomas G. 2005. "Measurements of Persistence." In *College Student Retention:
Formula for Student Success*, ed. Alan Seidman, 31–60. Westport: Praeger.
Reichert Powell, Pegeen. 2013. *Retention and Resistance: Writing Instruction and Students
Who Leave.* Logan: Utah State University Press.
Ruitenberg, Claudia W. 2011. "The Empty Chair: Education in an Ethic of Hospitality."
Philosophy of Education: 28–36. http://ojs.ed.uiuc.edu/index.php/pes/issue/view/29.
Sheridan, David, Jim Ridolfo, and Anthony Michel. 2012. *The Available Means of
Persuasion: Mapping a Theory and Pedagogy of Multimodal Public Rhetoric.* Anderson:
Parlor Press.
Wardle, Elizabeth, and Doug Downs. 2013. "Reflecting Back and Looking Forward:
Revisiting 'Teaching about Writing, Righting Misconceptions' Five Years On."
Accessed September 22, 2015. *Composition Forum* 27. http://compositionforum.com
/issue/27/reflecting-back.php.
Wardle, Elizabeth, and Doug Downs. 2014. *Writing about Writing: A College Reader.* Boston:
Bedford/St. Martin's.

9

RETENTION, CRITICAL PEDAGOGY, AND STUDENTS AS AGENTS
Eschewing the Deficit Model

Beth Buyserie, Anna Plemons, and Patricia Freitag Ericsson

Although common knowledge in composition studies has long held that first-year composition (FYC) plays an important role in student retention, proof for that belief is scarce. In Fall 2008, composition faculty and advocates from a number of student support units at Washington State University collaboratively designed and put into practice a unique retention and persistence program that has led us to validate this common knowledge. Known as the Critical Literacies Achievement and Success Program (CLASP), this retention approach affirms the experiences and academic assets of underrepresented students, provides theoretically-grounded pedagogical workshops for faculty, works in collaboration with a broad collection of campus support units, collects both quantitative and qualitative data, and has succeeded in garnering grant support. In essence, CLASP addresses student retention and persistence by actively supporting weekly student-faculty dialogue and critically reflective teacher pedagogy.

This chapter foregrounds the major tenets of CLASP's retention approach while illustrating them in a particular institutional setting. CLASP employs a two-pronged approach, with one prong focused on student learning and the other on faculty development. First, we reject a deficit model for the increasing number of students at Washington State University (WSU) who identify as low-income, of color, first-generation, or have other retention "risk" factors. Instead, we work to couple students' existing academic assets with opportunities to practice self-efficacy. Second, we engage faculty in critical pedagogy sessions that help them explore the connections between their pedagogy and the retention of underrepresented students. These approaches *together* make a difference

DOI: 10.7330/9781607326021.c009

that, we argue, either one alone would not. In this chapter, we outline CLASP's theoretically grounded pedagogy, which connects retention theory outside composition (Tinto 1993) with critical composition pedagogy (e.g., Ratcliffe 2005; Reichert Powell 2013; Villanueva 1997, 2004), drawing in additional significant voices from related fields (e.g., Bonilla-Silva 2014; Steele 2011). Our data on student retention, persistence, and skill transfer demonstrate the model's successes and areas for improvement, adding quantitative and qualitative information to the existing body of composition scholarship on retention.

Briefly, students in CLASP dialogue weekly with faculty during office hours, developing a practice of self-efficacy that better equips them to navigate the unspoken expectations of the university. At the same time, CLASP engages faculty in professional development opportunities that explore the connection between pedagogy and the retention of underrepresented students. Finally, CLASP also meets with educational opportunity programs (i.e., TRiO, Multicultural Student Services, and the College Assistance Migrant Program), closing the loop between those who support the students outside the classroom and those who teach in key introductory courses like English composition.

WHAT WE (DON'T) KNOW ABOUT STUDENT RETENTION AND FYC: A LITERATURE REVIEW

In March 2015, a WPA-listserv exchange on "FYC and retention" revealed that some Writing Program Administrators (WPAs) are paying attention to campus retention discourses. By delving into institutional research data, some WPAs (e.g., Nora Bacon of University of Nebraska Omaha and Michael Day of Northern Illinois University) reported that students who take FYC in their first year of college return at a rate nearly 10 percent higher than those who did not take FYC. While this rare data provides some correlation, it is not strong enough to prove causation. Additional support for our disciplinary belief in the importance of FYC for retention can be drawn from the National Survey of Student Engagement's (NSSE) focus on "High-Impact Practices" (NSSE 2015). Although FYC is not explicitly one of those practices, it is an integral part of all the practices listed as High-Impact. In fact, the definition of a High-Impact Practice can be easily mapped on to FYC best practices: High-Impact Practices "demand considerable time and effort, facilitate learning outside of the classroom, require meaningful interactions with faculty and students, encourage collaboration with diverse others, and provide frequent and substantive feedback" (NSSE 2015). Starting in

2013, the NSSE reinforced the importance of writing as an important facet of student engagement by providing institutions with an optional module on writing (NSSE 2015). All of the questions in this model are oriented toward an evaluation of FYC best practices pedagogy (NSSE 2015). These few examples, however, are not strong enough to fully support claims about the importance of FYC in student retention.

Arguing against our common understanding of the importance of FYC is 2009 research by Blythe et al., published in the *WPA: Writing Program Administration*. This research was based on previous insights that "more writing experience may not always be what academically marginal students need." The authors posit that "more writing is not always the answer to an academically marginal student's writing dilemma" (Blythe et al. 2009, 12). Overall, their research substantiated this insight and indicated writing courses themselves might not be the only successful intervention in student retention (Blythe et al. 2009).

Recent research by Pegeen Reichert Powell (2013) argues that retention should not be about keeping students at a particular university and instead about the good pedagogical practices teachers routinely employ. Reichert Powell (2013) claims that "the focus on the first year in retention literature does not always translate to a focus on pedagogy or to a reliance on the expertise of faculty who regularly teach first-year students" (8). CLASP stands in that gap, asking faculty to think critically about their role as classroom teachers in student retention. We agree with Reichert Powell's (2009) earlier argument that the composition classroom is particularly well suited to serve as a bridge between overly bureaucratic notions of student retention and strong pedagogical discussions. As Reichert Powell (2009) argues, the composition class can serve "as an interface between students' past and future educational experiences, as an introduction to the discourse practices of higher education, and as one of the only universal requirements at most institutions" (669). CLASP considers faculty pedagogy a key component of student retention. Therefore, we have worked to engage our entire FYC faculty in critical reflection about their pedagogy, helping faculty in our program understand the direct lines between how they teach and student persistence.

Reichert Powell's (2009, 2013) ongoing efforts to complicate the role of FYC in retention echoes those of Richard E. Miller (1998), who emphasizes how little we really know and understand about student retention, even as our discourse is peppered with vague references to "the student" (15). Miller claims that "invoking the ever-pliable student helps cover over the embarrassing fact that we know almost nothing about how students experience the culture of schooling or why some students fail and other succeed" (16). Students are simply perceived, in Miller's words, as "absolutely anonymous, deracinated, ahistorical, malleable, infinitely penetrable being[s]" (16). Reichert Powell (2013) might agree that this infinite malleability is a key characteristic of current retention discourse, as all our current approaches to retention view students "as a problem to be solved" (36).

CLASP was not initially designed to support claims about the importance of FYC in retention discourse, nor did we set out to complicate the sometimes questionable nature of retention discourse. Nevertheless, the program's emphasis on both critical pedagogy and intentional weekly dialogue during office hours between students and faculty has proven to be instrumental in navigating the intersections between FYC, underrepresented students (particularly students of color at a predominantly white university), and administrative conversations about student retention. We have found that the CLASP framework addresses the weaknesses in retention discourse—discussion about and around the student—by eschewing a deficit model and working to support students who are identified by the university as "at risk" for retention. By rejecting notions of deficit, this framework aligns with Reichert Powell (2013), who insists that the university share responsibility for student persistence—rather than placing the onus for this persistence solely on the students.

STUDENTS AS AGENTS: CONNECTING RETENTION THEORY WITH CRITICAL STUDENT ENGAGEMENT

While we reject the pitfalls of traditional retention discourse, we are aware that this discourse pervades campus discussions. A composition program can be a part of efforts to modify the conversation by inviting students "at risk" for retention into purposeful dialogue with faculty members. As student development scholars such as Alexander Astin, Arthur Chickering and Zelda F. Gamson, and Vincent Tinto have noted, underrepresented students (particularly first-generation college students) benefit from opportunities that develop and scaffold the bureaucratic skills that high-achieving students are more likely to employ without overt permission (implicit permission is typically afforded to students operating within positions of race and class privilege) (Astin 1999; Chickering and Gamson 1999; Tinto 1993). One such skill is the use of faculty office hours, a tradition most faculty consider standard and may only communicate via the syllabus or routine class announcements. Many faculty are unaware of the power dynamics inherent in office hours, believing (with good intentions) that students who want to meet will simply show up. To help make the power and potential of office hours understandable to a wider range of students, CLASP relies on institutional support to help underrepresented students better utilize and navigate faculty office hours (and later to help faculty reflect on their own power in this space). That institutional assistance comes from a variety of campus units, including the College Assistance Migrant Program, College Success Foundation Scholars, First Scholars, Multicultural Student Services, Native American Programs, Smart Start, TRiO, and Athletics. These units have full-time advisors whose job is to support their cohort of students. These advisors emphasize and reaffirm the importance of office hours, encouraging students to make weekly office-hour appointments with composition faculty, as well as guiding them through the initial process of generating potential weekly questions. The students themselves take the initiative to make and keep the appointments, as well as formulate specific critical questions in preparation for these meetings. The weekly office hour meetings foster dialogue with faculty as a means of promoting student agency, confidence, and institutional connectedness.

Our data from student and instructor focus groups suggest that CLASP students initially ask relatively "safe" questions about due dates, formatting, or grammar. By the end of the semester, however, students are often posing complex, engaged questions specific to particular writing projects and rhetorical situations. Weekly practice discussing course material one-on-one with faculty provides the students the opportunity to consciously reflect on their development as scholars. Following Bruce Horner's (1997) exhortations, teachers and students are encouraged to recognize that their courses have "social and historical locations" (524). By encouraging students to build academic relationships with faculty, students can begin to see the course pedagogy "as something in which they could actively participate" (524). These overt invitations for students are opportunities to practice self-advocacy and active course participation. Referencing CLASP's design as an example of "subversive complicity," Victor Villanueva (2013) claims that "The best learning is one-with-one; novice students' great fear is the one-with-one with professors. Through this program [CLASP], the professors get to discover the students as more than victims; the students get to discover the professors as less than geniuses" (105).[1]

THEORETICALLY-GROUNDED PEDAGOGY: CONNECTING
RETENTION THEORY WITH CRITICAL COMPOSITION PEDAGOGY

Because we believe that good pedagogy supports retention and persistence, the second prong of CLASP is a six-part critical pedagogies series that offers FYC faculty the opportunity to engage in ongoing reflexive conversations regarding teacher rhetoric, privilege, and power in the classroom. The series is part of the composition program's weekly Professional Development in Composition sessions, which are attended by instructors (who can earn Professional Development Certificates) and graduate students (who attend Professional Development sessions for credit). An average of thirty instructors participate in the CLASP pedagogy series every year. composition faculty's willingness in this series to critically examine teacher rhetoric, privilege, and power plays an important role in student retention and in the discourse of student retention, particularly the retention of low-income students and students of color at predominantly white, middle-class institutions. This pedagogy series is presented within the context of ongoing reflection and dialogue, recognizing that addressing issues of power is never complete. CLASP advocates from various student support units also attend these sessions to ensure that our conversations represent the students as whole persons, rather than as representatives from homogenous underrepresented groups. This series is intentionally designed to address an institutional system that often frames these student-faculty interactions as remedial.

Reichert Powell (2013) argues against the dangers of presuming retention is even possible or that can be supported with one-size-fits-all models. Nonetheless, Reichert Powell's strong claims about what we cannot do hardly negate the need for critical reflection and de-colonial action on the part of faculty. As three white faculty/WPAs working within a predominantly white institution, we are aware of composition's role in the linguistic colonization of students. A significant body of composition scholarship details the disconnections, silences and damages that occur in cross-cultural communication in the classroom (e.g., Ratcliffe 2005; Royster 1996; Villanueva 1997, 2004). As Stephanie Kerschbaum (2014) points out, underrepresented students are often still positioned "as outsiders needing to be better integrated into campus communities" (151), an assimilation move that marks difference as deficient. Her claim is important for composition's approach to retention: classrooms might be spaces to introduce students to academic discourse and push back against unexamined notions of difference and inclusion. The CLASP pedagogy series focuses on the problematic intersections of teacher rhetoric and cross-cultural intention.

Table 9.1. CLASP Pedagogy Series

Semester 1	Semester 2
Session 1: Pedagogies of Inclusion/Critical Pedagogies	*Session 4:* Rhetorical Listening and Responding to Student Writing
Session 2: Power, Privilege, and Student Participation	*Session 5:* Student Self-Reflection, Goal Setting, and Stereotype Threat
Session 3: Course Design and Critical Pedagogy	*Session 6:* Rhetorical Listening, Color-blind Racism, and Stereotype Threat: Considerations for Student-Teacher Conferencing

The six-part critical pedagogy series, offered during weekly Professional Development in Composition sessions, includes the elements depicted in Table 9.1.

In this series, to engage a busy FYC faculty in productive, ongoing questioning of pedagogy, we looked for scholarship that addressed particular aspects of privilege. Since WSU is approximately 70 percent white, considering Bonilla-Silva's (2014) work on color-blind rhetorics and Claude Steele's (2011) work on stereotype threat offers appropriate platforms for a larger conversation about the relationship between teacher privilege and classroom pedagogy. The decision to focus on race privilege was also supported by the CLASP campus partners, who articulated the frequency with which their students experience negative race-related encounters in the classroom. Systemic racism is an aspect of the college experience for many students and faculty are often unwitting actors in student stories about racist and racialized experiences. For our pedagogy series, Bonilla-Silva (2014) and Steele (2011) provide discussion ideas and pedagogical tools for starting difficult and protracted conversation about a fraught topic.

To avoid the pitfalls of discrete, reifying "diversity training" programs, teachers are also introduced to a methodology for listening rhetorically (Ratcliffe 2005). Each topic is selected for the possibilities it affords the discussion of teacher privilege in the classroom within a practical, pedagogical context. The pedagogical constructs of the series do not operate from a deficit model (neither teachers nor students are "broken"), nor is it an expert discourse. The sessions encourage the inclusion of lived experience and story telling between teachers, thus modeling and reinforcing a posture of rhetorical listening (Ratcliffe 2005). Ratcliffe's call to purposeful listening for presences, absences, and unknowns leads to the fundamental question that has always complicated/frustrated/stymied cross-cultural communication: "How may we listen for that which we do not intellectually, viscerally, or experientially know?" (29), a question prompted by the work of Jacqueline Jones Royster (1996). The work of Bonilla-Silva (2014) on color-blind racism and Steele (2011) on stereotype threat offer writing teachers some starting points for working toward a productive methodology that responds to Ratcliffe's (2005) fundamental question of how we listen for what we do not understand and for that which we have not been trained to hear.

To be specific, Bonilla-Silva (2014) gives teachers the language with which to interrogate the disconnections between cross-cultural intention and classroom practice and interrogate their own relationship with the dominant racial ideology. Bonilla-Silva's insight that "younger, educated, middle-class people are more likely than older, less-educated, working-class people to make full use of the resources of color-blind racism" (71) is particularly important for us because the demographic of WSU writing teachers is predominantly white, young, and educated. While Bonilla-Silva (2014) outlines the frames and rhetorical moves used by whites in the maintenance of a color-blind racism, Steele's (2011) research on stereotype threat describes the psychological responses by members of non-dominant groups in specific instances where they perceive a threat of being viewed in a stereotypic way. Steele suggests that performance is significantly and negatively affected in situations where members of a non-dominant group perceive the threat of being viewed in a stereotypic way. The work of Bonilla-Silva and Steele, taken together, gives faculty some concrete tools with which to listening with intent to students, consider how their rhetoric might maintain dominant ideology, and identify disconnections between teacherly intent and pedagogical practice.

CLASP DATA: FALL 2011–SPRING 2014

Speaking to the Bureau: Data and Retention Discourse

In a different era, it might have been enough for a composition program to emphasize pedagogy and go forward, but data-driven accountability and shrinking budgets demand that composition programs provide substantiated results. Composition scholars, Richard Haswell and Susan McLeod (2001) argue that "we need to think carefully about administrators [bureaucrats] as audience—what they do, what they want, and what kind of information they might need from evaluators to do their job. . . . As the academic equivalent of managers in a corporation [a bureaucracy], they have the job of maintaining the quality of the institution while working within budgets" (Haswell and McLeod 2001, 173). Part of the CLASP approach is a careful collection of retention data and reporting that data to administrators. This approach has allowed CLASP to become visible and valuable to the administration in ways that would not be possible without such data. Our work takes heed of Haswell and McLeod's argument that administrators have a primary need: "to make decisions about allocation of resources" (173). We are fully aware that as a bureaucratic entity dependent on the resources of statistical analysis, we need to provide the bureau's administrators the kind of data they need to justify the types of programs we want to run.

In Fall 2011, CLASP received a 3-year grant from College Spark Washington (a community grants program). This grant funding allowed us to design our assessment methods, develop and implement the CLASP Pedagogy Series, and prepare materials for dissemination and potential replication. Though CLASP continues, most of our data (including student and faculty pre- and post-course surveys, student and faculty focus groups, course grades, student demographic data, number of student-faculty conferences, retention rates, and progress toward graduation) was collected between Fall 2011 and Spring 2014. Because our data come from a particular institutional setting, we do not claim that our results are generalizable to outside populations, although we suspect they might be. Even though our data is persuasive, it is not absolute proof of CLASP's effectiveness. The situational and contextual interactions that take place in the pedagogy sessions and student-faculty meetings are not fully representable by numerical data. That aside, we include results that we have repeatedly presented to WSU faculty, advisors, and administration, other institutions, and at national conferences. This data-driven research has been invaluable in opening dialogue with upper-level administration, as well in helping help us consider how we might shape retention discourse at our institution.

Demographics and Retention

For the six semesters between Fall 2011-Spring 2014, CLASP served an average of 40 students per semester (240 students total). Eighty-four percent of the students were Pell-Grant eligible, and 80 percent were students of color. For the six-semester period, 1,920 student-teacher meetings during weekly office hours took place. CLASP students met with their FYC instructors an average of eight times during each semester. Each faculty member was assigned no more than four CLASP students to ensure that faculty could meet with students during regular office hours. Because of this limitation, the size of our program is always dependent upon the number of faculty teaching English 101 (typically about 25–30 instructors teaching over 50 sections per semester).

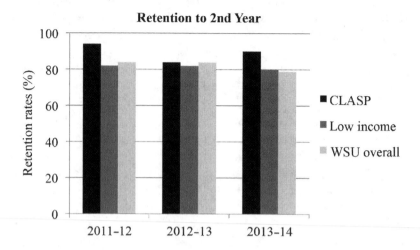

Figure 9.1. Retention to 2nd Year (CLASP Participants: 2011–12 = 93; 2012–13 = 77; 2013–14 = 71)

Figure 9.1 illustrates CLASP student retention rates from first to second year for the three years of our grant.[2] We realize the retention rates in Figure 9.1 are affected by a number of variables, so we do not attribute them solely to CLASP. At the same time, because our follow-up data shows positive results, we assume CLASP has played a significant role in the positive retention numbers for participants.

CLASP student retention rates from second to third year are illustrated in Figure 9.2.

Survey Data: CLASP and Control Group

For six semesters, CLASP students completed a pre- and post-course survey, responding to questions about their confidence in speaking with faculty and how likely they were to do so. Our results were positive, enabling us to meet or exceed our grant's benchmarks. In Fall 2012, the granting agency requested a survey of non-CLASP students to serve as a control group; the control group received no special instructions to meet with faculty, other than the general invitations to attend office hours that faculty typically extend to a class. That semester, CLASP students and faculty conferenced a total of 322 times in Fall 2012, with an average of 7.1 meetings per student.[3] No data was collected on the number of times non-CLASP students met with faculty.

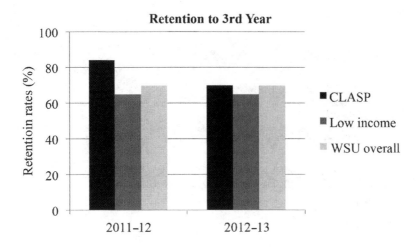

Figure 9.2. Retention to 3rd Year (CLASP Participants: 2011–12 = 93; 2012–13 = 77)

The figures below illustrate CLASP and control group responses to a series of statements about student confidence in meeting and talking with faculty.

> Question A: I am confident with my academic (college level) writing abilities. (Figure 9.3)
>
> Question B: I am confident talking with my instructor about my writing. (Figure 9.4)
>
> Question C: I am likely to approach my English instructor if I have a question. (Figure 9.5)
>
> Question D: I am like to meet with my future instructors to ask questions or dialogue about course concepts. (Figure 9.6)

CLASP students showed substantial growth in confidence, consistently surpassing the control group. The control group provided more positive responses on the pre-survey, but did not show the same improvement in positive responses on the post-survey.

In promoting the idea of students as agents, we are interested in whether students apply the skills learned in CLASP (including approaching a faculty member, using office hours, and developing strong questions as a starting point for dialogue) to their future courses. Figure 9.6 shows that, without exception, CLASP students indicated they were likely to be active agents in dialoging with faculty.

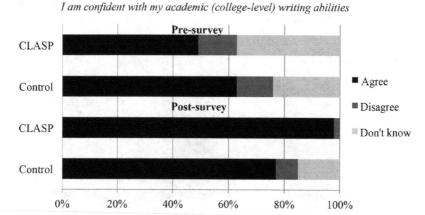

Figure 9.3. Question A Responses

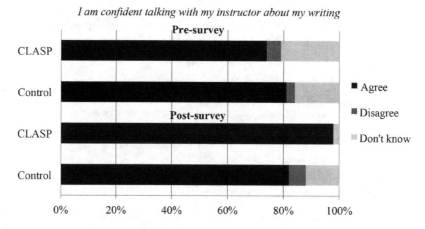

Figure 9.4. Question B Responses

After CLASP: Student Survey Results

Our data also show that students who learn to use faculty office hours in CLASP transfer this ability to their subsequent classes. We asked students who were one semester out of CLASP to respond to the following two statements:[4]

1. I met with instructors of my courses this semester.

2. I met with instructors of my courses this semester because of what I learned in CLASP.

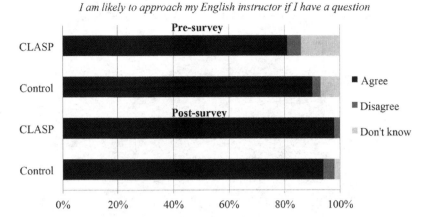

Figure 9.5. Question C Responses

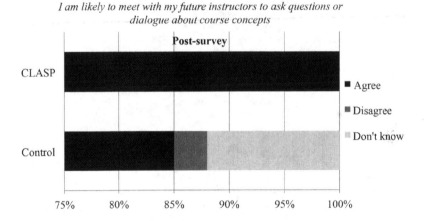

Figure 9.6. Question D Responses

Figures 9.7 and 9.8 show the average of responses to these two questions from the Fall 2011 and 2012 follow-up surveys:

Overall, our data suggest that students in the program understand that they can choose to be actively engaged in their own education, rather than subjects of it.

I met with instructors of my courses this semester

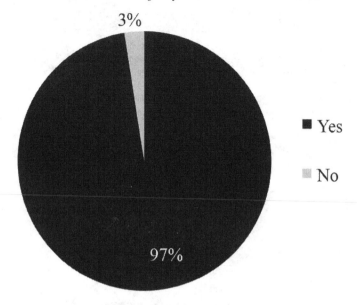

Figure 9.7. Question 1 Responses (averages from Year 2011–2012 Cohort)

I met with instructors of my courses this semester because of what I learned in CLASP

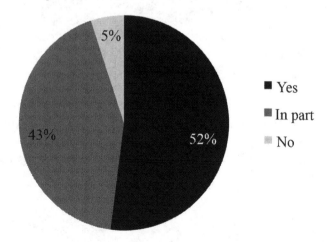

Figure 9.8. Question 2 Responses (averages from Year 2011–2012 Cohort)

FUTURE DIRECTIONS FOR CLASP: A REPLICABLE
AND CUSTOMIZABLE MODEL

We believe that the CLASP model can be implemented at other institutions, and its dual emphasis on student-faculty dialogue and teacher pedagogy can be used as a model for other populations. As evidence, we look to our own university. The composition program was CLASP's only academic partner at WSU for its first five years. In 2013, the Mathematics Department began participating in the structured weekly student-faculty dialogue (during office hours) component of CLASP, and is in the process of adding the key critical pedagogy piece. After a Retention Summit held in May 2014, eight additional academic departments joined CLASP, with nearly 60 participating faculty meeting with approximately 100 students per semester. To support the critical pedagogy component, and to continue collecting data, a campus-wide CLASP Director was hired in Spring 2015. As of Fall 2015, there are 10 academic units participating: Comparative Ethnic Studies, English, Entomology, Environmental Science, Geology, History, Human Development, Mathematics, Music, and Science.

Though our data has been instrumental to the successful growth of CLASP and serves the university bureaucracy well, we intentionally foreground theoretical and pedagogical frameworks that we believe will help turn retention and persistence discourse away from deficit models that deny student agency. Attention to faculty development that acknowledges student assets ought to be a key part of retention theory and practice. Likewise, retention efforts are well-served when they include sustained, critical faculty reflection regarding the relationship between power, privilege, rhetorical listening, stereotype threat, and the retention of underrepresented students.

Notes

1. The concurrent labor issues and the details of CLASP are addressed later in this chapter.
2. We thank Dr. Preston Andrews for his invaluable help with our data representation design.
3. The Fall 2012 CLASP cohort included 45 students from 20 sections of English 101; the control group included 119 students from five sections English 101.
4. 66% of students responded to follow-up survey in Fall 2011; 69% in Fall 2012.

References

Astin, Alexander. 1999. "Student Involvement: A Developmental Theory for Higher Education." *Journal of College Student Development* 40 (5): 518–29.

Blythe, Stuart, Rachelle Darabi, Barbara Simon Kirkwood, and William Baden. 2009. "Exploring Options for Students at the Boundaries of the 'At-Risk' Designation." *WPA. Writing Program Administration* 33 (1–2): 9–28.

Bonilla-Silva, Eduardo. 2014. *Racism without Racists: Color-Blind Racism and the Persistence of Racial Inequality in America.* 4th ed. Lanham, MD: Rowman & Littlefield.

Chickering, Arthur, and Zelda F. Gamson. 1999. "Development and Adaptations of the Seven Principles for Good Practice in Undergraduate Education." *New Directions for Teaching and Learning* 1999 (80): 75–81. http://dx.doi.org/10.1002/tl.8006.

Haswell, Richard, and Susan McLeod. 2001. "Working with Administrators: A Dialogue on Dialogue." In *Beyond Outcomes: Assessment and Instruction within a University Writing Program*, ed. Richard Haswell, 165–89. Westport: Ablex.

Horner, Bruce. 1997. "Students, Authorship, and the Work of Composition." *College English* 59 (5): 505–29. http://dx.doi.org/10.2307/378664.

Kerschbaum, Stephanie L. 2014. *Toward a New Rhetoric of Difference.* Urbana: CCC/NCTE.

Miller, Richard E. 1998. *As If Learning Mattered: Reforming Higher Education.* Ithaca: Cornell University Press.

NSSE. National Survey of Student Engagement. 2015. Accessed June 5. http://nsse.indi ana.edu.

Ratcliffe, Krista. 2005. *Rhetorical Listening: Identification, Gender, Whiteness.* Carbondale: Southern Illinois Press.

Reichert Powell, Pegeen. 2009. "Retention and Writing Instruction: Implications for Access and Pedagogy." *College Composition and Communication* 60 (4): 664–82.

Reichert Powell, Pegeen. 2013. *Retention and Resistance: Writing Instruction and Students Who Leave.* Logan: Utah State University Press.

Royster, Jacqueline Jones. 1996. "When the First Voice You Hear is Not Your Own." *College Composition and Communication* 47 (1): 29–40. http://dx.doi.org/10.2307 /358272.

Steele, Claude M. 2011. *Whistling Vivaldi: How Stereotypes Affect Us and What We Can Do.* New York: Norton.

Tinto, Vincent. 1993. *Leaving College: Rethinking the Causes and Cures of Student Attrition.* 2nd ed. Chicago: University of Chicago Press.

Villanueva, Victor. 1997. "Maybe a Colony: And Still Another Critique of the Comp Community." *JAC* 17 (2): 183–90.

Villanueva, Victor. 2004. "*Memoria* Is a Friend of Ours: On the Discourse of Color." *College English* 67 (1): 9–19. http://dx.doi.org/10.2307/4140722.

Villanueva, Victor. 2013. "Subversive Complicity and Basic Writing Across the Curriculum." *Journal of Basic Writing* 32 (1): 97–110.

10

RECONFIGURING THE WRITING STUDIO MODEL
Examining the Impact of the PlusOne *Program on Student Performance and Retention*

Polina Chemishanova and Robin Snead

Given the increasing public demand for accountability, expectations of demonstrating the "value added" outcome of a college education, and the decreasing state funding for public higher education, not surprisingly, issues of retention, student persistence, and graduation rank are among the current most studied areas in higher education. For years, retention and graduation rates have been used as metrics to measure institutional effectiveness and efficiency. Like many other colleges and universities, the University of North Carolina at Pembroke (UNCP) considers student persistence and retention an ongoing critical concern. Since 2008, the school has implemented a number of initiatives to improve retention and graduation rates, which were then among the lowest in the sixteen-campus UNC system. One of these retention initiatives included the development of the *PlusOne* program focused on improving student success in the composition classroom.

This chapter offers a critical case study of how UNCP's *PlusOne* program has allowed the writing program to reconceptualize approaches to retention and foster ongoing support for writing instruction and pedagogy. It provides an overview of its design and implementation, addresses the challenges and successes of this undertaking, and illustrates ways in which the *PlusOne* program reconfigured the writing studio model in an effort to establish a meaningful and sustainable retention-focused initiative that aimed to improve students' performance and success rate in first-year writing courses. The *PlusOne* program, we argue, represents a redefined and broadened focus on student persistence and retention and a viable means for offering critical support for student learning

DOI: 10.7330/9781607326021.c010

while also attending to issues of labor and faculty working conditions in first-year writing programs. While our narrative is grounded in local and institutional contexts, we offer it as one model for Writing Program Administrators (WPA) who are considering alternative methods of delivering supplemental instruction in first-year writing courses and improving the workplace of composition. Substantial change in faculty working conditions in higher education, we posit, can take place at the local level when framed in the context of student retention and persistence.

INSTITUTIONAL PROFILE

UNCP has been one of the constituent institutions of the University of North Carolina since the system's inception in 1972. The history of the institution, however, dates back to 1887 when the first state-supported college for American Indians in the nation, the Croatan Normal School for Indians, was founded to train teachers to educate the Native American population in the southeastern area of the state. Since that time, UNCP has become one of the most diverse institutions of higher education in the South and has been described by *US News and World Report* as one of the most diverse institutions in the nation with over half of the students self-identifying in a racial or ethnic minority group.

Today UNCP functions largely as a regional university within the UNC system. The university's rural location as well as the educational and economic characteristics of its primary service region (with resulting factors of poor academic preparation[1] and socioeconomic disadvantage) present significant challenges to student success. Sixty-eight percent of the students who attend the university graduated from high schools in a surrounding eight-county region, with seven of these eight counties being in the bottom quartile in unemployment in the state. Forty-three percent of the enrolled students identify either Robeson (39%) or Scotland (4%) Counties as their county of residence (Office of Institutional Research 2015a), which are among the ten most economically depressed areas of North Carolina.[2]

Educational attainment levels are also low in this region. Data from the National Center for Education Statistics' 2003 National Assessment of Adult Literacy indicate that as great as one-third of the population in Robeson County may lack basic prose literacy skills (NCES 2003), while Census data report that only 12.5 percent of the population aged twenty-five years or older has completed a Bachelor's degree. Over 50 percent of students admitted to UNCP are the first in their families to pursue college education, and therefore they may initially lack the contextual knowledge and awareness necessary for successful acculturation into the university environment (Conley 2008). Many students, then, arrive at UNCP both academically underprepared and without any real sense of what will be required of them to obtain a college education. For these students, the transition to college can be overwhelming and can pose significant problems for their retention.

EFFORTS TO IMPROVE PERSISTENCE AND RETENTION

In 2007, the University of North Carolina General Administration (UNC-GA), the governing body for the UNC system, identified retention and persistence as targeted areas for improvement following the US Department of Education's report of the Commission on the Future of Higher Education (US Department of Education 2006). Students admitted to UNCP in the fall of 2007 had an average high school GPA of 3.03 and a mean combined critical reading and mathematics SAT score of 949, below both the state mean of 1004 and the national mean of 1017. Retention and graduation rates at UNCP were among the lowest in the sixteen-campus UNC system. Based on data released by UNC-GA (University of North Carolina General Administration 2012), for the Fall 2007 cohort, the UNC system boasted a first- to second-year retention rate of 81.3 percent, higher than the national average of 79 percent. However, UNCP's retention rate was 67.4 percent, the lowest in the system as a whole and the lowest among our peer institutions within the system.

Since 2008, UNCP has engaged in a number of initiatives to improve student retention and graduation rates. These efforts have pulled largely from Vincent Tinto's research on student retention as well as George Kuh's work through the LEAP (Liberal Education and America's Promise) initiative with the Association of American Colleges and Universities. Both Tinto (2006) and Kuh (2008) identify the transitional first year of college as critical to student success, and both point to critical engagement and interaction between faculty and students as essential in developing persistence. Further, both address the known achievement gaps between underrepresented, low-income, or underprepared students and their majority, higher-income, or more adequately prepared peers as issues requiring focused attention. Kuh (2008) specifically suggests the need for "high-impact educational practices," which he defines as research-backed practices that increase rates of student retention and engagement. High-impact educational practices are "programs and activities [that] appear to engage participants at levels that elevate their performance across multiple and desired-outcomes

measures such as persistence" (14). High-impact activities include practices such as undergraduate research, global learning, capstone courses,
first-year seminars, internships, collaborative projects, learning communities, and service or community-based learning. Kuh (2008) asserts
that "historically underserved students tend to benefit more" from high-
impact practices, especially in the first year, in which such practices have
a "compensatory effect on first-year grades" and retention (17–19).

Given the known barriers to success faced by incoming students,
many of the initiatives to increase retention and persistence at UNCP
have involved traditional first-year experience efforts intended to aid
students in their transition from high school to college. These efforts
include an enhanced freshman orientation program and extensive revisions of the freshman seminar course aimed at both introducing students to the university environment and helping students to develop the
contextual skills, cognitive strategies, and academic behaviors (Conley
2008; Kuh 2008) needed to be successful. Additional initiatives that
focus beyond the first year alone include expanded academic advising,
the development of the HAWK ("Honing Academics with Knowledge")
early alert system designed for the early identification of and intervention with students who are experiencing academic difficulty, the utilization of upperclassmen as Academic Resource Mentors, and the availability of both professional and peer tutors free of charge to students
through the Academic Support Center.[3] Finally, UNCP encourages
integrated learning and enhanced scholarly engagement through seven
learning communities,[4] which have proven to increase student engagement and success during the first year and beyond.

FIRST-YEAR WRITING AS HIGH-IMPACT EDUCATIONAL PRACTICE

Given Kuh's (2008) definition, first-year writing at UNCP can be considered a high-impact educational practice. Kuh delineates several characteristics that make high impact activities "unusually effective" (15),
many of which are regular features of first-year writing courses. High-
impact practices are effective, among other reasons, because (1) they
require students to devote significant time, effort, investment, and commitment to purposeful tasks, (2) they are often writing-intensive activities, (3) they demand regular interaction with faculty and peers that
makes anonymity impossible, and (4) they involve frequent formal and
informal feedback from faculty and peers. In addition to the required
Freshman Seminar course, the two courses in first-year writing are the
only university courses required of every student who graduates from

UNCP. As such, every student who begins his or her collegiate career at UNCP engages in coursework through the composition program. Courses in first-year writing, therefore, are appropriate courses in which to study and imbed efforts targeting increased retention and persistence especially given abundant evidence indicating that attrition rates for students between the first and second year in college are the highest of all four years. Furthermore, as Pegeen Reichert Powell (2014) explains, the nature of the writing course with its relatively small class size and the individual attention that first-year writing faculty engage students in are "tremendous resource[s], deliberately or not, for retention efforts" across institutions of higher education (43). And while first-year writing courses often serve as gateway courses to Writing across the Curriculum/Writing in the Disciplines (WAC/WID) courses across the university, they could also act as gatekeeping classes if students are unable to complete them successfully in a timely manner and make progress toward graduation. Decreasing students' non-completion rates in first-year writing courses at UNCP is one way of impacting positively the attrition rates between first and second year.

Even before the 2007 UNC-GA mandate to improve retention and graduation rates, the composition program housed within the (then) Department of English and Theatre[5] at UNCP had begun to look closely at ENG 1050: Composition I and ENG 1060: Composition II, the foundational courses in the two-semester composition sequence required of all students as a part of the General Education program. Historically, many students did not pass these courses and therefore had to repeat them (some more than once), potentially increasing their time to graduation and/or the likelihood that they would drop out. In an effort to create a meaningful pedagogical response to students' performance in composition classes, in the spring of 2006 the English Department implemented a one-year pilot program, *PlusOne*, designed to provide additional writing instruction and support to students who were repeating the second semester composition course.[6] Students self-selected or were recommended for enrollment in *PlusOne* sections of ENG 1060, which were capped at twelve students and required co-enrollment in a one-credit-hour supplemental writing lab designated as ENG 1020: Laboratory in Writing. The writing labs involved smaller groups of students working with the instructor-of-record for the ENG 1060 course, reinforcing the work in ENG 1060 and allowing for increased interaction between the students and the course instructor in a workshop environment.

Results of the pilot program were encouraging. The failure rate for students enrolled in *PlusOne* sections of ENG 1060 was less than half of the non-*PlusOne* course failure rate. The program gained increased support from Academic Affairs and continued to run on a small scale through the fall of 2008. Continued success led to full program development and expansion in the spring of 2009 with funding through the Native American Serving Non-Tribal Institutions Grant (NASNTI).

PLUSONE PROGRAM DESIGN

The Native American Serving Non-Tribal Institutions Grant program, operated by the US Department of Education and authorized under the 2008 federal Higher Education Act, "provides grants to eligible institutions of higher education to enable them to improve their academic quality, increase their self sufficiency and strengthen their capacity to serve students" (UNCP n.d.) In October 2008, UNCP was awarded a two-year NASNTI grant for a project titled *Strengthening Institutional Capacity for Student and Faculty Advancement.* One facet of this project focused on strengthening academic support for students and included the full development of the *PlusOne* program with expansion into ENG 1050.

The *PlusOne* program was designed to loosely replicate Rhonda Grego and Nancy Thompson's Writing Studio program at the University of South Carolina (Grego and Thompson 1995). Their Writing Studio model within the first-year writing program included weekly small group writing workshops led by experienced writing group leaders. Four or five students from different sections of the first-year writing course would meet with a writing studio leader once a week to work on developing their writing skills and receiving help on writing assignments for their composition courses. Students were either placed in the Writing Studio based on their diagnostic writing within the first two weeks of the semester and a portfolio of previous writing or they self-selected to participate in the Writing Studio. Active participation and regular attendance were the basic requirements of the writing workshops, and students did not receive a grade for being part of the Writing Studio program. Assessment of the Writing Studio program indicated that during the first year 94 percent of the students participating in the program completed their composition course successfully; in addition, surveys of students and faculty indicated predominantly positive response to the small group writing workshops (Grego and Thompson 1995, 76–77).

A variation of the Writing Studio model was also piloted at the University of Texas at El Paso in an effort to improve students' opportunities for success in first-year writing. In "Predicting Success: Increasing Retention and Pass Rates in College Composition," Beth Brunk-Chavez

and Elaine Fredericksen examine the correlation between low placement and diagnostic tests scores and students' performance and success in composition courses. Acknowledging the limitations of the
state-imposed mandatory use of Accuplacer for placement purposes,
Brunk-Chavez and Fredericksen (2008) offer the implementation of
a writing lab as one possible solution to improving the success rate of
low-scoring students. Taking advantage of an existing writing lab course,
this initiative offered students who were considered at risk for failing the
first-year writing course based on their Accuplacer scores an opportunity
to enroll in a supplemental one-credit hour laboratory course taught by
a trained English instructor. Similar to Grego and Thompson's (1995)
Writing Studio, this initiative placed students in a small group learning
environment where students could receive individualized instruction
and writing help.

What differentiates the *PlusOne* program at UNCP from writing studio models at other institutions is that the writing labs are taught by the
same instructor as the co-requisite first-year writing course. This allows
instructors to synchronize their teaching activities between the composition and laboratory courses so that the weekly laboratory sessions build
on the classroom instruction to support each student's needs. In the
weekly small-group writing lab periods students can ask questions about
their particular work-in-progress and elicit advice specific to their own
writing, work one-to-one with the instructor or other students on shared
problems with a particular composition assignment, dissect difficult
readings, or exchange drafts for peer review and reader response. The
smaller class size encourages students to ask questions about their own
work and offer constructive criticism to others.

In the spring of 2009, twelve faculty in the Department of English and
Theatre taught *PlusOne* sections of ENG 1050 and ENG 1060. Each section involved a traditional three-credit-hour composition course, capped
at sixteen students, which was linked to three sections, each capped at
six students, of a one-credit-hour co-requisite, pass/fail laboratory course
designated as ENG 1020: Laboratory in Writing. According to the internal UNCP Spring 2009 *PlusOne* Program Report, 153 students participated in the program in that semester. As Table 10.1 shows, the successful completion rate for *PlusOne* students was 17 percent higher in ENG
1050 and 19 percent higher in ENG 1060 compared to their peers in
traditional, non-*PlusOne* courses (Guynn and Hicks 2009).

In addition to the quantitative student outcomes, a review of instructor and student evaluations conducted at the end of the Spring 2009
semester indicated that the *PlusOne* program was perceived to be a

Table 10.1. Student Performance and Success Rate in FYW classes in Spring 2009

Spring 2009	ENG 1050	ENG 1050 PlusOne	ENG 1060	ENG 1060 PlusOne
Total enrollment	331	60	624	93
No. of students with final grade of C or higher[a]	209	48	397	70
Success rate	63.14%	80%	63.62%	75.26%
Withdrawal rate	6%	5%	9%	6%
Average grade in course[b]	2.09 (4.00)	2.54 (4.00)	2.23 (4.00)	2.65 (4.00)

Notes

a. At UNCP students need to earn a grade of C or better in both ENG 1050 and ENG 1060.

b. The grade averages consist of the average of the grades of all students, excluding those who withdrew or otherwise did not complete the class.

success and should be continued. Instructors reported using lab time for instructional activities focused on "assignment comprehension, reading comprehension, prewriting and planning, drafting, organization, research, grammar and punctuation, summary and paraphrase, and citation and documentation" (Guynn and Hicks 2009, 1). Their comments reflected that students in the *PlusOne* sections performed better than their peers in traditional, non-*PlusOne* course sections, and they noted that the lab activities allowed students to develop a greater sense of community as writers. Students indicated that they found the lab sections "helpful" (Guynn and Hicks 2009, 2), particularly given the smaller class size, which allowed for more personal instruction and interaction. As the report indicated, "nearly all students reported that they would recommend the *PlusOne* program to their friends" (Guynn and Hicks 2009, 3).

Based on the data and feedback from the Spring 2009 semester, the department began to consider adjustments and revisions to improve the *PlusOne* program. Because some student participants in the ENG 1050 *PlusOne* courses desired to continue in the program in ENG 1060, it became necessary to distinguish two different lab courses—one to serve as the co-requisite for ENG 1050, and a second to serve as the co-requisite for ENG 1060—to allow students to repeat the writing lab for credit. Further, although students in the Spring 2009 courses did earn one hour of course credit for the lab, because of the pass/fail nature of the grading their performance in the lab did not count toward their grade-point average, which was a point of frustration for students. To address

each of these concerns, the Department of English and Theatre proposed, and the university approved, a change in title from ENG 1020:
Laboratory in Writing to ENG 1020: Laboratory in Writing I, the addition of ENG 1030: Laboratory in Writing II, and a change from pass/fail
to standard letter grading for both lab courses.

MOVING BEYOND RETENTION FOCUS IN *PLUSONE*

Initially, the *PlusOne* program targeted students who desired additional
writing support or who had been previously unsuccessful in completing the composition sequence but has since expanded its focus. Any
student who wishes to may enroll in a *PlusOne* section of Composition I
or Composition II; the *PlusOne* writing labs are mandatory, however, for
students enrolled in the College Opportunity Program (COP). At present, the *PlusOne* program serves three distinct segments of first-year
writing students: the academically at-risk students in the COP, the self-
identified students who seek additional writing support, and the pre-
nursing students whose acceptance into the highly competitive nursing
program depends on successful and timely completion of the first-year
composition sequence. It is not enough for pre-nursing students to simply successfully complete the first-year composition sequence with a final
grade of C or higher the first time they enroll in the courses; they must,
instead, excel in their general education studies to meet the requirements of guaranteed admission to the nursing program. To pre-nursing
students, the *PlusOne* component offers intensive writing support in
the form of the writing labs and increases their chances of higher academic achievement as evidenced in the aggregate data of pre-nursing
students performance in ENG 1050 and ENG 1060. Since Fall 2012, 407
pre-nursing majors have enrolled in a *PlusOne* section of ENG 1050 and
have completed the course successfully with a final grade of C or higher
with their average course grade being 2.90 compared to a 2.40 average
course grade for students in traditional ENG 1050 course. Of the 407
pre-nursing students, 294 or 72.2 percent elected to enroll in a *PlusOne*
section of ENG 1060 in the following semester even though they were
not required to do so. The 294 students who took ENG 1060 and the
co-requisite *PlusOne* writing lab ENG 1030 finished the second semester
composition course with an average course grade of 2.86 compared to
the average course grade of 2.71 that the remaining pre-nursing students who did not take the writing lab achieved. While final grades in
first-year writing courses are not necessarily good indicators of students'
writing abilities, they are the traditional measures used by universities

to signify whether or not students were successful in the course. The data indicate that pre-nursing students who completed the *PlusOne* version of the first-year writing courses performed better compared to the students in the traditional sections of the same course and pre-nursing students who opted out of the writing lab option in the second semester composition course.

STUDENTS' PERFORMANCE IN *PLUSONE* CLASSES

Since Fall 2009, the *PlusOne* program has continued to grow and to date has served a total of 3,028 students. One way to measure the effectiveness of the program is to analyze the performance of *PlusOne* students in the first-year composition courses in comparison to that of students enrolled in the traditional version of the same courses. As Table 10.2 illustrates, the supplemental instruction that the *PlusOne* program offers leads to improved performance and higher success rate in first-year writing courses. Between Fall 2009 to Spring 2015, 87.36 percent of the students who took the *PlusOne* version of ENG 1050 completed the course successfully with a final grade of C or higher compared to the 72.02 percent students who enrolled in the traditional format of the same course. Similarly, 80.89 percent of the students enrolled in ENG 1060 *PlusOne* received a satisfactory grade compared to 68.89 percent enrolled in the regular sections of Composition II.

As Table 10.2 indicates, the success rates of students who took the composition courses paired with the writing labs are 15.34 percent and 12 percent respectively higher than their peers in the non-*PlusOne* versions of the same courses. The data show that the *PlusOne* sections of ENG 1050 and ENG 1060 are meeting the target goal of an 80 percent passing rate as outlined in the NASNTI grant that funded the program originally.

STUDENTS' PERCEPTION OF THE *PLUSONE* PROGRAM

The positive impact of the writing lab courses on students' performance in first-year writing classes is echoed in their perception and evaluation of the *PlusOne* program, which provides a compelling argument for continuing this initiative. Between Fall 2009 and Spring 2015, 3,028 students have enrolled in ENG 1020 and/or ENG 1030. Representing a 39.40 percent response rate, 1193 of them have completed the *PlusOne* Student Evaluation Survey.[7] The results of the survey indicate predominantly positive perceptions of the program and overall student satisfaction with the supplemental writing instruction

Table 10.2. Student Performance and Success Rate in FYW classes

	ENG 1050	*ENG 1050* PlusOne	*ENG 1060*	*ENG 1060* PlusOne
Total enrollment: Fall 2009–Spring 2015	7,628	1,432	7,303	1,596
No. of students with final grade of C or higher	5,494	1,251	5,031	1,291
Success rate (in percentage)	72.02%	87.36%	68.89%	80.89%

Table 10.3. Responses to the survey question "How likely would you be to recommend to your friends to take a *PlusOne* class?"

Very likely	*Somewhat likely*	*Unsure/No opinion*	*Not at all likely*
684 (57.33%)	374 (31.34%)	100 (0.083%)	45 (0.038%)

that the *PlusOne* classes provide. As Table 10.3 illustrates, 88.67 percent of the respondents said that they are either very likely or somewhat likely to recommend the *PlusOne* class to their friends, which suggests they recognize the benefit that the writing labs offer in terms of supplemental writing instruction.

Furthermore, when asked how their participation in the *PlusOne* program has affected their performance in the composition class, students offered the following comments that are representative of an overall positive experience in the program:

- "Out of all my English classes in the past, this English class has been the most enjoyable and enriched class of them all. I owe this experience to the benefits received from the *PlusOne*. If it weren't for the extra hour of discussions, I probably would not had made it this far in the class."

- "My experience in the class gave me extra time and opportunity to ask questions about my writing."

- "The participation in the *PlusOne* class was very beneficial to me in my composition class. In the *PlusOne* class it gave me the opportunity to understand things one-on-one and also the instructor made the assignments more clear by going more in-depth what she was looking for."

- "It was helpful because it's like a 'to be continued' session of your English class. [I]t allows you to understand and ask anything you weren't able to in class."

Perhaps not surprisingly students identify the small class sizes and the personal attention from the instructor as one of the most valuable aspects of the *PlusOne* program. Included below are some of the comments attesting to that:

- "This class was a key component this semester in helping me with my work. [I]t gives you precious time with the teacher that helps you more with your work."

- "I was able to ask additional questions, get more one-on-one time with the instructor, and recollect past knowledge of composition skills."

- "I feel I have a personal relationship with my professor. I feel like I can email him with or ask him a question and he will give me a thought out response. I don't have that with many teachers."

- "I find the writing lab to be very helpful. I enjoy the one-on-one attention that the small class size provides. It has helped my writing grow. When I don't understand things in class, it is nice to talk to the teacher one-on-one about my writing or questions."

- "The writing lab is only a small class of 6 and you can have a lot of time with your peers and the professor."

Finally, when asked what changes they would like to make to the *PlusOne* program, one student recommended making all English classes *PlusOne* classes because then "maybe more people will enjoy writing" while another student suggested expanding the *PlusOne* program to include general education science and math classes as well.

Not all students, however, shared their peers' enthusiasm for the *PlusOne* program. Some students did not see the need for the required weekly meetings and instead advocated for a "drop in when you need help" approach to the writing labs. Others described the meetings as "boring," "too long," or "unhelpful" because they did not find the writing labs of 'value' to them. As one student noted, "I didn't really like the lab that much, but if someone needs it, the lab would help." This comment illustrates how students' perception of the "value added" of the writing lab affects their overall perception and evaluation of the program as a whole and results in somewhat conflicted statements as evident in the following comment from another student: "The *PlusOne* class I feel is helpful but is also just a waste of time. I feel that we could meet with our instructor on our own terms and not be around classmates when receiving help." Overall, however, student evaluation of the *PlusOne* program is overwhelmingly positive and reaffirms the connection between a high level of student-faculty interaction and student retention and success.

RETENTION INITIATIVES AND FACULTY WORKING CONDITIONS

The success of the *PlusOne* component in achieving student learning objectives has generated ongoing faculty and administrative support for the composition program. When federal funding for the program from NASNTI ended after the initial grant period, the university committed to continuing and expanding the *PlusOne* component of the first-year writing program. In 2010, UNCP administration allocated additional funding both to enable the Department of English and Theatre to meet student demand for *PlusOne* composition courses by offering additional sections and to convert three non-tenure track positions into tenure-track rhetoric and composition faculty positions. Strong institutional support, which means having tangible resources as evidence of commitment at all levels of institutional decision-making, is paramount for the sustainability of any retention initiative no matter how innovative. Simply designing and implementing a program to enhance student success is not enough because, as Tinto (2006) points out, "too few [institutions] are willing to commit needed resources and address the deeper structural issues that ultimately shape student persistence" (9). Instead, retention initiatives are often added to the existing faculty course load without an institutional system in place that recognizes and rewards faculty's commitment to and support in improving student retention. The design of the *PlusOne* program at UNCP and the demonstrated positive impact of the writing lab courses on students' performance illustrate why student success and retention initiatives grounded in first-year writing programs should attend to labor issues and faculty teaching loads. The ongoing administrative and financial support for the *PlusOne* program allows us to offer *PlusOne* sections of Composition I and II courses and the co-requisite ENG 1020 and ENG 1030 writing labs every semester without increasing faculty teaching responsibilities, which in turn helps to ensure continued faculty support for the initiative.

Furthermore, only recently have scholars begun to examine the connection between faculty working conditions, strong pedagogy, and increased student retention (Tinto 2006) despite evidence suggesting that "teachers' working conditions and students' expectations at any given institution are inextricably linked" (Reichert Powell 2014, 44). In fact, as Reichert Powell remarks, "the focus on the first year in retention literature does not always translate to a focus on pedagogy or to a reliance on the expertise of faculty who regularly teach first-year students" (8) yet retention data are frequently used to determine funding at the departmental, institutional, and state levels. Not surprisingly, then, according to Reichert Powell, "the broader discourse of retention intersects with the material and political contexts in which we do the work of writing program administration and composition instruction" (53), particularly given the erosion of faculty working conditions in higher education and the large number of contingent faculty teaching first-year writing courses.[8]

In light of recent research on the negative impact of faculty employment status on student persistence (Eagan and Jaeger 2008; Jaeger and Eagan 2011; Ronco and Cahill 2006; Schibik and Harrington 2004), retention initiatives must position issues of ethical faculty labor as ancillary to student persistence and performance if they are to become fully institutionalized to significantly impact student success in first-year writing courses. "Improving working conditions needs to be posed not simply as a labor issue," contends Joseph Harris (2000), "but also as a means of improving the quality of undergraduate education" (61). Amanda Godley and Jennifer Seibel Trainor also agree that "the key to improving working conditions for writing teachers is to make more savvy arguments based on student needs and market demand" (Godley and Trainor 2004, 173). Changes in institutional structures and implementation of ethical labor practices can be achieved at the local level when arguments for better working conditions for faculty teaching first-year writing courses are framed in the context of student persistence and academic performance. While it is highly unlikely that all first-year writing classes can be staffed with tenured or tenure-track compositionists, promoting serving the needs of students through strong pedagogy and better faculty working conditions is one way to improve the workplace of composition.

The design of the *PlusOne* program takes into consideration faculty working conditions and accounts for part of the instructors' course load for the semester as opposed to adding to one's teaching load. At UNCP where a four-course per term teaching load equals 100 percent full-time equivalent (FTE),[9] teaching the *PlusOne* writing labs counts as 25 percent of this workload. Thus, faculty members teaching a *PlusOne* section of Composition I as part of their four composition courses per semester teaching load, for example, have the following teaching responsibilities: two regular sections of Composition I (three credit hours each), one *PlusOne* section of Composition I (three credit hours), and three sections of ENG 1020: Laboratory in Writing I (one credit hour each). Since composition courses as UNCP are capped at twenty students, faculty members teaching a *PlusOne* section of composition a semester are in effect teaching no more than sixty writing students per term, which falls within CCCC Position Statement on Principles for the Postsecondary Teaching of Writing. This programmatic setup allows faculty members teaching the writing lab courses to provide intensive individualized writing support to these *PlusOne* students without the burden of an increased teaching workload. Provisions such as this one are crucial for the implementation *and* the sustainability of a retention initiative grounded in a first-year writing course because they support faculty buy-in and long-term commitment to the success of the program.

In addition, teaching a *PlusOne* section of ENG 1050 or ENG 1060 is open to all full-time faculty members in the department, regardless of their rank.[10] The non-tenure-track (NTT) English lecturer positions at UNCP, whose primary responsibility is teaching in the composition program, conform to MLA's recommended professional employment practices for non-tenure-track faculty members. Carefully chosen for their expertise and experience in the teaching of writing at the college level, the NTT lecturers serve on departmental and university-wide committees, have equal voting rights, and receive the same benefits and professional development funds as the tenured and tenure-track members of the department. Since the 2009 pilot of the *PlusOne* program, UNCP administration has continuously allocated additional funding to meet student demand for *PlusOne* composition courses by offering additional sections and hiring more NTT lecturers.

CONCLUDING THOUGHTS AND IMPLICATIONS FOR WPAS

Ultimately, the *PlusOne* program has positively impacted students' academic performance and persistence and has allowed us to identify one high impact pedagogical practice that supports students' development of writing abilities. The first-year composition sequence represents two of three courses required of all first-year UNCP students, and therefore can serve either a "gateway" or "gatekeeping" function, assisting or impeding retention and persistence. In addition, many of the challenges faced by students in our service region, including socioeconomic disadvantage, first-generation college student status, low levels of educational attainment among the population, and poor academic preparation often manifest themselves in students' writing ability and have hindered student performance in ENG 1050 and 1060. The success of the *PlusOne* program in improving student performance in first-year writing and increasing the rates of completion in these courses indicates that it represents one sustainable method for addressing these challenges and improving retention and persistence in our local and institutional context.

Developed originally as a way to improve student retention, the *PlusOne* program has grown into a research site that offers new implications not only for examining high impact practices and the teaching of writing but for reconfiguring traditional sites of writing instruction and exploring the intersections between initiatives and discourses surrounding student retention, faculty working conditions, and the first-year writing classroom. Such focus is timely in an era of declining budgets and increased accountability when public colleges and universities are increasingly pressured to educate students more effectively and efficiently while simultaneously improving retention and graduation rates and curtailing attrition rates. While the overall goal of retention may be achieved by university-wide efforts, there are unique circumstances faced by different academic units that suggest higher suitability for academic-anchored retention initiatives, and the *PlusOne* program is one such initiative that has showed promising results since its inception more than five years ago. It has fostered ongoing institutional and financial support for and emphasis on the teaching of writing and has transformed into an institutionally embedded, programmatic structure that holds promise for student success and retention.

Notes

1. In 2014, 74 percent of first-year students presented a high school GPA of 3.01 or higher and a mean SAT combined verbal and math score of 935 (Office of Institutional Research 2015b), which is significantly lower than both the mean state score of 1006 and the mean national score of 1010 based on the North Carolina SAT Report for 2014 (North Carolina Public Schools 2014).

2. According to April 2015 statistics from the North Carolina Department of Commerce (2015), Robeson County ranks 91 out of 100 counties with 8.0 percent of the population unemployed, while Scotland County ranks 99 out of 100 counties with a 10.0 percent unemployment rate. The US Census Bureau "State & County QuickFacts" indicate that the median household income is $29,806 in Robeson County and $29,592 in Scotland County, as compared to a median household income of $46,334 for the state of North Carolina. Over 30 percent of the population in these two counties lives below the federally defined poverty level (United States Census Bureau n.d.).

3. Through the spring of 2015, a supplemental instruction program offered additional academic support through weekly peer-facilitated review sessions in targeted, historically difficult courses. Due to both funding and concerns over utilization, the supplemental instruction program is being phased out beginning in the fall of 2015, and will be replaced with a Student Learning Assistance (SLA) program that requires identified students to attend weekly support instruction in various gateway courses.

4. The seven learning communities include The Esther G. Maynor Honors Living Learning Community, The Leadership Living Learning Community, *The Discover Nursing: Living Learning Leading Community (DNL³C), The Global Learning Community, The Soaring Ahead: Early College Learning Community, The Career Quest Learning Community, and The Strengthening our Ties: American Indian Learning Community.*

5. Since 2007, the Department has reunited with the Foreign Languages Department and is now the Department of English, Theatre, and Foreign Languages.
6. Faculty members in the College Opportunity Program (COP), a program for provisionally admitted students who are identified as at-risk, had always required their students to participate in supplemental, not-for-credit writing labs with both the ENG 1050 and ENG 1060 composition courses. The spring of 2006 (along with the pilot of the *PlusOne* program) was the first time the lab was formalized and offered as credit-bearing for ENG 1060 in COP. The COP writing labs, however, were not capped at six students.
7. While students in the COP program are included in the 3,028 total number of students who have taken ENG 1020 and/or ENG 1030, they did not complete the evaluation of the *PlusOne* program survey, which accounts for the lower response rate on the survey.
8. The 1999 MLA Survey of Staffing in English and Foreign Language Departments reveals that first-year writing instruction is delegated primarily to part-time and non-tenure-track faculty. Only 36.3 percent of faculty who teach introductory writing courses within English departments are full-time, tenured or tenure-track whereas contingent faculty (32% part-time faculty, 9.5% full-time, non-tenure-track faculty, and 22% graduate teaching assistants) account for more than two-thirds of instructors responsible for teaching freshman composition.
9. At UNCP, the normal teaching load for non-tenure-track lecturers, tenure-track assistant professors, and tenured professors is twelve semester hours (four courses) or the equivalent per semester. In Fall 2013 the university adopted a reduced 3/4 course teaching load for tenure-track assistant professors and gave tenured professors the opportunity to receive reassigned time for scholarship and service.
10. At UNCP teaching one or more sections of composition every semesters is part of the teaching load of all full-time faculty members in English, including non-tenure-track lecturers and tenured and tenure-track professors. The university does not employ graduate teaching assistants. In the past the composition program has relied on small number (three to four) of qualified part-time lecturers for last-minute staffing of first-year writing classes; all but one of these part-time lecturers are already employed by the university full-time with benefits in some other capacity (e.g., librarian).

References

Brunk-Chavez, Beth, and Elaine Fredericksen. 2008. "Predicting Success: Increasing Retention and Pass Rates in College Composition." *WPA* 32 (1): 76–96.

Conley, David T. 2008. "Rethinking College Readiness." *New Directions for Higher Education* (144): 3–13. http://dx.doi.org/10.1002/he.321.

Eagan, M. Kevin, and Audrey J. Jaeger. 2008. "Closing the Gate: Contingent Faculty in Gatekeeper Courses." In *The Role of the Classroom in College Student Persistence: New Directions for Teaching and Learning*, ed. John M. Braxton, 39–53. San Francisco: Jossey-Bass.

Godley, Amanda, and Jennifer Seibel Trainor. 2004. "Embracing the Logic of the Marketplace: New Rhetorics for the Old Problem of Labor in Composition." In *Tenured Bosses and Disposable Teachers: Writing Instruction in the Manages University*, ed. Marc Bousquet, Tony Scott, and Leo Parascondola, 171–85. Carbondale: Southern Illinois University Press.

Grego, Rhonda C., and Nancy S. Thompson. 1995. "The Writing Studio Program: Reconfiguring Basic Writing/Freshman Composition." *WPA. Writing Program Administration* 19:66–79.

Guynn, Anita, and Scott Hicks. 2009. *"PlusOne Program Report." Department of English and Theatre.* Pembroke: The University of North Carolina at Pembroke.

Harris, Joseph. 2000. "Meet the New Boss, Same as the Old Boss: Class Consciousness in Composition." *College Composition and Communication* 52 (1): 43–68. http://dx.doi.org /10.2307/358543.

Jaeger, Audrey J., and M. Kevin Eagan. 2011. "Examining Retention and Contingent Faculty Use in a State System of Public Higher Education." *Educational Policy* 25 (3): 507–37. http://dx.doi.org/10.1177/0895904810361723.

Kuh, George D. 2008. *High-Impact Educational Practices: What They Are, Who Has Access to Them, and Why They Matter.* Washington, DC: Association of American Colleges and Universities.

National Center for Education Statistics. 2003. "National Assessment of Adult Literacy." *US Department of Education Institute of Education Sciences.* https://nces.ed.gov/naal/.

North Carolina Department of Commerce. 2015. "North Carolina County Rankings: Preliminary Data for April 2015." *North Carolina Department of Commerce. Labor & Economic Analysis Division. NC Division of Employment Security.* http://www.ncesc1.com /pmi/rates/PressReleases/County/NR_April2015CountyRateRelease_M.pdf.

North Carolina Public Schools. 2014. *The NC 2014 SAT Report. NC Department of Public Instruction.* October. http://www.ncpublicschools.org/docs/accountability/report ing/sat/2014/satreport14.pdf.

Office of Institutional Research. 2015a. "Enrollment by County of Residence." *2014–15 Fact Book. The University of North Carolina at Pembroke.* http://www.uncp.edu/about-uncp /administration/departments/institutional-research/fact-book/2014-15-fact-book.

Office of Institutional Research. 2015b. "Freshmen at a Glance." *2014–15 Fact Book. The University of North Carolina at Pembroke.* http://www.uncp.edu/about-uncp/administra tion/departments/institutional-research/fact-book/2014-15-fact-book.

Reichert Powell, Pegeen 2014. *Retention and Resistance: Writing Instruction and the Students Who Leave.* Logan: Utah State University Press.

Ronco, Sharron, and John Cahill. 2006. "Does It Matter Who's in the Classroom? Effect of Instructor Type on Student Retention, Achievement and Satisfaction." AIR Professional File 100. Tallahassee: Association of Institutional Research.

Schibik, Timothy, and Charles Harrington. 2004. "Caveat Emptor: Is There a Relationship between Part-Time Faculty Utilization and Student Learning Outcomes and Retention." AIR Professional File 91. Tallahassee: Association of Institutional Research.

Tinto, Vincent. 2006. "Research and Practice of Student Retention: What Next?" *Journal of College Student Retention* 8 (1): 1–19. http://dx.doi.org/10.2190/4YNU-4TMB-22D J-AN4W.

UNCP. n.d. "The Native American-Serving Non-Tribal Institutions." *The University of North Carolina at Pembroke.* http://www.uncp.edu/about-uncp/administration/departments /native-american-serving-nontribal-institutions-nasnti.

United States Census Bureau. n.d. "State & County QuickFacts." *US Department of Commerce.* http://quickfacts.census.gov/qfd/index.html.

University of North Carolina General Administration. 2012. "The University of North Carolina Retention and Graduation Report." *The Board of Governors of the University of North Carolina.* https://www.northcarolina.edu/sites/default/files/retention_gradua tion_report_2012.pdf.

US Department of Education. 2006. *A Test of Leadership: Charting the Future of U.S. Higher Education.* A Report of the Commission on the Future of Higher Education. U.S. Department of Education. http://www2.ed.gov/about/bdscomm/list/hiedfuture /reports/final-report.pdf.

11

RETENTION RATES OF SECOND LANGUAGE WRITERS AND BASIC WRITERS
A Comparison within the Stretch Program Model

Sarah Elizabeth Snyder

INTRODUCTION

Although many basic writing programs enroll second language (L2 or multilingual) writers, there is no evidence to suggest that basic writing program design is also beneficial for L2 writers. One program that currently enrolls L2 writers in a basic writing program model is the Stretch Program at Arizona State University (ASU). Being one of the most innovative, successful, and researched basic writing programs in the United States, it has been emulated by many other institutions. To date, the Stretch Program design has been shown to improve retention of first language basic writers (Glau 1996, 2007). However, there is no evidence currently that the same can be said for L2 writers who enroll in separate L2 sections of the Stretch Program. Therefore, this partial replication study of Glau (2007) concerning the Stretch Program examines the retention rates of L2 writing and basic writing cohorts to determine whether basic writing program design can also be beneficial for L2 writers. Specifically, I analyze the Fall 2012 cohort Stretch retention data for basic writing and L2 writing student populations. I then compare those results to the traditional model of first-year composition (FYC) for mainstream and multilingual students, as well as past studies of the Stretch Program.

REVIEW OF LITERATURE
Program Model Theory for L2 Writers and Basic Writers

Scholars have long discussed if both L2 writers and basic writers can be served appropriately by the same first-year composition courses or if each

DOI: 10.7330/9781607326021.c011

group has to have specialized courses to be given the optimal conditions to succeed (McKay 1981; Nattinger 1978; Roy 1984, 1988). Silva (1994) started a similar discussion regarding which program models would be best for L2 writers, concluding that as many models as are feasible for the institution should be offered. Regardless of theoretical discussion, Matsuda (2003) demonstrated through historical evidence that, when these populations were introduced to universities, one reaction was to put both basic writers and L2 writers in the same composition classrooms seemingly without regard to the differences in linguistic background between the two populations. Not paying explicit attention to differences associated with linguistic background is an issue because, according to Matsuda (2006), "[a]n image of students becomes problematic when it inaccurately represents the actual student population in the classroom to the extent that it inhibits the . . . ability to recognize and address the presence of differences" (639). Linguistic differences more often than not also connote socioeconomic and geographic differences as well, which may affect student retention. The problem then arises when basic writing programs are "designed primarily for U.S. citizens who are native speakers of a variety of English" (Matsuda 2006, 649) but are enrolling L2 writers. I contend that program design should be included in this consideration.

Matsuda (2003) further stresses "the importance of defining basic writers in ways that include all students who are subject to the disciplinary and instructional practices of basic writing" (69). Programs designed for basic writers that enroll L2 writers are making the assumption that *what is good for basic writers is also good for L2 writers.* Although these programmatic assumptions often have very good intentions and a heightened awareness of students' needs, good intentions are not enough—the assumption needs to be evaluated. One method of programmatic evaluation is retention research, which has been an important indicator of the success of basic writers and basic writing programs (e.g., Baker and Jolly 1999; Glau 1996, 2007; McCurrie 2009; Peele 2010; Webb-Sunderhaus 2010). Retention research of programmatic innovations have confirmed the worth of good intentions for basic writers in basic writing classes. However, there are no studies that use retention research to confirm or deny these good intentions for L2 writers who are enrolled in basic writing program models.

The Stretch Program at Arizona State University
The Stretch Program has served as an exemplary prototype for basic writing program models as well as retention research. During its

twenty-year tenure, a number of articles have cited the Stretch Program as an influential model for their institution-specific basic writing curriculum (e.g., Blakesley 2002; Goen-Salter 2008; Malenczyk 1999; Matzen and Hoyt 2004; Pavesich 2011; Peele 2010; Rigolino and Freel 2007). According to Pavesich (2011), along with other models of FYC surveyed, the Stretch Program provided "more nuanced procedural alternatives to the mainstreaming/segregation binary of the basic writing crisis in the sense that [the models] seek variously articulated middle spaces between mainstreaming and marginalizing" (95). In addition, Shapiro (2011) has commended the Stretch Program, among others, for "presenting a variety of course configurations for accomplishing curricular goals" (24). Over twelve colleges and universities have published about their curricula inspired by the Stretch model ("Stretch Award" 2014). It has also enriched conversations about student placement and its effect on retention (e.g., Ericsson and Haswell 2006; Matzen and Hoyt 2004). Through its contributions to the field of basic writing, the Stretch Program has indeed made a positive impact on the field of rhetoric and composition, expanding the populations of students that can (and should) be served through higher education, and improving our ability to serve our students.

Arizona State University's Stretch Program was created to help "change the way the profession talked about the students who didn't fit" into the university's first-year composition setting, referring to basic writers (Bartholomae 1993, 21, quoted in Glau 1996, 79). From 1987, in order to enroll at ASU, basic writing students needed to pass a remedial course, ENG 071, at a community college in order to get into ENG 101, the first course of the university-level FYC sequence ("Stretch Award" 2014). Many of the students taking ENG 071 at the community college were not coming to ASU afterwards (Schwalm 1989), and the Stretch Program sought to change that. The Stretch Program was created in 1992 as a pilot, and was in full operation by 1994, to bring basic writing students back into the university setting (Glau 1996).

As its name suggests, the Stretch Program changed the course configuration of ASU's "traditional" first-year composition to "stretch" ENG 101 over two semesters (WAC 101 and ENG 101) in order to encourage higher achievement and retention for basic writing students. Retention in the series of Stretch studies (Glau 1996, 2007) including this study is defined as retention from first semester to second semester, although for FYC, and most students, it is the same as retention from the first class to the second class (e.g., WAC101/7 to ENG 101/7 and ENG 101/7 to ENG 102/8). The program creates a situation where students take three

Table 11.1. Current First-Year Composition Course Offerings at Arizona State University*

		First Semester	Second Semester	Third Semester
Stretch	Mainstream (L1)	WAC 101	ENG 101	ENG 102
	Multilingual (L2)	WAC 107	ENG 107	ENG 108
Traditional	Mainstream (L1)	ENG 101	ENG 102	
	Multilingual (L2)	ENG 107	ENG 108	
Accelerated[†]	Mainstream (L1)	ENG 105		

* *Basic writers are often found in mainstream Stretch classes, and L2 writers are most often found in multilingual classrooms.*

† *Accelerated classes are not included in this analysis.*

FYC classes, (WAC 101, ENG 101, and ENG 102) as opposed to two FYC classes (ENG 101, ENG 102) in the traditional FYC model, much like many other composition programs in the United States. As of 2015, at ASU, there are three models (Stretch, traditional, and accelerated) of FYC. The Stretch and traditional models both have parallel mainstream and multilingual sections that fulfill the same FYC requirement for the student (WAC 101 and WAC 107; ENG 101 and ENG 107; ENG 102 and ENG 108). See Table 11.1 for an overview of the current FYC offerings at Arizona State University.

Summary of Previous Findings Regarding the Stretch Program

A wealth of information has been provided on the pass and persistence rates of Stretch and traditional student populations. Between academic years 1993 and 1994, Glau (1996) found positive indicators for retention of students from WAC 101 to ENG 101 in general. Specifically, this first report found that Stretch retained 21.53 percent more students than ASU would have if ENG 071 were still in place ("Stretch Award" 2014). Positive results were also confirmed in the ten-year study by Glau (2007). In both studies, students who took the Stretch Program passed ENG 101 at a higher rate than traditional students. Stretch students were also found to pass ENG 102 (the third class in the FYC sequence that is not related to the Stretch Program) at a slightly higher rate. The reported qualitative data collected from students in the form of an open-ended survey, revealed that the students felt their writing improved because of the program ("Stretch Program" 2014). Students also ranked the extra time as the "best thing" about the program. Other perceived advantages included having the same teacher, and the same classmates over two semesters ("Stretch Program" 2014).

L2 Writers in the Stretch Program

L2 writers have always been present in the Stretch Program and were absorbed directly into the mainstream Stretch sections.[1] In 1997, when the population of international students at ASU grew enough to fill their own class sections, the Stretch Program was expanded to include specialized Stretch multilingual writing classes. Created under the same premises that the Stretch basic writing courses were, the multilingual Stretch course had only a brief additional rationale that "[L2 writers] especially benefit from more time to work on their writing" (Glau 2007, 34). As well documented and well researched as the Stretch Program is for basic writers (Glau 1996, 2007; "Stretch Award" 2014), L2 writers' presence and retention in the Stretch Program has never been documented, nor researched for the program's effect. Thus, through retention data, this study examines the concept of using one model for both mainstream and multilingual students in the Stretch Program at ASU. The analysis will determine the effect of the program on students in mainstream and multilingual sections of the Stretch Program, and will explore whether the model implemented to help basic writers is also benefiting L2 writers.[2]

THE CURRENT STUDY: THE FALL 2012 STRETCH COHORT ANALYSIS

Method

As a partial replication study of Glau (1996, 2007), this study analyzed institutional data from the Fall 2012 cohort of Stretch and traditional FYC students at ASU. Institutional data were analyzed by sorting student indicators. Indicators described: *Residency*, the tuition and residency status of the student at the most recent term in the data set, which has three categories: Arizona resident, non-Arizona resident, and international; *Stretch*, students who had taken the first course in the Stretch Program (either WAC 101 or WAC 107) of which the opposite is *Traditional* (students who did not take any Stretch courses). The data also contained grade, term, term of completion, number of attempts, and GPA records for all student activity in any of the FYC courses (i.e., WAC 101, WAC 107, ENG 101, ENG 102, ENG 107, and/or ENG 108).

In order to have comparable analyses of the 2012 cohort data with the earlier articles (Glau 1996, 2007), Glau's (2007) "Step Model" was used as the method of analysis for the cohort data from Fall 2012 to Fall 2013 for student retention rates. The Step Model captures the cohorts that enter each course and their pass and persistence rates, creating a

---

A number of students register for WAC 101/107 [student profile]

   A percentage of these students pass WAC 101/107 [pass rate]

      A percentage of these students register for ENG 101/107 [persistence rate]

         A percentage of these students pass ENG101/107 [pass rate]

            A percentage of these students register for ENG102/108 [persistence rate]

               A percentage of these students pass ENG 102/108 [pass rate]

Figure 11.1. Step Model (adapted from Glau 1996, 2007)

measure of "retention." A student needs to earn a grade of C or above to "pass" a class, and enroll in the subsequent course the semester immediately following to "persist." The Step Model "compare[s] those students who moved into the next class not as a percentage of those [who had] originally started the sequence, but as a percentage of those who continued" (Glau 1996, 84). The Step Model is displayed in Figure 11.1. Although previous Stretch studies included student perception survey data, no survey data was collected for this study.

Research Questions

This partial replication study of Glau's (1996, 2007) Stretch reports, also analyzes the semester-to-semester retention rates of Stretch and traditional mainstream students. However, this study will also compare the populations of mainstream writers to multilingual writers within the Stretch Program, and then the Stretch Program to the traditional FYC program. The research questions are as follows for the cohort/time period of Fall 2012 to Fall 2013:

1. What is the current multilingual student profile of the Stretch Program?

   a. What are the proportions of multilingual students as described by international, Arizona resident, and non-Arizona resident tuition status in the Stretch and traditional FYC student profiles?

2. Can the same program model, the Stretch Model, comparably serve both multilingual and mainstream students?

   a. What are the retention rates (pass and persistence) in Stretch mainstream and multilingual sections?

   b. How do the retention rates of Stretch mainstream and multilingual sections compare to each other?

3. How does the Stretch Model of FYC compare to a more "traditional" model?

a. What are the retention rates (pass and persistence) of traditional mainstream and multilingual sections?

b. How do the retention rates of traditional mainstream and multilingual sections compare to those of Stretch mainstream and multilingual sections?

The study then compares this data to the historical results of Glau (1996) and Glau (2007).

Population

A total of 64,085 students who enrolled or earned a grade in any FYC class at ASU between Fall 2007 and Spring 2014 were included in the raw data set. Criteria for inclusion in this analysis required the students to have started the FYC sequence (Stretch or traditional) at ASU in Fall 2012. Exclusion criteria included all other populations (e.g., accelerated, transfer, AP, CLEP students), and all other cohorts besides Fall 2012–Fall 2013. These inclusion/exclusion criteria narrowed the raw data set to 5,801 students who had taken the beginning course of their respective placement in Fall 2012.

RESULTS

Student Profile of the Stretch Model

Regarding the first research question in this study, the overview of the student profile shows the Fall 2012 cohort included 949 students in WAC 101, 344 students in WAC 107, 4,238 students in ENG 101, and 270 students in ENG 107. It is interesting to note that there are more Stretch multilingual students than there are traditional multilingual students in this cohort. Out of the four groups, multilingual students in the traditional FYC course are the smallest population, whereas mainstream students in the traditional FYC course are the largest population—roughly fifteen times larger than the traditional multilingual population. As can be seen from Table 11.2, the majority of both WAC 107 and ENG 107 classes are international students. This is in contrast to international students comprising a small amount of the traditional classes, WAC 101 and ENG 101.

To further identify L2 writers and basic writers, the data was sorted by the class choice and residency status of the student. International residency status was separated from those of Arizona resident and

Table 11.2. Population of Students by Tuition Status

| Tuition Status | Stretch | | Traditional | | |
	Mainstream (WAC 101)	Multilingual (WAC 107)	Mainstream (ENG 101)	Multilingual (ENG 107)	Total
AZ Resident	552	10	2,494	6	**3,062**
Non-AZ Resident	384	7	1,711	9	**2,111**
International	13	327	33	255	**628**
Total	**949**	**344**	**4,238**	**270**	**5,801**

non-Arizona resident to estimate the proportions of each population in each initial class/cohort: WAC 101, WAC 107, ENG 101, and ENG 107. Although the L2 writing population and the international student population at ASU are not synonymous, they overlap significantly. A range of placement possibilities exist for L2 writers as students are placed by test scores into the Stretch or the traditional model, and then self-placed into the appropriate mainstream (WAC 101, ENG 101, or ENG 102) or multilingual (WAC 107, ENG 107, or ENG 108) courses with the help of academic advisors. Thus, international L2 writers are also found in mainstream courses. In this data set, there were 628 international students, and 46 (7%) of those students chose to take either the mainstream sections of Stretch (thirteen students) or the traditional mainstream FYC (thirty-three students). These students possibly did not prefer to have L2 writing support, either because they were native speakers of English from a foreign country (seventeen students were from Canada, and two were from Australia), or because they felt that their English skills were sufficient, among other reasons. Other countries represented by the thirty-three international students by frequency were China (seven), South Korea (six), Zimbabwe (three), India (two), and Ghana, Sweden, Spain, Norway, Switzerland, and Argentina with one student each. This data echoes Costino and Hyon's (2007) research suggesting that "neither linguistic labels nor residency status will necessarily predict which class a student feels will be the best fit for him/her" (78). The other 327 international students who took WAC 107 and the 255 international students who took ENG 107 add up to 582 students, and they represent 93 percent of the total number of international students. In addition, the 582 international students accounted for 94 percent of the total population (614) in the multilingual sections.

Multilingual students also had tuition designations other than international—Arizona resident and non-Arizona resident. Although these

L2 writing students were considered "resident" for tuition purposes, they may not be considered resident multilingual or Generation 1.5 students, defined as "students [who] graduate from US high schools and enter college while still in the process of learning English" (Harklau, Losey, and Siegal 1999, preface). Matsuda, Saenkhum, and Accardi (2013) reported that in Fall 2008, WAC 101 teachers at ASU perceived at least one resident multilingual student in 80 percent of classes surveyed. Furthermore, their study reported that, according to teacher perceptions, "resident multilingual students comprised about 91% (n = 141) of multilingual students enrolled in traditional sections, whereas international students accounted for about 78% (n = 123) of enrollment in multilingual sections" (73).

In this study, Arizona resident and non-Arizona resident tuition students were found in the multilingual sections of FYC. In the Stretch multilingual subcohort, 17 out of 344 students were Arizona or non-Arizona residents. In the traditional multilingual cohort, fifteen students were Arizona or non-Arizona residents. These resident-tuition students who self-identified as L2 writers comprised 5 percent of the combined WAC 107 and ENG 107 populations (32 out of 614 students). Ideally, the Stretch data would be analyzed for the resident multilingual writer population at ASU, although it is not feasible in this study because the data needed to confidently identify this population (e.g., language background, US high school records) was not collected. Resident multilingual students are surely in this data set, although it is an inherent difficulty to identify them.

Retention Rates of the Stretch Model

The second research question guiding this study was "*Can the same program model, the Stretch Model, comparably serve both multilingual and mainstream students?*" To answer this question, the retention rates of Stretch mainstream and multilingual sections were analyzed through the Step Model for pass and persistence rates. The results are shown in Table 11.3. For the Stretch mainstream students who started in WAC 101, the Fall 2012 cohort data shows that 89 percent passed. In Spring 2013, 88 percent persisted to ENG 101, and 91 percent of students passed. In Fall 2013, 64 percent enrolled in ENG 102, and 85 percent passed. For Stretch multilingual students, 93 percent passed WAC 107. In Spring 2013, 97 percent of students persisted to ENG 107, and 96 percent of them passed. The records then show that in Fall 2013, 74 percent enrolled in ENG 108, and 97 percent passed ENG 108.

Table 11.3. Stretch Model Pass and Persistence Rates

Semester		Mainstream (WAC 101)	Multilingual (WAC 107)
Fall 2012	Enroll in WAC 101/7	100%	100%
	Pass WAC 101/7	89%	93%
Spring 2013	Enroll in ENG 101/7	88%	97%
	Pass ENG 101/7	91%	96%
Fall 2013	Enroll in ENG 102/8	64%	74%
	Pass ENG 102/8	85%	97%

When comparing the Stretch mainstream and multilingual populations, the data indicates that Stretch multilingual students are passing at a higher rate than Stretch mainstream students. Stretch mainstream students passed WAC 101 at a rate of 89 percent, whereas 93 percent of Stretch multilingual students passed WAC 107. Ninety-one percent of Stretch mainstream students have passed ENG 101. In comparison, 96 percent of Stretch multilingual students passed ENG 107. The difference becomes most striking when ENG 102 and ENG 108 are compared, as 85 percent of Stretch mainstream students have passed ENG 102 and 97 percent of Stretch multilingual students have passed ENG 108.

Comparing the Stretch Program's persistence data, or the number of students who enroll in the next class in the immediately following semester, also shows that students in multilingual sections of Stretch persist more than the students who take mainstream sections of Stretch. In Fall 2012, 88 percent of students who passed WAC 101, went on to take ENG 101 in Spring 2013, and 97 percent of students who took WAC 107 in Fall 2012, went on to enroll in ENG 107 in Spring 2013. Showing a pattern, perhaps the biggest difference between the mainstream and multilingual tracks of Stretch is exhibited in the persistence rate of students to ENG 102 versus ENG 108. Sixty-four percent of Stretch mainstream students who passed ENG 101 enrolled in ENG 102, whereas 74 percent of Stretch multilingual students who passed ENG 107 enrolled in ENG 108 in Fall 2013.

Retention Rates of the Traditional Model

In order to evaluate the effectiveness of the Stretch Program, the results of the Stretch Program data should also be compared to a baseline, or the traditional model's data set. Thus, the third research question that

Table 11.4. Traditional Model Pass and Persistence Rates

Semester		Mainstream (ENG 101)	Multilingual (ENG 107)
Fall 2012	Enroll in ENG 101/7	100%	100%
	Pass ENG 101/7	89%	95%
Spring 2013	Enroll in ENG 102/8	89%	79%
	Pass ENG 102/8	92%	97%

this study addressed was, "*How does the Stretch Model of FYC compare to a more 'traditional' model?*" Table 11.4 shows the data analysis for the traditional model's data set. The traditional multilingual population exhibits higher rates of passing in comparison to the traditional mainstream population, as 95 percent passed ENG 107 and 89 percent passed ENG 101. Furthermore, 97 percent of students passed ENG 108 and 92 percent passed ENG 102. As there are only two classes in the traditional FYC model, there is only one persistence rate to report for each traditional track: out of the students who passed their respective classes in Fall 2012, 89 percent of ENG 101 students persisted to enroll in ENG 102, and 79 percent of ENG 107 students persisted to enroll in ENG 108.

To compare Stretch and traditional data, the combination of Tables 11.3 and 11.4 show that while Stretch mainstream students in the current data set have passed ENG 101 at a rate of 91 percent, traditional mainstream students are passing ENG 101 at a rate of 89 percent. Stretch multilingual students have passed ENG 107 at 96 percent and traditional multilingual ENG 107 students have passed at a rate of 95 percent. Pass rates of the final class in the sequence, ENG 102 or ENG 107, are the lowest for Stretch mainstream students who took ENG 102 (85%). Traditional mainstream students passed ENG 102 at 92 percent, and both Stretch and traditional multilingual students who took ENG 108 passed at 97 percent.

Persistence rates between ENG 101/7 and ENG 102/8 for Stretch and traditional students were as follows: traditional mainstream students exhibited the highest rate of persistence as 89 percent of ENG 101 students enrolled in ENG 102 in the Spring 2013 semester. The next highest persistence rate was demonstrated by the traditional multilingual students, as 79 percent enrolled in ENG 108. Stretch multilingual students persisted at 74 percent to ENG 108, and last, 64 percent of Stretch mainstream students persisted to ENG 102.

DISCUSSION: COMPARISON TO PREVIOUS FINDINGS
Student Profile

Due to the absence of data on students in multilingual sections in Glau (1996, 2007), no comparison of student profile can be made, although it can be noted that Stretch mainstream cohorts are consistently getting larger. Multilingual student populations represented 10 percent of the total ASU Writing Programs Fall 2012 cohort. For comparison, although the true number of multilingual students at ASU cannot be projected, according to the 2012 Open Doors report, ASU enrolled 5,616 international students. In 2012, ASU broke enrollment records to reach 73,373 students in Fall enrollment ("Enrollment at ASU Breaks Several Records" 2012). Thus, the international student population is 7.65 percent of the total ASU population. The international student population has only been projected to rise in the future.

Pass Rates

The previous studies (Glau 1996, 2007) were both able to show that Stretch students pass ENG 101 (with a C or above) at a higher rate than traditional students, and the data for this study supports that claim as well. Although Stretch mainstream students have passed ENG 101 at a slightly lower percentage (91%) than their Stretch peers from 1994 to 2004 (93%), and the 1994 Stretch cohort (also 93%), Stretch mainstream students are still passing ENG 101 at a higher rate than their traditional mainstream counterparts. In addition, of particular interest, is the multilingual population, which exhibits the highest pass rate of all populations for ENG 107 at 96 percent in Stretch and 95 percent in traditional. Overall, it can be seen that the pass rates of students show that Stretch Program students, both mainstream and multilingual, have higher success rates than students in traditional sections of ENG 101/107 (see Table 11.5).

A concern was raised in Glau (2007) that this higher Stretch pass rate may be due to grade inflation because the students had the same teachers for two semesters. If there were some teacher bias as a result of having the students longer in Stretch sections, a sharp drop in pass rates of ENG 102/108 might be expected. Table 11.6 shows the pass rates of ENG 102 and ENG 108 students who took Stretch and traditional FYC courses. Stretch was demonstrated to help students pass at a higher rate in the previous reports. In this study, with data from the 2012 cohort, students are still passing ENG 102 and ENG 108 at high rates, comparable to previous data. However, Stretch mainstream students pass ENG

Table 11.5. Historical Comparison of ENG 101/107 Pass Rates

	1994 Cohort (Glau 1996)	1994–2004 (Glau 2007)	2012 Cohort (This Study)	
	Mainstream (ENG 101)	Mainstream (ENG 101)	Mainstream (ENG 101)	Multilingual (ENG 107)
Stretch	93%	93%	91%	96%
Traditional	88%	89%	89%	95%

Table 11.6. Historical Comparison of ENG 102/108 Pass Rates

	1994 Cohort (Glau 1996)	1994–2004 (Glau 2007)*	2012 Cohort (This Study)	
	Mainstream (ENG 102)	Mainstream (ENG 102)	Mainstream (ENG 102)	Multilingual (ENG 108)
Stretch	81%	88%	85%	97%
Traditional	66%	85%	92%	97%

* Results adapted from "Stretch Award" 2014, 2.

102 at a rate of 85 percent, which is 7 percent lower than the pass rate of traditional mainstream students taking ENG 102. Despite the slight dip, 85 percent is still a high percentage, as the data from the ten-year analysis showed an 88 percent pass rate, higher than the first cohort's pass rate of 81 percent. The traditional mainstream students, however, seem to be excelling, passing at 92 percent. Most interestingly, both Stretch and traditional multilingual students are passing ENG 108 at 97 percent. This data shows that Stretch multilingual students pass their final FYC class at the same rate as traditional multilingual students. The data does not represent a sharp drop in pass rates for multilingual nor mainstream Stretch students. In fact, the data shows relatively positive growth over a historical timeline for mainstream students and very high pass rates for multilingual students.

Persistence Rates

Student persistence data for this study compared with the historical data from the previous studies is shown in Table 11.7, which shows the persistence of each group of students from their first semester class to their second semester class. The 2012 cohort data shows Stretch students continue to have high rates of persistence from their first semester class (WAC 101/107) to their second semester class (ENG 101/107),

Table 11.7. Persistence Rates from First Semester to Second Semester

	1994 Cohort (Glau 1996)	1994–2004 (Glau 2007)	2012 Cohort (This Study)	
	Mainstream	Mainstream	Mainstream	Multilingual
Stretch	82%	91%	88%	97%
Traditional	66%	87%	89%	79%

and traditional mainstream students' persistence rates at 89 percent, slightly surpassing their Stretch counterparts, who persist at 88 percent. This has not been the pattern of previous Stretch data, as a more striking difference has historically been recorded. However, a 1 percent difference between Stretch and traditional mainstream students indicates that Stretch students are still persisting at comparable rates to their traditional peers.

Multilingual Stretch students currently have the highest persistence rate (97%) in the history of the Stretch Program, which is much higher than the persistence rate of their traditional counterparts, who persist at 79 percent. There is no historical data to compare to, however, it is important to notice that Stretch multilingual students have the highest persistence rate from first semester to second semester in the 2012 cohort. Although the traditional multilingual students' persistence rate (79%) is surprisingly low, other factors besides the program should be taken into account for mainstream multilingual students who are 95 percent international students. For instance, some international students may only stay for a semester based on exchange program requirements. Data that might be able to illuminate this situation (i.e., degree-seeking/non-degree seeking status) was not collected for this study.

Further persistence analysis of the 2012 Stretch cohort reveals that persistence drops between the second and third semesters. In other words, 64 percent of the Stretch mainstream students who pass ENG 101 return to take ENG 102, and 74 percent of Stretch multilingual students who pass ENG 107 return to take ENG 108. The Stretch persistence rates from second to third semester are much lower in comparison to the first-to-second semester retention of traditional students who only need to take two classes (already reviewed in Table 11.7). Mainstream traditional students persist 25 percent more than mainstream Stretch students from ENG 101 to ENG 102. Mainstream multilingual students persist 5 percent more than multilingual Stretch students.

CONCLUSION

Overall, the claims that Glau's (1996, 2007) reports have made have also been supported by the data from the Fall 2012 cohort. The claim of improved student success concerning pass rates seems to be validated for all Stretch students—and students in multilingual sections are achieving at the highest rates in both Stretch and traditional models. Stretch multilingual writers seem to be enjoying the highest pass rates in WAC 107, ENG 107, and ENG 108 when compared to any other population—a testament to the preparation and continuing education that ASU provides for its teachers. All of these relatively high pass rates reflect positively on the Stretch Program, as well as the ASU Writing Programs in general, and they also indicate that the Stretch Program is still creating a necessary and important space for students who may not fit as easily into the university setting.

The Stretch Program persistence data also supports a claim of higher retention than traditional FYC from first semester to second semester for both mainstream and multilingual students. Persistence from second to third semester, however, seems to be problematic for Stretch students, and are the lowest percentages recorded for the Stretch Program to date. Although their pass rates are high, students in Stretch multilingual sections experienced a 26 percent drop in persistence from second to third semester. Likewise, Stretch mainstream students who passed ENG 101, persisted at the lowest rate of 64 percent to ENG 102. This is not to say that the rest of the students who passed ENG 101 and 107 never enrolled (see "Limitations"). It is possible that these students return later on in their undergraduate careers to pass ENG 102 and ENG 108. Considering the current analysis of the Fall 2012 cohort, the Stretch Program seems to be a successful space for most basic and L2 writers, although it deserves more data-driven research to be sure.

Implications

Linda Adler-Kassner and Susanmarie Harrington (2012) remind us that, "threats to the basic-writing narrative thus become threats to basic-writing students" (Adler-Kassner and Harrington 2012, 14–15) and this research should not be seen as a threat. It should be seen as dedication to excellence by writing programs and their administration, student access, and student success. The perennial question with any initiative in a writing program is, "Is what we are doing to help different populations of students *actually* helping them?" As student performance data can be read many ways based on which epistemological orientation is held, we run into political and ethical quagmires when the images of student populations are reified by the interpretation of data. For example, this research seems to have uncovered multiple conundrums of retention: on one hand, the students who persist are passing their classes, but not all students who are passing their classes are persisting. This data should be used only to improve our awareness of students' needs and understanding of implications for composition programs and models.

Another seemingly controversial issue is that of giving more time to Stretch students, seen in light of the mixed passing and persisting rates of Stretch mainstream and multilingual students. This may be related to the program design as students in previous studies criticized the Stretch Program for making them "lag behind their peers" (Glau 1996, 88). Although WAC 101/107 are now offered for university graduation credit, the three-course Stretch sequence may still be creating a lag as FYC is a mandatory pre-requisite for many other classes, and students typically finish off-sequence (in their third semester instead of their second), which may create a ripple effect for their other coursework. It may also affect international students' strict four-year scholarship packages, or alternatively their self-funding. On the other hand, if the Stretch Program had not been in place, these students may never had been at ASU and able to be retained in the first place. The low persistence rates could also signify issues that may be out of the Writing Programs' control.

It is unlikely that any retention analysis of institutional data only will be able to completely parse the program's effect versus curricular and extracurricular influence. Although students must take some responsibility for their actions, it is the program's responsibility to treat each student as ethically as possible by striving to increase persistence rates—and alternatively to figure out why persistence may not be an option for these students. This data should encourage writing program administrators to further endeavor in creating spaces for Stretch mainstream and multilingual students to succeed and persist at the same (or better) rate as their traditional FYC peers for variables that can be controlled.

Limitations

As with many studies, this study has limitations. Using the Step Model from Glau (1996, 2007), and therefore a more rigid definition of retention as "semester-to-semester" does not capture the actual number of students who passed FYC classes in the Fall 2012 cohort. This is because there are so many class session options. At ASU, and many other institutions, there are often three sessions per semester (one long session and two shorter sessions), which is also mimicked in summer sessions. The students who took and passed WAC 101 in Fall 2012, dispersed themselves into the next four semesters, Fall 2012 (session B), Spring 2013, summer 2013, and Spring 2014. Furthermore, the students who passed ENG 101 in Spring 2013, enrolled in six different following semesters, and that number of semesters was only cut short by the time period that the data was captured, which ended in Fall 2014. In short, seventy-eight additional Stretch mainstream students enrolled in their subsequent classes in semesters not captured by the definition of retention in the Step Model, and sixty-five of them passed—another 7 percent to be added to the pass rate. The enrollment patterns for Stretch multilingual sections differed slightly from that of Stretch mainstream, however the most difference in enrollment patterns is shown by multilingual traditional populations, who deviate less from the semester-to-semester enrollment pattern that the Step Model catches. Although semester-to-semester retention is important, as ideally all students should be able to pass the classes in the sequence on the first try, and semester-to-semester retention has implications for overall retention and graduation from university. In future studies of this kind, a modified definition of retention may be used to capture the true number of students who are passing the classes. Furthermore, it may more accurately reflect the good work that many writing programs are doing. An indicator of the number of times a class has been attempted overall may also be helpful to triangulate the success of the model, while balancing the model against the individual factors that affect student success.

Finally, as it is a study of one cohort from Fall 2012 to Fall 2013, the whole population should be analyzed to see if the cohort data is an accurate representation. When resolved, the limitations of this study will improve future studies, furthering our techniques and knowledge in the area of first-year composition retention for L2 writing, basic writing, and traditional writing students.

Acknowledgments

I am deeply grateful to Dr. Paul Kei Matsuda, Dr. Shirley Rose, Dr. Gregory Glau, and Dr. Todd Ruecker, for their insightful feedback and invaluable support on earlier drafts of this manuscript.

Notes

1. Gregory Glau, phone call with author, July 1, 2014.
2. Due to the challenges identifying US resident L2 students from institutional data that does not include the language background of students, the analyses in this project focused primarily on international L2 students.

References

Adler-Kassner, Linda, and Susanmarie Harrington. 2012. "Creation Myths and Flashpoints: Understanding Basic Writing through Conflicted Stories." In *Exploring Composition Studies: Sites, Issues, and Perspectives*, ed. Kelly Ritter and Paul Kei Matsuda, 13–35. Logan: Utah State University Press.

Baker, Tracey, and Peggy Jolly. 1999. "The 'Hard Evidence': Documenting the Effectiveness of a Basic Writing Program." *Journal of Basic Writing* 18 (1): 27–39.

Bartholomae, David. 1993. "The Tidy House: Basic Writing in the American Curriculum." *Journal of Basic Writing* 12 (1): 4–21.

Blakesley, David. 2002. "Directed Self-Placement in the University." *WPA. Writing Program Administration* 25 (3): 9–40.

Costino, Kimberley A., and Sunny Hyon. 2007. "A Class for Students Like Me: Reconsidering Relationships among Identity Labels, Residency Status, and Students' Preferences for Mainstream or Multilingual Composition." *Journal of Second Language Writing* 16 (2): 63–81. http://dx.doi.org/10.1016/j.jslw.2007.04.001.

"Enrollment at ASU Breaks Several Records" 2012. Sept 13. Accessed April 12, 2016. https://asunow.asu.edu/content/enrollment-asu-breaks-several-records.

Ericsson, Patricia Freitag, and Richard H. Haswell. 2006. *Machine Scoring of Student Essays: Truth and Consequences*. Logan: Utah State University Press.

Glau, Gregory R. 1996. "The 'Stretch Program': Arizona State University's New Model of University-Level Basic Writing Instruction." *WPA. Writing Program Administration* 20 (1/2): 79–91.

Glau, Gregory R. 2007. "Stretch at 10: A Progress Report on Arizona State University's Stretch Program." *Journal of Basic Writing* 26 (2): 30–48.

Goen-Salter, Sugie. 2008. "Critiquing the Need to Eliminate Remediation: Lessons from San Francisco State." *Journal of Basic Writing* 27 (2): 81–105.

Harklau, L., K. M. Losey, and M. Siegal. 1999. *Generation 1.5 Meets College Composition: Issues in the Teaching of Writing to U.S.-Educated Learners of ESL*. Ed. Linda Harklau, Kay M. Losey, and Meryl Siegal. Mawah, NJ: Lawrence Erlbaum Associates.

Malenczyk, Rita. 1999. "Productive Change in a Turbulent Atmosphere: Pipe Dream or Possibility?" In *Administrative Problem-Solving for Writing Programs and Writing Centers*, ed. Linda Myers-Breslin, 146–64. Urbana, IL: National Council of Teachers of English.

Matsuda, Paul K. 2003. "Basic Writing and Second Language Writing: Toward an Inclusive Definition." *Journal of Basic Writing* 22 (2): 67–89.

Matsuda, Paul K. 2006. "The Myth of Linguistic Homogeneity in U.S. College Composition." *College English* 68 (6): 637–51. http://dx.doi.org/10.2307/25472180.

Matsuda, Paul K., Tanita Saenkhum, and Steven Accardi. 2013. "Writing Teachers' Perceptions of the Presence and Needs of Second Language Writers: An Institutional Case Study." *Journal of Second Language Writing* 22 (1): 68–86. http://dx.doi.org/10.1016/j.jslw.2012.10.001.

Matzen, Richard N. Jr., and E. Jeff Hoyt. 2004. "Basic Writing Placement with Holistically Scored Essays: Research Evidence." *Journal of Developmental Education* 28 (1): 2–34.

McCurrie, Matthew Killian. 2009. "Measuring Success in Summer Bridge Programs: Retention Efforts and Basic Writing." *Journal of Basic Writing* 28 (2): 28–49.

McKay, Sandra. 1981. "ESL/Remedial English: Are They Different?" *English Language Teaching Journal* 35 (3): 310–5. http://dx.doi.org/10.1093/elt/XXXV.3.310.

Nattinger, James R. 1978. "Second Dialect and Second Language in the Composition Class." *TESOL Quarterly* 12 (1): 77–84. http://dx.doi.org/10.2307/3585793.

Pavesich, Matthew. 2011. "Reflecting on the Liberal Reflex: Rhetoric and the Politics of Acknowledgement in Basic Writing." *Journal of Basic Writing* 30 (2): 84–109.

Peele, Thomas. 2010. "Working Together: Student-Faculty Interaction and the Boise State Stretch Program." *Journal of Basic Writing* 29 (2): 50–73.

Rigolino, Rachel, and Penny Freel. 2007. "Re-Modeling Basic Writing." *Journal of Basic Writing* 26 (2): 51–74.

Roy, Alice Meyers. 1984. "Alliance for Literacy: Teaching Non-Native Speakers and Speakers of Nonstandard English Together." *College Composition and Communication* 35 (4): 439–48. http://dx.doi.org/10.2307/357796.

Roy, Alice Meyers. 1988. "ESL Concerns for Writing Program Administrators: Problems and Policies." *WPA. Writing Program Administration* 11 (3): 17–28.

Schwalm, David E. 1989. "Teaching Basic Writing: The Community College on the University Campus." *WPA. Writing Program Administration* 13 (1/2): 15–24.

Shapiro, Shawna. 2011. "Stuck in the Remedial Rut: Confronting Resistance to ESL Curriculum Reform." *Journal of Basic Writing* 30 (2): 24–52.

Silva, Tony. 1994. "An Examination of Writing Program Administrators' Options for the Placement of ESL Students in First Year Writing Classes." *WPA. Writing Program Administration* 18 (1/2): 37–43.

"Stretch Award." 2014. Accessed November 10, 2014. http://english.clas.asu.edu/wp-stretchaward.

"Stretch Program." 2014. Accessed November 11, 2014. http://english.clas.asu.edu/wp-stretch.

Webb-Sunderhaus, Sara. 2010. "When Access Is Not Enough: Retaining Basic Writers at an Open-Admission University." *Journal of Basic Writing* 29 (2): 97–116.

12

THE *KAIROTIC* CLASSROOM
Retention Discourse and Supplemental Instruction in the First Year

Sarah E. Harris

Though education researchers have long been interested in retention, the public and political discourse surrounding graduation rates, time to degree, and the general ability of colleges and universities to keep students enrolled has seen a substantial increase over the last two decades. This discourse has wide-ranging effects on our institutions, but one of them has been the steady erosion of developmental education at four-year colleges and universities, resulting in the paradoxical effect of students being pushed to enroll in first-year courses for which they may not be prepared. The fight to keep basic writing curricula in higher education has long been a subject of concern for scholars in that area—it has, as Webb-Sunderhaus (2010) points out, been seen as an issue primarily of access, "tied to the discontinuation of affirmative action and open-admission policies" (98). However, rather than focusing on admissions, the call to eliminate or relocate basic writing programs at both two- and four-year institutions has shifted in recent years to focus on language common to retention metrics and time-to-degree, with public stakeholders arguing that all courses at the university should "count." As the discourse around retention in higher education becomes more common in politics and public policy, time-to-degree is increasingly used as a rationale for eliminating basic writing and other developmental programs, providing students with access to college while mainstreaming them into first-year courses for which they may be underprepared.

For instance, in the state of Indiana, where I currently work and teach, the state's public universities reached an agreement with the Ivy Tech community college system in 2008 that would effectively eliminate associate's degree programs at the state's public, four-year institutions.

DOI: 10.7330/9781607326021.c012

The agreement was the culmination of years of pressure from the state legislature to establish a full community college system in Indiana and remove remedial education from four-year colleges and universities, in order to decrease the necessary general education credit hours students would take at these institutions and simplify time to degree.

Increasing the graduation rates of students who enroll in our institutions is not, on its face, a problematic goal—most of us want our students to remain in the university, to do well, and to graduate. But allowing the discourse around college "success" to be defined solely by numbers like graduation rates leaves out what students are actually doing and learning in our classrooms. Reichert Powell (2013) argues that faculty must begin to pay attention to retention initiatives on their campuses because they can "provide an important check to ensure that we retain a focus on teaching and learning rather than on simply keeping students in seats" (7). I want to go further and argue in this chapter that the increased attention to retention in public discourse and on our campuses serves as a potential moment of *kairos* for writing program administrators (WPAs) and writing instructors—an opportunity, as Reichert Powell suggests, which "arises from the forces at work" for both teachers and students (13). If we can recognize the discourse on our campuses as an opportunity to frame and construct the narrative on student success in the first year, we may then also construct opportunities to access institutional resources for our students and our courses that will align with learning outcomes and, in the process, encourage students to persist, even if the resources we draw on fall outside of a traditional developmental curriculum. Though the case study provided here will be necessarily local, my hope is that it will provide a useful frame through which other program administrators and writing instructors might think about their own institutional contexts, finding ways to both recognize and construct opportunities within the limitations of their own particular spaces and contexts.

THE INSTITUTIONAL CONTEXT

Before I introduce my own institutional context and the pilot tutoring program we implemented in the first semester composition course as both a response and a *kairotic* opportunity arising from cutbacks in basic writing at our campus, I want to begin by more broadly defining the rhetorical moment in which we were operating. Scholarship on *kairos* positions the term as either "associated with propriety or decorum," meaning either "understanding an order that guides and shapes rhetorical action," or enacting the opposite through a focus on "the timely, the spontaneous, the radically particular" (Miller 2002, xiii). Miller argues that any concept of *kairos* which includes only one of these ideas is "impoverished," and urges instead keeping them in "productive tension" (xiii). By embodying the tension between what is proper and what is radical, *kairos* functions as both an ability to recognize "the particular opportunity in a given moment," and to *construct* a moment (Miller 1994, 83). Miller explains that when time is seen as continuous, *kairos* functions as a "constructive power," where "one has the opportunity to make a change at any time" (Miller 1994, 83). When time is seen as discontinuous, then opportunities exist at particular disruptive moments.

Kairos is an important concept for understanding the discourse on retention, because we are living through a moment of emphasis on retention that contains the possibilities of both continuity and disruption. Retention research, for instance, has been continuous in higher education since the 1970s, arising in response to events that also shaped composition studies, as college campuses began admitting more diverse student populations. However, as Reichert Powell (2013) points out, "the current financial climate in higher education is prompting even more interest in the reasons students leave," and retention has become one of the most researched areas in higher education (35). Thus, retention has been a continuously building area of interest in higher education, from which local exigencies can be constructed as a way to gain access to resources or shape a campus climate. If retention policy and discourse is already occurring as disruptive discourse at an institution, however, it may be necessary to find the opening through which to create change. At my institution, Indiana University East, a mix of institutional interest in retention and challenges facing our writing program led me to look for opportunities to improve student learning that would fit our particular moment, and capitalize on the available possibilities in the potentially disruptive framing of an institution-wide retention initiative. There was a narrow window during which to propose projects, before projects were likely to be proposed to me from the top down, a position that will be familiar to many WPAs. Though my local context has been shaped by the disruption to our writing program caused by a variety of outside forces, and the narrative that follows will be one of disruption and *kairotic* response, I want to be clear that disruption is not necessary for others to create moments for *kairos* in their own programs or institutions.

When I began as writing program director at my institution in the Fall semester of 2013, our writing program faced an array of challenges. Our campus, a regional commuter campus with an enrollment of about four thousand students, had been through significant changes. Student enrollment has nearly doubled in a few short years; as recently as 2007 our enrollment was at around 2,200 students; now we have over just over four thousand undergraduates, with about 130 graduate students; during the same period we transitioned from an associate's degree granting institution to what the official institutional history describes as a "full-fledged baccalaureate and masters degree institution." Associate's degree admits were halted in 2008 and the final campus associate's degree was granted in 2011. Along with the growth in enrollment came changes and challenges for our writing program—in particular, even as student need increased, internal and external pressures of various kinds, including the state of Indiana's emphasis on credit hours and time-to-degree and a change in our writing placement process,[1] led to declining enrollment in our preparatory stretch course, Principles of Composition (W130), which has little institutional support and is currently under-enrolled. Our campus general education sequence in writing consists of a two-course required sequence, with Reading Writing and Inquiry I (W131) as the standard first course, followed by a range of possible second writing courses that vary by students' program enrollment. W130 serves as a preparatory stretch course students may elect to take prior to W131—it is credit bearing, but counts as elective credit. Prior to the implementation of directed self-placement on our campus, students with an SAT verbal at or below 430 were placed in W130. In Fall 2013, 79 new first-year undergraduates with an SAT verbal below 420 were enrolled, but we were able to offer only four sections of W130, with a total of 42 students enrolled in the course—well below the available caps for these sections, with one section enrolling only six students. Most new students were advised directly into W131 by their academic advisors, who are less likely to see the value in an "extra" course and are focused on maintaining students' progress toward their degree in accordance with state and institutional pressures. The number of offered sections and enrolled students has declined ever since—in Fall 2015, we were able to offer only two sections of the course.

The result has been a steady climb in the overall D, F, and withdrawal (DFW) grades awarded in our first-year writing (FYW) courses, which is now over 30 percent. The same year I joined the campus, we also recruited a new chancellor, who instituted a campus-wide focus on student success and retention. So though there was a window of opportunity to tackle the pass rate of our courses, there was also little support for additional credit hours in general education, whether developmental writing or studio-model "plus" courses.

Not only recognizing, but analyzing and constructing this opportunity for change was key to accessing new resources for our program. I began by examining the data on course DFW grades, looking to make a case for more robust placement methods to support and sustain W130, but instead found that there was little available data to justify a placement-based solution to student support. There was no pattern I could find that would predict which students would earn DFW grades, whether I looked at admissions data or at the instructor-scored diagnostic essays students wrote in the first week of classes. In addition, I learned through participation in institution-wide retention retreats and action groups that the writing program's retention rate was frequently in line with other courses targeting primarily first-year students; first-year seminar, for instance, also had a high DFW rate.

This confluence of circumstances led me to investigate methods of retention that were targeted at courses, rather than a particular group of students; if there was no very good way of identifying the students who were at-risk of dropping or failing the course for writing-related reasons, then perhaps our campus needed a method of intervention available to the general student body; this investigation led me to research on Supplemental Instruction.

THE SUPPLEMENTAL INSTRUCTION MODEL

Supplemental Instruction (SI) is a model of embedded course tutoring combined with study-sessions that began at the University of Missouri-Kansas City in the 1970s. The model was developed as a targeted solution for "difficult" or challenging courses, defined partly as those with DFW rates above 30 percent. Often, these courses are large lecture courses considered "gateways," difficult classes in math and sciences, for instance, that might be required either as part of general education or as prerequisites for a particular major.

Supplemental Instruction was explicitly designed to target courses, not students or instructors. It was meant to bypass some of the arguing about where to lay blame for low pass rates and instead get to solutions that would impact courses directly. Under the SI model, students who have been successful in the targeted course are recruited as SI leaders. They receive training in the model's instructional methods, which "integrate study skills with the course content" (Arendale 1994, 13). SI leaders attend class, meet with students in weekly outside-of-class study sessions, and meet regularly with the course instructor to review course content and plan possible interventions. In a typical course with SI support, an SI leader would attend class and announce the focus of that week's study session—usually a concept being studied in class or preparation for an upcoming test or assignment. Then the SI leader would meet students who chose to attend the session outside of class in a designated space, leading a review session with planned study activities like a Jeopardy game or "think, pair, share," an activity where study session attendees review a question, discuss it in pairs, and then share results with the larger group. So in a history class, for example, the SI leader might announce a review session on politics and power in the American Revolution to help students' prepare for an upcoming quiz, then meets with students outside of class to review relevant material by leading a quiz game focused on key events and figures from that time period.

The research on SI shows consistently that students who attend sessions improve their course grades, and there have been modest effects on overall course retention. One possible critique of the model is that these effects, particularly those of higher average grades, might be shaped in part by the kind of students who are likely to attend SI sessions in the first place; are the higher average GPAs a result of SI, or a result of isolating the GPAs of better-performing, more motivated students for comparison? There are, however, some studies of SI which indicate students identified as "at-risk" who regularly attend SI sessions in designated courses outperform better prepared students who do not, indicating some measurable impact on vulnerable populations (Ogden et al. 2003; Shaya, Petty, and Petty 1993).

Related research on embedded course tutoring in writing instruction emerges from writing center literature. Work with embedded tutors at Rider University, for example, has drawn on SI principles in design and assessment, and in the early 1980s SI was adapted for use in composition courses by the Point Loma College Learning Center; in both of these instances, the program was based primarily in a campus writing center and the embedded course tutors ran occasional classroom workshops and met one-on-one with students in the writing center to engage in discussion about student drafts based on a co-working model (McMillin 1992; Titus et al. 2014). Each of these examples function as slight adaptations of the SI model, which traditionally relies on content-based review sessions held in groups, rather than one-on-one work between the SI leader and students in the course. As I'll discuss in the next section, this difference may have significant impacts on how students, both SI leaders and session attendees, perceive and self-define successful learning experiences.

Because there was already an existing SI program on our campus, run out of the Office of Academic Support, I was well placed in our institutional context and space to advocate for a retention pilot program embedding SI leaders in first-year writing courses; using the *kairotic* disruptive moment of our campus retention initiative as a rationale for the pilot allowed me to secure funding to increase the number of SI leaders available to us from the Academic Support office. In Fall semester of 2014, therefore, we embedded SI leaders in four sections of the first course in our FYW sequence, Reading, Writing and Inquiry I (W131), with three course instructors participating in the pilot program.

THE MOST IMPORTANT THING: CONSTRUCTING
THE RESULTS OF OUR PILOT PROGRAM

In line with national data on SI, the GPAs of students in the pilot sections who attended SI, as compared to the students enrolled in those same sections those who did not attend sessions, ranged from 1.00—1.60 points higher, on average; that is, the students who attended SI sessions saw an increase in their course grade of about one letter grade. Though one isolated course grade is not necessarily indicative of retention rates, on our campus, data show that students with higher GPAs also have higher rates of retention. For instance following fall semester of 2013, the overall fall to spring retention rate of beginning students for the campus was 88.3 percent, however students with a GPA below 2.0 in that first fall semester were retained at a rate of 69 percent. Following fall of 2014, the semester of our pilot program, the overall fall to spring retention rate for beginning students was 82.8 percent, with students earning below a 2.0 retained at a rate of 52.8 percent. The increase in fall to spring retention associated with higher GPA was considered important enough by campus stakeholders that one key campus action group on retention was tasked with creating and enacting retention strategies to target at-risk students in the first year. That action group provides our program with the opportunity to construct a moment for change—today's opportunity to tie the increase in GPA associated with our pilot semester to campus retention data will serve as a compelling reason to secure funding for our support program in future years, without regard to how our current campus action groups may eventually be restructured.

GPA data are useful in the context of creating an opportune moment to increase campus support for our writing courses, but in addition I wanted to look at whether SI support had any impact on the overall passing rate for Reading Writing and Inquiry I. To do this, I looked at the DFW rates for the previous fall semester in which participating instructors taught the course, and compared that rate with the DFW rate for

Table 12.1. Pilot Program Retention Data, Reading Writing and Inquiry I

	*Fall 2013 DFW Percentage**	*Fall 2014 DFW Percentage*
SI Pilot Instructors	36.6%	30.6%
All sections	32.1%	37.2%

One of the pilot instructors did not teach the course in fall 2013; in that instance, data from fall 2012 were used to calculate the average.

those same instructors with SI leaders attached to their sections. My goal was to eliminate, as far as possible in the small sample size, extraneous factors that might be contributing to changes in DFW rates, such as assigned instructor or semester of enrollment (DFW rates are higher for this course in the spring semester, when there are fewer sections offered and many students may be taking the class a second time). The result of this comparison was a modest decrease in the overall percentage of DFW grades, with three sections showing a direct improvement compared to the prior semester, and all sections showing a lower DFW rate than the average across all W131 sections (see Table 12.1).

Though the preliminary data presented in Table 12.1 are in line with the larger body of research on SI, I want to stress that this is a very small data set, and though the numbers are moderately encouraging we will need to collect more information over time to determine whether this is a real, sustainable impact. Though the data sample is small, however, it does serve as one element of a rhetorical strategy designed to take advantage of a key point of focus for retention on our campus. Evidence of improvement in DFW rates and student GPAs can be used to show key stakeholders, like the campus action committee, that initiatives like this one have a measurable impact on retention and are worthy of continued, sustained, funding and support. However, the initiative cannot be defined solely through data; instead, we need to turn to more qualitative measures designed to illustrate for key stakeholders what a program like Supplemental Instruction does for student learning. Without qualitative data on learning outcomes, we risk making grades or "bodies in seats" the sole outcome of our initiative, rather than a beneficial side effect of what students have learned to do in our curriculum.

Therefore, in addition to looking at course data, I also conducted case study interviews with three student participants in the pilot program—two SI leaders, Mike[2] and Jara, and a student, Chris, who attended study sessions. Interview participants were solicited from the pilot sections and were asked a set of open-ended questions designed to encourage a dialogue on session strengths and students' own definitions of success.

Mike and Chris both described primarily positive experiences with SI, while Jara's experience was more mixed, but the three interviews taken together provided an important context for narratives about successful participation in SI. These students' own descriptions of the lived experience of this program, which methodologically are too small a sample size to serve as concrete evidence, can provide a key context for the data on the success of our pilot. Much as Reichert Powell (2013) does in her book, I want to invite these students to "participate in the discourse on retention" on our campus, and to add their voices to the conversation on student success (20). Interview responses are presented in italics through the remainder of this chapter.

As a student in W131, Chris described SI as a resource that allowed him to succeed in the course even when personal circumstances might have interfered. On his choice to participate in SI, he explained that *last semester I was out quite a bit due to family issues [. . .]. So SI really helped me out in [. . .] getting to you know do my papers better, or just in general learning something that I either wasn't there for or I didn't understand at the time.* Chris was the kind of student who might not show up in traditional placement measures as "at-risk," the kind of student who made the data points I initially examined for writing placement so murky; one of the reasons it was so difficult to predict which students would earn DFW grades in their writing courses in order to sustain placement in W130 was because of the many students like Chris who enroll at campuses like ours. His difficulty was not with writing practice, but with family life and regular access to the institution, a common issue for students at commuter campuses in particular.

Later, when he was asked whether his SI participation impacted how he approached his writing class, Chris referred to the value of SI as one of access when he again brought up the classes he had missed: *Because of my lack of being there had I not caught up things would have been, things would have gone very south. But this semester I think the things I learned last semester transferred over a little bit, so I don't feel the need to do it, unless I actually am struggling with something.* Chris, by his own admission and unprompted, pointed to the knowledge transfer and study skills SI provided for him— both transferrable course skills (he later mentioned having learned to take notes as he read, a skill he was still using, and feeling more proficient with APA style compared to some of his peers in his second writing course), and transferrable study skills, including the ability to self-diagnose when he was struggling and seek help.

Chris speaks directly to the experience of one type of student we particularly hoped to reach with the SI pilot program—a student who may not have shown up in more traditional measures of academic risk. But he also pointed to interesting factors that may have influenced what he learned in the class, and his perception about how and why that knowledge transferred to other courses. As he was describing why he felt SI sessions were successful for him, he set up a contrast between a studio or lab course, and the writing SI sessions he attended:

> So I, for a while I had math and I had math lab to go with it. And math lab was a lot more, even though it was a room full of people it was a lot more of a singular experience where you had to ask the teacher to help. Whereas with SI, being able to talk to other people, and then being able to talk to the instructor about the thoughts you had, I would say just was more effective, just in general, because if I understand something in one way, and that person understands it in a different way, if the two of us can't find a way where we both understand it then we can at least talk to the teacher or the SI instructor [. . .] I think just the ability to talk to more than one person was probably a big help.

Chris points here to something all three students referenced in their discussions of SI—that it provided opportunities to talk and network with other students that they considered a key component of their learning success. As writing instructors, many of us think of our classrooms as spaces that are already set up to provide that opportunity, but students may persistently see the space of the classroom as one of teacher authority, or may feel unable to openly communicate in that space for fear of saying the wrong thing—even when they are talking with other students in activities or small groups, they may be doing so performatively, acting primarily for the instructor.

Mike, one of the SI leaders, also emphasized opportunities for interactive learning. When asked what factors he felt made an SI session successful, Mike answered, *I think the most important one is their ability to interact with other people. Because, when they're sitting through the lecture they don't always get the opportunity to interact.* When asked to elaborate, Mike pointed to examples of many kinds of classes he'd attended where he felt the students interacted with one another very little, and in consequence finding ways in most of these courses to talk to classmates outside the context of the course. For instance, in describing one math class, Mike said,

> I'm in a math class right now where everybody comes in and they sit down, and at the end there's a person who stays after the class and he continues to work on his homework, and I'm like 'hey you want to work on homework and explain this,' and he's like 'yeah,' and I say 'Okay, so what's this about,' and then he'll say 'did you get this answer for this problem,' and then we just kind of work together a little bit.

However, for students not as proactive as Mike, or students like Chris who for one reason or another cannot regularly be in class or may not be able to stay late, there is value in providing a kind of scaffolding for these out-of-class interactions, especially at a commuter campus like ours, where students are less likely to encounter one another spontaneously in common or community spaces outside of classrooms.

Both of these students' own descriptions of their experiences indicate there is value for them in the process of learning; in describing success in these sessions, they point to interactions, conversations, and opportunities, rather than grades; their experiences reinforce the necessity of including students' own definition of success and learning in the conversation around retention. Chris, for instance, mentions an ability to persist and complete the class, but also values opportunities to interact with other motivated students, pointing out the value in SI's emphasis on voluntary participation when he says that, *In class you're either, you'll either have the person who's intently watching or you have the person who's not really paying attention. Whereas in SI everyone was there for the same reason so everyone was you know, willing to contribute on some level at least. So it was a little bit different.* This points to an issue with which I want to end this chapter—the necessity of student agency and choice in the success of retention initiatives, if those initiatives are to truly aid and encourage learning.

SOMETIMES YOU JUST GET A WEIRD CLASS: MOTIVATION AND THE *KAIROTIC* CLASSROOM

Though I've focused on fall semester in this chapter, our SI pilot continued into the spring, and we continue to expand and improve the program with additional sections assigned SI leaders and a new initiative in progress focused on adding assistance to our online course sections. Ultimately, our goal is to add support to every section, with SI leaders attached to all W131 courses, though recruiting the necessary number of student workers has been a challenge on our small campus.

The most interesting take-away, for me, has been the role of agency and choice in the success of these students. It's clear to me that the SI program is useful for students who take advantage of it, and that we need to find ways to increase attendance in the SI study sessions without negating the role of choice in this process; I don't think requiring students to attend is a workable solution because, as Arendale (1994) points out, students who are "at-risk" "perceive that tutorial help, far from relieving them of their academic burden, increases the burden as they must now answer to a tutor in addition to the course professor" (16). I spoke with SI leader Jara about session attendance in the writing course she was assigned to; she told me that she did not *get a lot of attendance* at her regular SI sessions, so the course instructor developed an individual conference model with points assigned as an incentive, and students met with both Jara and the course instructor for one-on-one conferences prior to submission of their unit papers. Unlike the course that Mike was assigned to, Jara felt that students in the course were not motivated to do well in the class; she reported that *there are a few students who actually do their work on time and turn stuff in, but a lot of them, they don't turn [work] in on time, they don't come to class, [. . .] probably less than half of the class regularly comes.* Students who opt out of class work and activities are losing valuable feedback and instructional time that may bar them from traditional definitions of success in the course, and despite opportunities to catch up on work through SI sessions, as Chris did, many students in Jara's course section were choosing not to engage. Though the spaces for learning were available, they did not feel as convenient or as "opportune" for these students; it is important for the future success of our SI initiative to consider why that might be so.

One possible explanation for these students opting out is the difference between the voluntary, interactive atmosphere Chris and Mike describe, and the points-based, one-on-one interaction Jara described. One-on-one tutoring in the conference model, where students send their essay to the SI leader, who reads them and then relates suggestions in a short meeting—as Jara did in this instance—is much more in line with traditional tutoring practices than it is with the Supplemental Instruction model. Though both have their benefits, in the case of our students, the ability to create shared, collaborative space for learning may be more important for learning than direct tutoring feedback. Both, I suspect, would result in the data outcomes we saw as a result of the pilot. But Reichert Powell (2013) encourages writing teachers to use retention as an opportunity to consider pedagogy through the lens of *kairos*, to consider a way of teaching that is "flexible and inventive enough to determine what reading and writing tasks a student might need right now" (119). We should think more carefully, Reichert Powell argues, about educating the student who is right in front of us in the present moment; if that student might leave, then we have to think more fully about what they would leave us with. She argues that "our goal should not be to *prepare* a student to live the life of an intellectual, worker, and citizen, but rather to invite the student to *participate* now as reader and writer of the world" (118). If success for our students, now, in this moment, means providing opportunities to participate in intellectual community, and teaching students how to make those communities possible outside the space of the classroom, then SI can be one way to do so. SI, as Arendale (1994) points out, has the potential to be proactive rather than reactive; it starts with the first day of class, and students don't need to wait until they are doing poorly to attend and benefit from conversations (17).

I don't think we can simply sit back and count on the success of SI attendees to motivate other students in the course, something Arendale (1994) suggests will happen. But neither can we force students into the program. As Jara's example illustrates, required attendance may increase GPAs, but it may not lead to the curiosity and conversation that creates a deeper impact. One way of adapting the one-on-one conference model is suggested by McMillin (1992), who adapted SI for composition courses by focusing on paired interaction, with SI leaders holding one-on-one tutoring sessions in the campus learning center. McMillin presents a tutoring dialogue, for use during one-on-one conferences, that focuses on the SI leader as a "co-worker," emphasizing the SI principles of "discovery of learning in a non-threatening environment" and "an awareness of process" (McMillin 1992, 34). The dialogue emphasizes student control, with the SI leader always asking what the student wants to focus on, and obtaining verbal agreement before looking for anything else in the essay. It emphasizes good tutoring practices of student ownership over their own work, with the SI leader never commenting on the work without the student present. The goal of the dialogue appears similar to the way Mike described working with a fellow student in his math class, with sample exchanges like "Ok, if I find anything else that needs work, do you want me to point it out? [. . .] Yes. I want to find all the errors I can" mimicking the example exchange Mike describes, *I'm like 'hey you want to work on homework and explain this' and he's like 'yeah.'*

Jara, in describing the ideal of a successful SI session, also defined student success through multiple interactions, saying *the more help they have with the drafting and revision process the better they're gonna do. Because the more people they have read through it, the more people that you know give them feedback, as long as they actually do something with that feedback of course, the better they're going to get.* But sometimes attendance in sessions will not allow for this happy possibility. If so, the next best thing may be to allow some looseness into the conference model, so that the aim of the SI leader is not only to make writing corrections but also to model the benefits of peer interaction and conversation.

There may be very little institutions can do to prevent all students from leaving when the reasons students leave are complex and may be determined "before they step foot on our campuses," but that data and discourse on retention assumes the current structures of our institutions must remain intact (Reichert Powell 2013, 106). It is true that, as Jara puts it, *I think sometimes you just get a weird class,* and instructors do not always have control over the forces that are impacting their students' lives. But we do have an opportunity, to both recognize and construct a moment that will allow us to change those structures, even if only in small ways. When disruptive events occur in the "multiple places" our students inhabit while they are in our classroom, we can shift our attention, as Reichert Powell (2013) advocates, to new *kairotic* opportunities, new spaces that might assist our students in disruptive times (116). And when disruptive moments occur in our own campus discourses, we must be just as active in finding ways to investigate and shape our institutions, so that we can create opportunities for success in the many collaborative, interactive ways our students describe and envision it.

Notes

1. A full description of the rationale for changes in writing program placement is beyond the scope of this article. However, initially ACT and/or SAT test scores were used in combination with grades in high school writing courses designated as "college preparatory" to place students in writing courses. Placement was completed by hand by a member of the English faculty, using individual student transcripts. However, this method became unsustainable as campus enrollment increased, and the campus moved to a self-placement model.
2. All student names are pseudonyms.

References

Arendale, David R. 1994. "Understanding the Supplemental Instruction Model." *New Directions for Teaching and Learning* 1994 (60): 11–21. http://dx.doi.org/10.1002/tl .37219946004.

McMillin, Jan. 1992. "Adapting SI to English Composition Classes." In *Supplemental Instruction: Improving Student Success in High-Risk Courses,* ed. Deanna C. Martin and David R. Arendale, 34–37 Columbia: National Resource Center for the Freshman Year Experience.

Miller, Carolyn R. 1994. "Opportunity, Opportunism, and Progress: Kairos in the Rhetoric of Technology." *Argumentation* 8 (1): 81–96. http://dx.doi.org/10.1007/B F00710705.

Miller, Carolyn R. 2002. *Foreword to Rhetoric and Kairos: Essays in History, Theory and Praxis.* Ed. Phillip Sipiora and James S. Baumlin, xi–xiii. Albany: SUNY Press.

Ogden, Peggy, Dennis Thompson, Art Russell, and Carol Somons. 2003. "Supplemental Instruction: Short- and Long-Term Impact." *Journal of Developmental Education* 26 (3): 2–7.

Reichert Powell, Pegeen. 2013. *Retention and Resistance: Writing Instruction and Students Who Leave.* Logan: Utah State University Press.

Shaya, Stephen B., Howard R. Petty, and Leslie Isler Petty. 1993. "A Case Study of Supplemental Instruction in Biology Focused on At-Risk Students." *Bioscience* 43 (10): 709–11. http://dx.doi.org/10.2307/1312343.

Titus, Megan L., Jenny L. Scudder, Josephine R. Boyle, and Alison Sudol. 2014. "Dialoging a Successful Pedagogy for Embedded Tutors." *Praxis (Bern)* 12 (1). http://www.praxisuwc.com/titus-et-al-121.

Webb-Sunderhaus, Sara. 2010. "When Access Is Not Enough: Retaining Basic Writers at an Open-Admission University." *Journal of Basic Writing* 29 (2): 97–116.

13

ENHANCING ALLIANCES AND JOINING INITIATIVES TO HELP STUDENTS
The Story of How We Created Developmental Learning Communities at Texas A&M University–Corpus Christi

Susan Wolff Murphy and Mark G. Hartlaub

INTRODUCTION

Improving first-year student persistence, especially at a regional, public, Hispanic-Serving Institution (HSI), is an ethical imperative determined by our university's mission and vision; by our institutional and state history; by our individual callings as faculty; by the field of composition's long-standing dedication to access, equity, and empowerment; and by the grotesque consequences of student failure, including debt. First-year student persistence is a multi-faceted, never-ending challenge that requires teams of people coordinating efforts and resources. It is certainly not the sole purview of a writing program administrator (WPA), and cannot be accomplished solely by her efforts. There are many large-scale retention and persistence initiatives that enable the coordination of resources and encourage campus-wide interdisciplinary and inter-departmental cooperation. At Texas A&M University-Corpus Christi (TAMU-CC), we attempted to improve our first-year student persistence by combining several campus-wide initiatives, including our long-standing learning communities program; an accreditation-mandated, five-year quality enhancement plan (QEP);[1] and the national learning improvement initiative, Liberal Education and America's Promise (LEAP), from the Association of American Colleges & Universities (AAC&U). With these initiatives, we designed and implemented, from 2010 to the present, developmental learning communities (DLCs) that have been shown to improve the likelihood that first-year students who are identified as at-risk will finish their first semester in good academic

DOI: 10.7330/9781607326021.c013

standing. Our collaboration, which included many faculty, staff, and administrators, enabled us to identify many of the disparate parts of student support networks and coordinate them. During this process, Susan, coordinator for composition, became the QEP director. Mark, psychology department chair and faculty member, served on the QEP advisory committee and became one of our pioneering faculty to teach in a developmental learning community. Using the DLC example, we will show what can be achieved when WPAs participate in and/or lead campus persistence initiatives that build networks of support that may be particularly effective for Hispanic students.

THE TROUBLED WATERS OF COMPOSITION

Histories of composition demonstrate how the course is entangled with the processes and policies that both provide gateways to college success and weed out "underprepared" students (Rose 1985). Sharon Crowley, among many others, has articulated how the universal requirement of a writing course is problematic for many reasons, including its relationship to "people who have differing histories and traditions and languages and ideologies" (Crowley 1998, 9), which is particularly troubling at an institution designated to serve students whose cultural and linguistic heritages differ from those who are privileged. Compositionists have been advised to pay attention to the ways in which our courses, our assessments, and our assumptions may work for or against the students we serve who may be ethnically, racially, linguistically, economically, or otherwise marginalized (Horner and Trimbur 2002; Inoue and Poe 2014; Kells and Balester 1999; Kirklighter, Cárdenas, and Wolff Murphy 2007). There are several ways that composition can mitigate the dangers of the first-year transition for students, including collaborating with other student success initiatives. Borrowing resources and impetus from campus initiatives and realizing the importance of campus-wide networking are not new ideas, especially in the field of Writing across the Curriculum (WAC) (Townsend 2002; Walvoord 1996) and composition linked to learning communities (Zawacki and Williams 2001).[2] There can be dangers in joining retention initiatives; Peegan Reichert Powell (2014) warns WPAs to educate themselves about these efforts in order to protect the interests of our students and our programs (7). As she points out, retention initiatives frequently arise in non-academic departments and may focus on keeping students at an institution, rather than on the quality of their learning. Decisions made in other units can damage or change first-year composition, one of the most universally required courses (e.g., replacing a writing course with a first-year seminar course) (Reichert Powell 2014, 8). We agree with Reichert Powell's caution; however, we would argue that if a WPA is involved in as many campus conversations about retention and success as possible, and if there is mutual respect and collaboration on a campus, that involvement might stave off the dangers, or reap large benefits to a writing program administrator.

THE ROLE OF THE WPA

A longstanding WPA has the theoretical grounding in student learning and pedagogy and often has the practical know-how and relationships across campus to implement a project focused on improved student persistence. What may hold her back, however, can be a lack of budget, time, and administrative clout. These can be provided by a campus-wide initiative, such as those described below. WPAs in leadership roles can use their grassroots knowledge, "street cred" with faculty, and relationships with support systems and campus networks to help make campus retention initiatives more effective for students and faculty and less disruptive to systems already in place. Three different initiatives helped bring the DLCs to fruition; Susan and Mark have both participated in and/or led, to greater or lesser degrees, all of these.

FIRST INITIATIVE: LEARNING COMMUNITIES

Learning communities have been demonstrated to improve the success of first-year students at both two- and four-year institutions (Kuh 2008, 15). Research on learning communities has shown that they are helpful for student learning (Hansen, Meshulam, and Watson 2010; Lichtenstein 2005) and that the first-year seminar instructor is especially critical in the process (Jozwiak and Hartlaub 2012). Recognizing that we represented an HSI, our QEP planning committee members were especially interested in learning communities because of their effectiveness with Latino students (e.g., Sandoval-Lucero, Maes, and Chopra 2011) and those who are historically under-represented, at-risk, and/or academically underprepared (Huerta and Bray 2013; Kuh 2013; Nosaka and Novak 2014). Having a writing course in a learning community is vital for contextualizing the students' research, reading, and writing activities. The linked writing course may help students "recontextualize" learning (Nowacek 2011) and may help students learn threshold concepts in both writing and general education courses (Adler-Kassner, Majewski, and Koshnick 2012). Due to pressure from the federal government and accrediting organizations, administrative leaders—seeking to improve their institutions' rates of retention and persistence of first-year students, especially those who come from at-risk categories—are paying attention to learning communities and other data-supported initiatives, such as those from AAC&U.

SECOND INITIATIVE: LIBERAL EDUCATION AND AMERICA'S PROMISE (LEAP)

Learning communities are one of these High-Impact Practices advocated for by AAC&U, a national data-supported initiative to improve student learning in higher education. Texas and other states have committed to becoming LEAP states, so many campuses in Texas are embracing the various initiatives of the AAC&U (e.g., High-Impact Practices, VALUE rubrics, Inclusive Excellence). Data show that Latino students who participate in multiple High-Impact Practices (which include first-year seminar and learning communities) have improved graduation rates (O'Donnell 2013, 19). All of this attention to learning outcomes, student success, and assessment means that TAMU-CC is continuing to put resources toward faculty development and assessment of the pedagogical approaches identified as High-Impact Practices and in pursuit of the Essential Learning Outcomes. The initiatives of the QEP aligned with these goals perfectly, and the alignment has allowed us to "hang" the QEP professional development onto the AAC&U frameworks and use their materials, even extending the reach and focus of the QEP beyond students in their first year to all students, including graduate and online students.

THIRD INITIATIVE: THE QUALITY ENHANCEMENT PLAN (QEP)

As part of our Southern Association of Colleges and Schools Commission on Colleges (SACS-COC) accreditation, TAMU-CC is required to complete a Quality Enhancement Plan (QEP) every ten years. In 2009, largely because of the data we were facing about our low first-year retention, the campus decided to focus on enhancing the first-year students' academic experience. Our first step was to identify courses in which our students struggled the most. A large database was constructed in which we tracked student performance (i.e., GPA) in all first- and second-year Core Curriculum classes. It turned out that students did most poorly in courses in history, political science, biology, and developmental mathematics.

Once these disciplines and courses were identified, the faculty who taught them formed work groups to redesign the courses to improve student learning and performance in them. Both the groups working on the History and mathematics courses decided to address the needs of underprepared students by forming smaller learning communities. These groups were brought together to design the developmental learning communities, which linked developmental mathematics, history, seminar, and English. As these involved multiple academic departments as well as state-mandated "college readiness" placement exams, developmental education compliance monitoring, tutoring, and advising, they constituted the most complex, and as it turns out, the most effective interventions to arise out of the redesign projects funded by our QEP.

THE INSTITUTIONAL CONTEXT

TAMU-CC enrolls just over 11,000 students and offers undergraduate, master's, and doctoral degrees. As a regional, public, Hispanic-Serving Institution (HSI) whose mission and funding have origins in a civil rights legal challenge (Acosta 2010; Flack 2003),[3] and which enrolls 48 percent first-year Hispanic (mostly Mexican American) students (TAMU-CC 2015).

TAMU-CC has had a long history of focusing on quality undergraduate education and providing structures to help students succeed. The First-Year Learning Communities Program (FYLCP) has been a feature of the first-year experience since 1994, and have always been tightly integrated with the First-Year Writing Program (FYWP). These programs have operated collaboratively for twenty years and have been physically located in the same office for more than ten years. Our learning communities are all connected by integrative work and faculty meet regularly. The university's mandate that all full-time, first-year students take two semesters of first-year seminar makes its learning communities program comprehensive, which is unusual. Universal enrollment means that the High-Impact Practices of learning communities and first-year seminars are provided for every student. By enrolling all students in learning communities, we eliminated the possible "selection bias" of learning communities, where only those students whose backgrounds and/or inclinations might encourage them to choose an optional, educational enhancement experience do so (Hawkins and Larabee 2009, 194). In this way, we ensure that underprepared students or those who might not be familiar with college, like first-generation students, will receive the benefits of the learning communities program. Research has shown that the more High-Impact Practices that students, especially Latino/a students, experience, the more successful the student is likely to be (O'Donnell 2013).

As our enrollment grows, the scope of offering learning communities to all first-year students continues to expand. For example, in Fall 2014, 1,900 first-year students were enrolled in one of nineteen learning communities. Approximately 1,300 students were enrolled in a linked section of Composition I (68%). In Spring 2015, of 1,400 students in learning community courses, approximately 900 students were enrolled in Composition II linked to a learning community (64%). TAMU-CC remains committed to offering all first-year students this beneficial learning community experience.

THE RETENTION PROBLEM

Despite our learning communities program and first-year seminar courses, TAMU-CC has struggled to retain its first-year students like many other colleges and universities. Our first-time freshmen one-year retention rate was approximately 57 percent in 2005, and that was a serious drop from a few years before. Our six-year graduation rate with the 2004 cohort (which consisted of 1,133 first-time in college, full-time undergraduate students seeking a bachelor's degree) was just 38 percent. Although our six-year graduation rate was not significantly different than other universities of our size in our region, there was obviously room for improvement.

Likewise, our D/F/W rate (i.e., percentage of students receiving a D, F, or withdrawing) is also a concern. In some classes, D/F/W rates were as high as 50 percent, especially among our first-year students. We have recently experienced a large influx of first-year students, but it came at the cost of college readiness. A greater percentage of our students started coming to us lacking the skills necessary to succeed in college (according to measures such as SAT/ACT scores, high school rank and GPA, and our own admission standards). That meant more assistance, developmental coursework, and consequently more resources would need to be directed toward the first-year students and the first-year program in general. Combine the increase in students with the lack of preparedness, and it is clear that educating and retaining these students was going to be a difficult task. In the next section, we will describe how we leveraged resources, designed schedules, reduced course size, placed and enrolled students, chose a curriculum, offered support services, and measured the results.

THE DEVELOPMENTAL LEARNING COMMUNITIES (DLCS)

The creation of a developmental learning community was a collaboration between the faculty in history, English, seminar, and mathematics. The DLC was our first attempt at linking developmental coursework,[4] but we were very familiar with the processes of building learning communities.

The Caveat

There are a few factors that made the implementation of these developmental learning communities easier for us than it may be at other campuses: we have a well-established and comprehensive learning community program that was already well-integrated with a well-established writing program, both of which have dedicated, full-time faculty who enjoy working in them; and we had an accreditation-based, first-year student focused quality enhancement plan (QEP) that provided resources. The DLC would be possible without these; however, it would require more work. Coordinating whatever resources exist can empower a WPA to attempt these kinds of bigger programs and build support networks for at-risk students.

Leveraging Resources

The power and financial resources given to an accreditation project, however temporary, allow campuses to make changes to improve the retention and success of first-year students. We brought experts to campus who provided workshops on teaching, college success skills, and reading. The QEP provided funding for additional peer supplemental instructors for history and math, provided course releases for the faculty teaching the sixty-seat lecture courses in the DLCs,[5] and provided travel funding for professional development events, conferences, and campus visits. This travel allowed us to gather information about other schools with similar programs and compare our successes and challenges to theirs. In many ways, this initiative provided resources to which the faculty and administrators involved did not otherwise have access.

Building Schedules

In learning communities, we co-enroll students in courses on the same days with coordinated times, so they move from one course in their learning community to the next, with minimal interruptions. Students value large lecture the highest, equating the size and sometimes rank/

Table 13.1. DLC Sample Week

Monday	Wednesday	Friday
10:00–10:50 Lecture	10:00–10:50 Lecture	10:00–10:50 Lecture
11:00–11:50 English	11:00–11:50 English	11:00–11:50 English
12:00–12:50 Mathematics	12:00–12:50 Mathematics	12:00–12:50 Mathematics
01:00–01:50 Seminar	01:00–01:50 Seminar	

esteem of the professor above the faculty they find in seminar and English composition, so we started each day with the large lecture. We sandwiched mathematics between the other courses, so students were less likely to skip that class (Table 13.1). The DLC met three times a week in order to have more frequent contact with the students.

We use a combination of permissions, co-requisites, cross listing, and blocking in Banner (our student information management system) to set up the schedules, to restrict access of the learning community sections to the students we identify, and to mandate concurrent enrollments in all linked sections. In this way, we can ensure appropriate students are receiving this intervention.

The learning communities have to be built so the teaching schedules are also workable and preferably employ the smallest number of faculty. Keeping the teaching teams small helps the faculty coordinate assignments and collaborate on learning goals and activities to support them. In addition, the members of the teaching teams found it much easier and more efficient to track student progress with a smaller number of students.

Reducing Course Size

Although there is some debate about the effect class size has on student learning (Hornsby and Osman 2014), most experts agree that smaller sections work better, especially for students who are at risk because of a lack of adequate academic preparation (Chapman and Ludlow 2010). Therefore, we kept the DLCs smaller than the regular learning communities, so the "large lecture" course is capped at sixty, instead of ranging from 150 to 275. Due to limited faculty, the developmental mathematics courses are capped at thirty students.[6] Mathematics supplements its modular courses with peer learning assistants who work alongside the faculty member. For the writing and seminar courses, because we recognized that our student population was an at risk, underprepared population, even though they were not enrolled in a developmental English course as part of the DLC, we negotiated smaller class sizes for English and seminar by using the suggested numbers from the National Council of Teachers of English (2014). We managed to cap those courses at 20.

Placing and Enrolling Students

We used mathematics placement tests to identify and enroll students into the DLCs because we knew that it was one piece of information that summer orientation staff could easily access and use, and because we knew that we had approximately five hundred students each summer who were not college ready in mathematics. We had to eliminate any students who had credit for English or the lecture involved (history or psychology). We did not use reading or writing placement in any way.[7]

In order to fill the seats in this developmental learning community, the WPA visited with the advisors to explain the program. Even so, we found we had to actively recruit students by expressing the advantages, particularly to parents, of taking this learning community. The advantages included the small class size; close contact with faculty; focused mentoring; extra supplemental instruction, including peer mentors within the math classes; and the self-paced, module-based math classes. Parents found small class size and mentoring attractive; however, students were less impressed with the help provided, but seemed to appreciate the idea having a smaller lecture course.

Recruiting Faculty

The WPA must determine who should teach the writing class in a developmental learning community. We have found that faculty must be dedicated to students and work well with their learning community partners, and given the commitment level for the DLC work, they should be full-time, permanent faculty. We believe it would be exploitive to ask adjunct and graduate faculty to do the kind of intensive work with students that is required by the DLC teaching. The DLC English instructors must be willing to work closely with the faculty in the lecture and seminar courses. We all commit time to sending emails and/or conferencing with students about their missing work, missing class, abbreviated drafts, possible learning issues, family, and other concerns. We are very intrusive in our mentoring of students; in other words, we do not hesitate to track down students, to alert support services, and/or to talk about students' difficulties in our meetings. We identify who has the closest relationship to a student and nominate that person to reach out when there is trouble. Susan, a WPA, has tried to choose faculty for the DLCs who have been trained to teach developmental writers in graduate coursework and/or those who have been trained for and worked in writing centers. While students are still held to a high standard in their coursework, faculty are often more successful when they are flexible when it comes to life issues interfering with the students' ability to get work done on time. They must also be willing and able to assess when learning is not happening, when a lesson needs to be revised, redone, changed, reinforced, or broken down into smaller parts, and to complete that redesign and check again on the students' understanding. Faculty must be willing to abandon their expectations when it comes to what students "should" know, and respond to what their students actually know. They must constantly check for prior learning, but to not balk at a wide range of experiences or a seeming lack of experience altogether. Faculty working with the students in these learning communities must, like all first-year instructors, approach their students with caring, respect, and high expectations, and provide plenty of support along the way.

Choosing a Writing Curriculum

Once we enrolled students in the DLCs, we had to decide what to teach in the linked composition courses to value our students' home languages and literacies and to help them transition to the university. During conversations preparing for the QEP, faculty had identified reading as a barrier to student success. Having read Kuh (2008), we knew that supporting, but also challenging, students was vital to their engagement and success. In composition, Ann Beaufort (2007) demonstrated how the reading and writing in composition courses was sometimes less challenging than in other disciplines. In addition, Alice Horning and others have discussed the importance of integrating reading into composition as a means of supporting students (Carillo 2015). To assign more complex readings, composition adopted the writing-about-writing curriculum and textbook (Downs and Wardle 2007), and faculty in many core disciplines began to teach reading processes and make reading assignments count for points in their classes, usually by creating reading guides, quizzes, discussion posts, journals, and/or other low-stakes assignments. A commitment to supporting and challenging students in first-year composition is vital to engaging students in their college academic experience; however, it is also important to value the knowledges, languages, and literacies they bring with them.

As the scholarship in writing-about-writing has developed, we have modified our curriculum, deliberately adding reflective pieces and key concepts (Yancey, Robertson, and Taczak 2014), and modifying the threshold concepts (Adler-Kassner and Wardle 2015). What is particularly heartening about this curriculum in our Hispanic-Serving Institution (HSI) environment is how the assignments we use (the literacy narrative and discourse community ethnography) enable faculty to learn more about their students' histories with literacy and discourse, and the assignments we have adapted help us to help students develop metacognitive awareness of their choices as writers (Ruecker 2015, 157; Yancey, Robertson, and Taczak 2014).

We value our students' diverse national, linguistic, and cultural heritages by modifying the traditional, individually focused literacy narrative into a multi-generational literacy narrative that requires students to investigate the literacy experiences of three generations of their family histories. Frequently on our campus, this means students are interviewing family members who speak only Spanish, as well as those whose family situations prevented the continuation of schooling due to work or the demands of family. The literacy narrative from the DLCs is revised into a poster and presented as part of the "First-Year Writing Display" during Hispanic Heritage Month.

The second major assignment, the Discourse Community Ethnography (DCE), also helps students identify, research, and value their linguistic and cultural heritages, even as they are using Standard Edited English and academic language conventions (Ruecker 2015, 158). In the DCE, students research the ways their communities use language to get things done. They investigate how those discourses vary. In this way, they bring their personal and professional experiences into the academic arena, analyze them from an academic perspective, and present to others as an expert. At the end of the Fall semester, we have a two-day First-Year Symposium where all first-year students in composition (about 1,500 students) present their DCE research. DLC student presentations have included such diverse sites as a Spanish-language evangelical church and a salon that provides hair care for African American women.

Writing has played a key role in the DLCs, particularly in collaboration with the first-year seminar courses, as a place where students discuss and plan their goals and reflect and provide evidence of their learning in midterm and final portfolios that integrate work from all the courses in the learning communities. As Reichert Powell (2014) and Ruecker

(2015) emphasize, small class contact with first-year students provides a great opportunity to work closely with students in group work and conferencing. Conferencing with students allows faculty to discuss not only their difficulties and progress in writing and research but also their progress in the module-based mathematics courses, their grades in all their courses, study habits for the lecture course, and their general transition to college challenges. In the DLCs, the writing curriculum is supplemented by the seminar instructors, who work on reading comprehension, study strategies, practicing writing processes, and addressing writing anxiety, as one might if one were teaching developmental writers.

Offering Support Services

The DLC faculty coordinate closely with the writing center, taking classes into the center for an orientation/peer review session and providing incentives for using its services. Sometimes sessions are used as evidence of learning and/or revision/editing in portfolios. We also partner with the library's information literacy instruction, taking classes into the computer lab to find sources and for their discourse community ethnographies.

While the DLCs have taken years to imagine, create, and implement, the basic premise is simple: we are creating smaller, more intrusive learning environments for students who need them in order to help these students successfully make the transition from high school to college. Ostensibly, we did a simple thing: we added developmental math to an existing learning communities program; however, as we have offered this structure over the years and now as we begin to attempt to expand it, we realize that there is a diversity of elements that work together to help students succeed, and we continue to attempt to refine and improve them.

RESULTS OF THE DLCS

The practice of linking developmental mathematics with credit-bearing courses to form a DLC, has been shown, at least preliminarily, to reduce the numbers of students on probation and to improve student retention. At our university, approximately 35 percent of the students who enter as first-year students needing developmental math are on academic probation at the end of the first semester (i.e., a cumulative GPA of below 2.0). The reduction of the percent of students on probation is evident in the data from the Fall 2013 DLC titled, Tetrad H,[8] which consisted of a first-year seminar course, an English composition course, remedial math, and General Psychology. At the end of the Fall 2013 semester in Tetrad H, only 12 percent of the students were on academic probation. It should be noted that in this case GPA is a legitimate measure of overall academic performance because it includes courses outside of the learning community as well as those within it, so it is not just a reflection of grade inflation. However, more comprehensive data are also available.

These data from Tetrad H are supported by a larger correlational study that used "univariate and multivariate analysis" with "pre-college" data from the students enrolled in the FYLCP in Fall 2010, 2011, and 2012, and included Tetrad N, the first developmental learning community TAMU-CC instituted (Sperry 2014, v).[9] Sperry's dissertation demonstrated that

> [t]here were no statistically significant differences in the retention and probation rates among the different learning communities despite their significantly differing incoming student populations. This is perhaps most noteworthy when Tetrad N is considered; this group contained students with the most incoming risk factors including, but not limited to, the lowest SAT scores, the greatest financial need, and the lowest high school percentiles, all of which were predictors of retention or probation status. (Sperry 2014, 77)

This analysis also demonstrates how we successfully captured an at-risk population for this intervention by using the mathematics as a placement mechanism (SAT, financial need, high school percentiles).

We have also measured the impact of our DLCs with the direct measure of student learning, using assessment of student work. All first-year students involved in the learning communities must complete an assignment that attempts to integrate all the parts of the learning community. The integrative assignments vary, but all require the synthesis of information and/or skills from multiple classes. Each year, the director of the Core Curriculum asks each learning community to assess the percentage of students who successfully completed the integrative assignment at a grade of 75 or better (i.e., 75%, 80%, etc.). The students in Tetrad H did not perform any differently from students in other learning communities, in that their pass rate (96.6%) was similar to the pass rates in the other learning communities.

The grade distribution in the large lecture class in Tetrad H was different than in some other learning communities (Table 13.2). For example, below are the grade distributions from the large lecture PSYC class in 2012 and the PSYC class in Tetrad H.

Table 13.2. Grade Distributions from Psychology Classes

Grades (f)	Spring 2012 (regular LC) N = 161	Fall 2013 (Tetrad H) N = 56	Fall 2014 (Tetrad H) N = 74
A (%)	36 (22.4)	5 (8.9)	6 (8.1)
B (%)	59 (36.6)	28 (50.0)	23 (31.1)
C (%)	37 (23.0)	11 (19.6)	30 (40.5)
D (%)	12 (7.5)	7 (12.5)	9 (12.2)
F (%)	17 (10.6)	5 (8.9)	6 (8.2)
GPA (SD)	2.53 (1.22)	2.38 (1.10)	2.19 (1.03)

As can be seen in Table 13.2, students did indeed tend to do better in the learning community that was not designated for those students needing remedial work. As expected, there were fewer in the developmental learning community than in the regular learning community. However, the overall GPA for both of the developmental learning communities was above 2.0, which means that the average student is not on academic probation after the first semester. Given these various forms of evidence of the success of the DLCs, the First-Year Learning Communities Program is arguing for the expansion of the DLC program in order to meet the needs of our incoming student population.

RECOMMENDATIONS FOR DLCS

Having offered the DLCs for several semesters and having consistent evidence that they help students persist by earning higher grades and avoiding probation in the first semester,[10] we have several recommendations for WPAs who may wish to consider offering these on their campuses.

1. Small class size is important to enable faculty to follow up on students who miss class or do not turn in assignments. It also prevents students from feeling anonymous in lecture.

2. Small and dedicated teams of faculty are vital to success. At-risk students need focused attention and intrusive advising. They need faculty who will track them down, even after long absences, to work with them and help them succeed. They also may need to be told, "Drop this class and try again next semester."

3. Faculty and staff must be familiar with the kinds of level of familial and economic demands that are typically made on students at an HSI. This familiarity feeds back into their advising, conferencing, and even lesson

plan/homework design. Experience and stability, meaning full-time positions and salaries, help with this goal.

4. Instruction in college systems and resources is crucial. Campus resource scavenger hunts, setting short-range goals, navigating software packages, and time-management lessons are all things we included in the DLCs.

5. Technology is vital to linking courses properly and restricting enrollments to those students being targeted.

6. Especially at an HSI, but we would argue anywhere, curriculum should be designed to highlight students' home cultures and languages and to scaffold their learning with a fair amount of repetition and an allowance for back tracking if faculty discover that students need more time.

7. Conferencing can be used to ask specific questions about their progress to get past the initial, "I'm okay, it's all good," response. "What module are you on in math?" or "How did you answer question 3 on the History exam?" or "Have you completed your literacy narrative interviews?" gets much more specific information to which faculty can respond.

IMPLICATIONS FOR THE FUTURE

As TAMU-CC continues to grow, we are proposing increases in staffing and other resources to expand the DLC offerings so we can enroll more students who need them. Currently, we can enroll about 180 students per year; we'd like to be able to enroll all alternatively admitted students, which would mean expanding capacity to about 1,200 students/year. We are also piloting and assessing DLCs with developmental English instead of developmental mathematics, following the Accelerated Learning Program (ALP) model (Adams et al. 2009). In general, the impact of the success of the DLCs has encouraged faculty to adopt some of its curricular, pedagogical, and advising strategies, in terms of being more intrusive with assistance, more culturally and linguistically aware, and more attentive to scaffolding skills, especially reading strategies.

WPAs can use their connections, know-how and resources to make retention and other kinds of student success initiatives more effective by avoiding the duplication of existing services, negotiating various programs and departments to find collaborators, and relying on pre-existing relationships and trust. WPAs need to seek out these initiatives and pursue leadership roles in them in order to achieve access to resources that will help them, their programs, and their students. When collaborating with other programs and initiatives, writing program administrators can provide both philosophical and practical leadership, and, as

Reichert Powell (2014) has suggested, a critical lens. WPAs can participate in interventions like the developmental learning communities to
enhance alliances, meet student needs, and increase student success.
Even though we will not solve every problem or retain every student, we
can hopefully better meet their needs, expand our reach and resources,
and extend the influence and uses of writing on our campuses.

Notes

1. The accrediting agency is the Southern Association of Colleges and Schools Commission on Colleges (SACS-COC). The QEP has been a part of SACS-COC accreditation since 2004.
2. Scholarship on linking writing courses in learning communities is gathered online
   in the "Linked Writing Courses" WPA/CompPile Research Bibliography (LaFrance
   2010) and can also be discovered in the CompPile.org site, using keywords "linked"
   and "learning-community."
3. In 1987, the Mexican American Legal Defense and Educational Fund (MALDEF)
   filed *LULAC et al. v. Richards et al.*, a class-action lawsuit that charged the State
   of Texas with discrimination against Mexican Americans in south Texas because
   of inadequate funding of colleges. Even though it was overturned by the Texas
   Supreme Court, this case led to the South Texas Border Initiative, which increased
   appropriations for colleges in south Texas, where the greatest numbers of Latino
   and low-income students are, to provide higher education equity in the state.
   (Acosta 2010; Flack 2003).
4. More recently, we have piloted a link to developmental English, modeled on the
   "Accelerated Learning Program" by Adams, Gearhart, Miller, and Roberts (2009).
5. While TAMU-CC funds a course reassignment (release) for faculty teaching one
   hundred–plus seat sections in learning communities to compensate them for team
   coordination, meetings, etc., the campus did not normally fund smaller learning
   community course reassignments.
6. Each section of mathematics is made up of a combination of 1.5 of the English/
   seminar courses.
7. Our reading/writing college readiness placement was not practical for this purpose. First, we did not have enough students to fill the developmental learning
   communities, and second, we had a large number who are international students
   and/or non-native speakers of English. Because of their very specific needs, these
   students are placed into a different learning community-based intervention. The
   DLCs rarely enroll non-native English speaking students; however, we find that
   many are second or third generation English speakers, and that there is a strong
   presence of students who speak Spanish at home.
8. On our campus, we label our learning communities, depending on how many
   classes are linked, as "dyads" "triads" or "tetrads," followed by a letter, like "Triad
   B." Our DLCs are Tetrad H (psychology) and Tetrad N (history).
9. Tetrad H was not implemented until Fall 2013, and therefore was not a part of
   Sperry's dissertation; however, the patterns of the success in the students in these
   developmental learning communities (Tetrad N and H) have been relatively consistent, according to internal institutional data.
10. Unfortunately, some of the evidence of success is university data and unavailable for
    us to share.

References

Acosta, Teresa Palomo. 2010. "Mexican American Legal Defense and Educational Fund." *The Handbook of Texas*. Austin: Texas State Historical Association. https://tshaon line.org/handbook/online/articles/jom01.

Adams, Peter, Sarah Gearhart, Robert Miller, and Anne Roberts. 2009. "The Accelerated Learning Program: Throwing Open the Gates." *Journal of Basic Writing* 28 (2): 50–69.

Adler-Kassner, Linda, John Majewski, and Damian Koshnick. 2012. "The Value of Troublesome Knowledge: Transfer and Threshold Concepts in Writing and History." *Composition Forum* 26. http://compositionforum.com/issue/26/troublesome-know ledge-threshold.php.

Adler-Kassner, Linda, and Elizabeth Wardle, eds. 2015. *Naming What We Know: Threshold Concepts in Writing Studies*. Logan: Utah State University Press.

Beaufort, Anne. 2007. *College Writing and Beyond*. Logan: Utah State University Press.

Carillo, Ellen C. 2015. *Securing a Place for Reading in Composition*. Boulder: University Press of Colorado.

Chapman, Lauren, and Larry Ludlow. 2010. "Can Downsizing College Class Sizes Augment Student Outcomes? An Investigation of the Effects of Class Size on Student Learning." *Journal of General Education* 59:105–23.

Crowley, Sharon. 1998. *Composition in the University*. Pittsburgh: University of Pittsburgh Press.

Downs, Douglas, and Elizabeth Wardle. 2007. "Teaching about Writing, Righting Misconceptions: (Re) Envisioning 'First-Year Composition' as 'Introduction to Writing Studies.'" *College Composition and Communication* 58 (4): 552–84.

Flack, Teri. 2003. "Presentation on South Texas Border Initiatives." *Report for the House Border and International Affairs Committee*. http://www.thecb.state.tx.us/reports/PDF /0592.PDF.

Hansen, Michele, Susan Meshulam, and Brooke Watson. 2010. "Assessing the Effectiveness of a Learning Community Course Designed to Improve the Math Performance of First-Year Students." *Journal of Learning Communities Research* 5:1–24.

Hawkins, Viannda M., and Heather J. Larabee. 2009. "Engaging Racial/Ethnic Minority Students in Out-of-Class Activities on Predominantly White Campuses." In *Student Engagement in Higher Education: Theoretical Perspectives and Practical Approaches for Diverse Populations*, ed. Shaun R. Harper and Stephen John Quaye, 157–78. New York: Routledge.

Horner, Bruce, and John Trimbur. 2002. "English Only and U.S. College Composition." *College Composition and Communication* 53 (4): 594–629. http://dx.doi.org/10 .2307/1512118.

Hornsby, David, and Ruksana Osman. 2014. "Massification in Higher Education: Large Classes and Student Learning." *Higher Education* 67 (6): 711–9. http://dx.doi.org /10.1007/s10734-014-9733-1.

Huerta, Juan Carlos, and Jennifer L. Bray. 2013. "How Do Learning Communities Affect First-Year Latino Students?" *Learning Communities Research and Practice* 1(1). http://washingtoncenter.evergreen.edu/lcrpjournal/vol1/iss1/5/.

Inoue, Asao B., and Mya Poe, eds. 2014. *Race and Writing Assessment*. New York: Peter Lang Publishers.

Jozwiak, Joseph, and Mark Hartlaub. 2012. "'Getting Them Through': 'Professional' Seminar Leaders and Student Performance." *Learning Communities Journal* 4:127–44.

Kells, Michelle Hall, and Valerie Balester. 1999. *Attending to the Margins: Writing, Researching, and Teaching on the Front Lines*. Portsmouth, NH: Heinemann.

Kirklighter, Cristina, Diana Cárdenas, and Susan Wolff Murphy. 2007. *Teaching Writing with Latino/a Students: Lessons Learned at Hispanic-Serving Institutions*. Albany: State University of New York Press.

Kuh, George D. 2008. *High Impact Educational Practices: What They Are, Who Has Access To Them, And Why They Matter.* Washington, DC: Association of American Colleges and Universities.

Kuh, George D. 2013. "Taking HIPs to the Next Level." In *Ensuring Quality and Taking High-Impact Practices to Scale,* ed. George D. Kuh and Ken O'Donnell, 1–14. Washington, DC: Association of American Colleges and Universities.

LaFrance, Michelle. 2010. "Linked Writing Courses." In *WPA-CompPile Research Bibliographies No. 14,* ed. Dylan Dryer and Rich Haswell. http://comppile.org/wpa /bibliographies/Bib14/LaFrance.pdf.

Lichtenstein, Marsha. 2005. "The Importance of Classroom Environments in the Assessment of Learning Community Outcomes." *Journal of College Student Development* 46 (4): 341–56. http://dx.doi.org/10.1353/csd.2005.0038.

National Council of Teachers of English. 2014. "Why Class Size Matters Today." http://www.ncte.org/positions/statements/why-class-size-matters.

Nosaka, Taé, and Heather Novak. 2014. "Against the Odds: The Impact of the Key Communities at Colorado State University on Retention and Graduation for Historically Underrepresented Students." *Learning Communities Research and Practice* 2(3). http://washingtoncenter.evergreen.edu/lcrpjournal/vol2/iss2/3.

Nowacek, Rebecca S. 2011. *Agents of Integration: Understanding Transfer as a Rhetorical Act.* Carbondale, IL: Southern Illinois University Press.

O'Donnell, Ken. 2013. "Bringing HIPs to Scale." In *Ensuring Quality and Taking High-Impact Practices to Scale,* ed. George D. Kuh and Ken O'Donnell, 15–22. Washington, DC: Association of American Colleges and Universities.

Reichert Powell, Pegeen. 2014. *Retention and Resistance: Writing Instruction and Students Who Leave.* Logan: Utah State University Press.

Rose, Mike. 1985. "The Language of Exclusion: Writing Instruction at the University." *College English* 47 (4): 341–59. http://dx.doi.org/10.2307/376957.

Ruecker, Todd. 2015. *Transiciones: Pathways of Latinas and Latinos Writing in High School and College.* Logan: Utah State University Press.

Sandoval-Lucero, Elena, Johanna B. Maes, and Ritu V. Chopra. 2011. "Examining the Retention of Nontraditional Latino(a) Students in a Career-Based Learning Community." *Journal of Hispanic Higher Education* 10 (4): 299–316. http://dx.doi .org/10.1177/1538192711414909.

Sperry, Rita A. 2014. "Prediction of Retention and Probation Status of First-Year College Students in Learning Communities Using Binary Logistic Regression Models." PhD diss., Texas A&M University-Corpus Christi.

TAMU-CC. 2015. "Student Headcount by Ethnicity" and "Student Headcount by Geographic Source." In *Factbook Pivot Tables.* http://pir.tamucc.edu/Internal%20 Resources/Factbook%20Pivot%20Tables.html.

Townsend, Martha. 2002. "Writing Across the Curriculum." In *The Allyn & Bacon Sourcebook for Writing Program Administrators,* ed. Irene Ward and William J. Carpenter, 264–74. New York: Longman.

Walvoord, Barbara E. 1996. "The Future of WAC." *College English* 58 (1): 58–79. http://dx.doi.org/10.2307/378534.

Yancey, Kathleen Blake, Liane Robertson, and Kara Taczak. 2014. *Writing across Contexts: Transfer, Composition, and Sites of Writing.* Logan: Utah State University Press.

Zawacki, Terry Myers, and Ashley Taliaferro Williams. 2001. "Is It Still WAC? Writing within Interdisciplinary Learning Communities." In *WAC for the New Millennium,* ed. Susan H. McLeod, Eric Miraglia, Margot Soven, and Christopher Thaiss, 109–40. Urbana: NCTE.

14

UNDERGRADUATE MENTORS AS AGENTS OF ENGAGEMENT
Peer Advocates in First-Year Writing Courses

Michael Day, Tawanda Gipson, and Christopher P. Parker

FIRST-YEAR COMPOSITION AND RETENTION

Faced with declining enrollments and decreasing persistence to graduation, many colleges and universities are struggling to discover and implement new strategies that will attract new students and provide existing students not only with academic support but also with activities that will help them engage in the campus community. Our public state university is one such school; for the past few years, we have been greeted with headlines reading "Overall Enrollment Down at NIU [Northern Illinois University]." We have witnessed a shocking 20 percent decline in enrollment in just the past six years. Recently, new top-level leadership came on board and identified student retention as a key priority to ensure the health and well-being of our university in the years to come. In so doing, the administration followed a national trend of intense focus on retention in an age of accountability in which state funding for public institutions is increasingly based on graduation rates.

At a university-wide retention summit in November 2013, faculty, student, support, and administrative leaders collaborated for a full day, brainstorming possible ways to increase retention rates. Mentoring came up repeatedly in our discussions, since it is widely recognized that students crave connection with faculty and others in the campus community and that forging these connections can make a difference in retention. According to Vincent Tinto (1999), "the more frequently students engage with faculty, staff, and their peers, other things being [equal], the more likely they are to persist and graduate" (3). Tinto points to the first year of college as the period that this connection is most tenuous but also most important. Thus it was no surprise that our

DOI: 10.7330/9781607326021.c014

discussion turned to the first year and one of the classes almost all first-year students must take. We agreed that because of their relatively small size, opportunities for individual attention, and collaborative workshop focus, First-Year Composition (FYComp) classes offer an ideal site for initiatives to increase retention.

Much of the research in retention supports our focus on the first year of college. Upcraft, Gardner, and Barefoot (2005) note that there is "overwhelming evidence that student success is largely determined by student experiences during the first year" (1). Referencing the work of Randi S. Levitz, Lee Noel, and Beth J. Richter (Levitz, Noel, and Richter 1999, 6), Reichert Powell mentions the high attrition rate between the first and second years of college and the fact that this attrition rate is a strong indicator of eventual graduation rates dictates that "efforts at improving retention after the first year will have a positive ripple effect on rates in subsequent years" (Reichert Powell 2013, 7). For example, Pascarella and Terenzini (1991, 2005), Cuseo (2010), Crissman Ishler and Upcraft (2005), and other researchers point to the strong influence of first-year interventions such as first-year seminars on retention and student success. On the local front, our analysis of student retention during the 2009–2014 timeframe revealed that the probability of our students leaving our university is highest in the first year.

Leaving aside for the moment the question of whether retention initiatives can actually make a difference in the complicated reasons that cause students to leave, we agree that initiatives that improve the quality of academics and the campus community are worthwhile. In his "principles of effective retention," Tinto (1993) suggests that retention efforts be "committed to the students they serve," . . . be "committed to the education of all, not just some of their students," and be "committed to the development of supportive social and educational communities in which all students are integrated as competent members" (146–48). Thus, whether or not we believe we can affect retention in any meaningful way is secondary to our goal of supporting students and engaging them in the academy.

With strong encouragement from university leadership and support services, our FYComp program held a retention summit in January 2014 involving every teacher and administrator in the program, as well as key stakeholders from across campus. We were pleased that the then-new president and provost both attended and played active roles in discussion and deliberation. But we also had welcome input from Faculty Development and Instructional Design, the Office of Student Academic Success, and the Office of Assessment Services in addressing pressing issues relating to student engagement. So as not to lower morale, we first concentrated on the strengths of our program, including the dedicated teachers, strong faculty development, frequent individual conferences, and homegrown assessment through electronic portfolios. Then the program director gave a short presentation featuring examples of first-year retention initiatives from other institutions, including extra lab tutorial sessions (Brunk-Chavez and Fredericksen 2008), electronic portfolios (Clark and Eynon 2009; Eynon, Gambino, and Torok 2014), and mentoring (Henry, Bruland, and Omizo 2008).

To develop a broad a sense of possibility for change, the group then made a "wish list" of all the efforts that they thought might allow our FYComp program to help with retention, not limiting themselves to current financial and contractual limitations. Not surprisingly, issues such as class size, instructor teaching load and contingent status, and classroom/computer lab technology and comfort came up right away, and the president and provost made it clear that they were listening. As with most constructive/productive brainstorming workshops, the summit ended with a look at steps we could take in the short term future, keeping in mind Jennifer L. Crissman Ishler and Lee M. Upcraft's admonition that "First-year student persistence is very much institution specific, thus, not all strategies will work at all institutions. Institutions must develop initiatives consistent with their mission, resources, students, faculty, leadership, and other characteristics" (Crissman Ishler and Upcraft 2005, 32). Participants agreed that since first-year students crave personal interaction, "high touch" (Naisbitt 1999) initiatives such as increasing the number of one-on-one conferences could make the biggest difference. They made a commitment to using the university's early warning system (mentioned by Don Hossler and Douglas K. Anderson as another effective retention strategy [Hossler and Anderson 2005, 75]), MAP-Works[1] surveys and software to help students get help when needed, and renewed their commitment to making the FYComp electronic portfolio a focal point for helping students connect the learning in their various classes with their lives, co-curricular activities, and future careers.

More to the point, the summit participants were also intrigued by the possibility that peer mentors might improve retention by helping students engage not only with their coursework, but also with their classmates and the wider university. In the past few decades, research has shown that interaction with peers is crucial to success in the first year of college. Citing the findings of Astin (1993) and Hirsch (1980), Crissman Ishler, and Upcraft (2005) propose that "Peer relations are critical for support, confirmation of one's identity, opportunities for socialization, and persistence" (38). Furthermore, in addition to the well-documented problem of homesickness, first-year students may suffer from "friend-sickness" (Paul and Brier 2001; Paul and Kelleher 1995; Crissman Ishler and Schreiber 2002), needing a replacement for interactions with peers at home. Astin (1993) has reported "a large body of research attesting to the positive influence of upper-level students on the cognitive development of first-year students." However, according to Barefoot (2005), "the use of upper-level undergraduates in co-teaching roles is very infrequent across all first-year classes" (54).

Some of the mentoring programs already in place at other schools, such as Brigham Young University, the University of Texas at El Paso, and the University of Hawaii have been shown to make a difference. For example, the University of Texas at El Paso employs upper-level peer leaders in first-year seminars. To improve these mentoring programs, they created a Student Leadership Institute to provide organization and support (Natalicio and Smith 2005). At the University of Hawaii, graduate students were introduced into four sections of FYComp, where they helped build rapport, build students' self-confidence, and "opened the door for more general teaching about how to 'be a student' at the college level—a skill perhaps more effectively conveyed by a peer than an authority figure" (Henry, Bruland, and Omizo 2008, 22).

Our university already has several mentoring initiatives in place, in first-year experience programs such as Themed Learning Communities and University Experience. But stakeholders identified the need for a new retention effort focusing on peer mentoring. For the first time since our involvement in the Foundations of Excellence in the First Year of College five years ago, we found an administration willing to support a new first-year initiative: the Peer Advocate (PA) program. As Jay Chaskes and Ralph Anttonen remind us, campuses interested in supporting first-year student success and persistence must form a coalition, and "perhaps the most crucial members of that coalition are those who are directly responsible to manage the institution" (Chaskes and Anttonen 2005, 201). Our partnerships with other campus offices were important, but without strong support from the president and provost, we could not have moved forward with the PA program.

THE PEER ADVOCATE PROGRAM

When funding came through for an initial pilot of eighteen peer mentors placed in first-year writing classes at the start of the Spring 2014 semester, the provost asked us to develop the program immediately and implement it as soon as possible. We had to scurry to recruit applicants, pair mentors with classes/teachers, develop a training schedule and a set of guidelines, create and populate a Blackboard site for communication and reporting, and much more. We were lucky to have a great deal of assistance from support staff in the Office of Student Engagement and Experiential Learning (OSEEL), who allowed us to use a modified version of their application form and training materials, as well as to draw from their pool of student leaders to assign as peer mentors.

Because we did not wish to disrupt the classes that were already well under way, we chose to assign peer mentors to a set of eighteen classes over which we have direct control: those taught by first-year teaching assistants as part of our composition teaching practicum, English 600. Since we oversee their day-to-day classroom activities and assignments, we were able to adjust the curriculum of both English 600 and the classes they were teaching to accommodate the new mentoring program. We briefed them on the role of mentors and had them help us develop plans for using the mentors effectively in our second-semester FYComp classes.

To differentiate our program from other peer mentoring initiatives on campus and to keep our focus on the central role of mentors as engagement agents, we call our mentors Peer Advocates (PAs). In their chapter in *Challenging and Supporting the First-Year Student*, Chaskes and Anttonen (2005) discuss the concept of advocacy across a spectrum of campus roles, but mostly in terms of higher administration. In describing the "common knowledge, set of strategies, and skill set shared by those who successfully advocate on behalf of first-year students" (192), Chaskes and Anttonen stress that advocates are "change agents" (192) who do not "emphasize control, coordination, or supervision" (193), and "navigate the 'organized anarchy' of the academy in order to effect programmatic change" (193). Although our PAs do not have administrative power to make change, they advocate by working from the bottom up, employing skills similar to those recommended by Chaskes and Anttonen: having passion, caring, being an active listener, being creative and flexible, having a good sense of humor, and being patient but persistent (203).

As we developed our program, our evolving definition of peer advocate was an advanced undergraduate student with a 3.0 GPA or better who has been successful in writing classes, is deeply involved in the campus community, and who has demonstrated leadership skills. It is important to emphasize here that PAs are not writing teachers or tutors.

Unlike the peer tutors envisioned by scholars like Kenneth Bruffee (1984), who function as writing coaches, the PAs' primary role is to keep students involved in both the class and the campus community through helping with group work and class projects, hosting study sessions, and inviting students to events on campus. We discuss the PA roles and activities in more detail below.

The campus community agreed that we did an excellent job getting the pilot PA program up and running so quickly, and the process taught us quite a bit about how to do it better in the future. Because of the hasty implementation, not to mention that we began in the second, not the first semester of first-year writing, the effect on retention was unclear at best. Further, in the written and spoken comments, a few FYComp teachers and students expressed some resentment at having an extra undergraduate student in the class. "We're adults; we don't need baby-sitters!" was the sentiment of these students. In turn, some of the PAs and their teachers expressed frustration at the hurried organization of the program, the difficulty in planning interactions with first-year students, and the low attendance at mentoring events. Even so, there were plenty of success stories, and for the first time in many years, FYComp received welcome publicity in the form of campus news articles and frequent mentions in speeches by the president and provost. That first semester provided us with plenty of feedback and a good laboratory to plan for the following year, when we were funded to continue the pilot with an expanded number of classes. In Summer 2014, we developed a much more comprehensive application and interview process, and in Fall 2014, we placed PAs into thirty first-year composition classes. For the second semester of this pilot, we again tapped the classes of eighteen new graduate teaching assistants, but we were also able to begin placing PAs in classes taught by full-time instructors and advanced graduate students. With more time to prepare and more strategies in our repertoire, we found that the fall semester PA program ran more smoothly. The PAs worked well with their cooperating teachers and were better integrated into the daily rhythm of the classes.

PEER ADVOCATE ROLES AND ACTIVITIES

To prepare for their roles, PAs attended a morning half-day session of the pre-semester OSEEL mentor training orientation (for all mentors) and focused on the FYComp curriculum and classes in the afternoon session. They had weekly meetings with program coordinators and the cooperating class instructor, and were required to attend class at least once a week. They held pizza parties, led study sessions, connected students to campus resources, invited students to campus events, contacted students on social media, helped with group work in class (including preparation for the annual Showcase of Student Writing), and helped students register for classes the following semester. To emphasize the professional development and evaluative aspects of the program, PAs also had to write regular reflections, and keep detailed activity logs. Some PAs opted for internship credit; in this role they helped lead the program and completed extra projects, raising their time commitment from six to ten hours per week.

BENEFITS

Although the logistics involved in developing and sustaining the PA program were considerable, the benefits were significant as PAs reminded first-year students of the resources available to them by talking to them in person. They demonstrated our university's commitment to student success by acting as role models, they served as a resource for class work, they helped resolve issues and problems, and they helped students connect with each other and the campus community. In their comments, students said that the PAs helped them feel supported as they make the difficult transition from home and high school to independent campus life.

We must also consider the experience of being a PA as a kind of professional development for more advanced undergraduates. Henry, Bruland, and Omizo (2008) point out that their peer mentors "could benefit enormously themselves by witnessing first-hand an instructor's approach to course design, writing assignments, and classroom activities" (19). The undergraduate students who served as PAs, many of whom will teach at some point, not only gained the opportunity to work with a faculty member and collaborate with other student leaders; they also got a chance to work independently and creatively, testing their own ingenuity. The leadership and counseling experience they got just from mentoring served them well in preparing for lifelong learning and careers, and gave them the opportunity to document the experience in their own resume or portfolio.

Another benefit of the PA program is in its ability to attract high-quality, motivated students and keep them motivated and engaged—at our institution, not somewhere else. According to Diana S. Natalicio and Maggy Smith, "Rewarding students for their participation in the SLI allows UTEP to keep its very best students on campus in positions where they can help others succeed" (Natalicio and Smith 20015, 172). We must remember that retention applies not only to first-year students but also to advanced students who are striving to create and enhance their professional identities. Being a peer advocate is not only a job, it is also a reward, a source of support, a professional development activity, and a very attractive line on the resume.

Campus-wide, our PA program's initiative provided a good model for other peer mentoring programs, which often struggle to find an effective approach. Over the course of the first three semesters, through inventing and reinventing our PA program organizational structure, we hit upon a structure of small-team cohort support that leads to large-team support and events that include all the PAs and many students. Weekly meetings not only introduced PAs to new resources and strategies and help them plan events but also gave them a space to share their successes and challenges, using that information to plan what to do next. And this sort of sharing continued in social media such as Facebook and Twitter, where the PAs also planned and coordinated events for the first-year students. In its blending of the grassroots efforts of FYComp faculty with top administration and inter-office campus support, the PA program was also a good example of the sort of "coalition building" that Chaskes and Anttonen (2005, 200–201) claim is crucial to making institutional change through first-year programs. Finally, our assessment of the program, which included frequent reflections by PAs and surveys by PAs, cooperating teachers, and first-year students, not only provided us with data to improve the PA program but also served as a model for other mentoring programs.

ASSESSMENT AND EVALUATION

Since the early days of the project, we have been collaborating with our school's Office of Assessment Services to measure the impact of our peer advocates on student success, connection to the university community, and persistence. First-year students were surveyed before and after their peer advocate experience, and peer advocates and their cooperating teachers were surveyed at the end of the semester. Students provided self-assessments of their learning, self-efficacy, connection to the university, and use of campus resources. We compared scores of PA and non-PA students on the major program assessment, the electronic portfolio. Finally, we also tracked retention and GPA for the students in PA and non-PA classes.

We collected data from FYComp classes in Spring and Fall 2014 in support of the program evaluation. We addressed the following questions:

1. What is the impact of the PA program on students' connection to the university?

2. What is the impact of the PA program on student learning?

3. What is the impact of the PA program on student retention?

4. What is the impact of the PA program on students' use of academic and extracurricular resources?

5. What factors moderate the effects of the PA program on student outcomes?

6. What comments did students and PAs make about the program?

Sample and Method

We conducted evaluations of the PA program in both the Spring and Fall semesters of 2014 using slightly different study designs and survey instruments. At the end of the Spring 2014 semester, we surveyed all students enrolled in English 104 (in class) regarding their perceived learning during the semester, their level of connection to the university, and their use of academic and non-academic resources during the semester. We also asked students in PA sections about the quality of their relationship with the PA assigned to their class section and the support they received from the PA. Of the 1,496 students enrolled in English 104 during the Spring 2014 semester, we received surveys from 893 students (a 60% response rate). For Fall 2014 we used a pre and post evaluation design. We gave students the surveys online during class time at the beginning and end of the semester. Of the 1,712 students enrolled in English 103, 922 students completed pre and post surveys (a 54% response rate). We also collected other data from Registration and Records, including gender, ethnicity, GPA, ACT composites, and final grades. In addition, we surveyed the peer advocates and course instructors at the end of both semesters. In considering the results presented below, it is important to note that the PA intervention was applied to different classes with students who were in the second (spring) and first (fall) semester, respectively.

Instruments

The Spring 2014 student survey instrument included twenty-five items given to all students, with an additional twelve items for students enrolled in PA sections. Measures included: learning, connection to the university, resource use (academic and extracurricular), and PA relationship quality. With the exception of the section on resource use, we used a five-point, "strongly disagree" to "strongly agree" Likert scale. We used a binary "yes/no" scale for resource use questions. The Fall 2014 student survey instrument included additional measures, but for the purposes of this evaluation, we will only be discussing the following measures: learning (self-reported and actual), connection to the university, use of academic and extracurricular resources, and PA relationship quality (see appendix).

Results

We ran independent sample *t*-tests to determine if there were any group differences in learning or connection to the university. Results from Spring 2014 showed no statistically significant differences between PA and non-PA groups in retention, student learning (either self-reported or actual), or connection to the university.

However, there are other clues that PAs may have made a bit of a difference in self-reported learning, connection to the university, and academic resource use. When we look at the Pearson correlations among variables, we find statistically significant positive correlations between PA relationship quality and all three variables [relationship quality vs. self-report learning, $(r = 0.311, p < 0.001)$; relationship quality vs. connection, $(r = 0.145, p = 0.014)$; relationship quality vs. academic resource use, $(r = 0.132, p = 0.032)$]. Specifically, students who reported a more positive relationship with their PA reported that they used academic resources more often, saw greater gains in their writing skills, and reported a stronger connection to NIU.

There were no statistically significant differences in the fall between PA and non-PA groups for use of academic and extra-curricular resources or student retention. However, students enrolled in PA sections produced higher levels of self-reported student learning [non-PA $(M = 3.92, SD = 0.85)$; PA $(M = 4.06, SD = 0.71)$; $t(507) = 2.13, p = 0.034)$], reported higher levels of overall support [(non-PA $(M = 4.00, SD = 0.74)$; PA $(M = 4.17, SD = 0.60)$; $t(507) = 2.86, p = 0.004)$], and greater sense of connection to the university [(non-PA $(M = 3.65, SD = 0.88)$; PA $(M = 3.80, SD = 0.80)$; $t(507) = 1.99, p = 0.047)$] (see Figure 14.1).

Actual Learning

At the end of each semester, students are required to complete an electronic portfolio of work that demonstrates their growth over the semester. As part of the First-Year Composition program assessment process

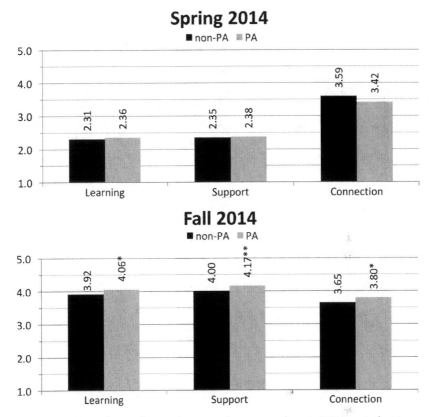

Figure 14.1. Comparisons of peer advocate and non-peer advocate FYComp students' perceptions of learning, support, and connection to the university, Spring and Fall 2014. *p < 0.05, **p < 0.01.

(aimed at program improvement), a team of English faculty reviewed a sample of 275 portfolios and rated them using a departmentally developed rubric, which consisted of ten criteria in the spring on a scale of 1 to 6 and six criteria in the fall on a scale of 1 to 4. The rubric change was due to the university's desire to incorporate the Association of American Colleges and Universities VALUE rubrics into its assessment practices. This new rubric was partially aligned to the Critical Thinking and Written Communication VALUE rubrics. Results showed no statistically significant differences in the scores of those who had PAs versus those who did not for Spring 2014; however, for Fall 2014, results indicate that students in the PA sections spent more time reflecting on their work [non-PA (M = 2.22, SD = 0.80); PA (M = 2.46, SD = 0.75); t(273) = 2.54, p = 0.012)].

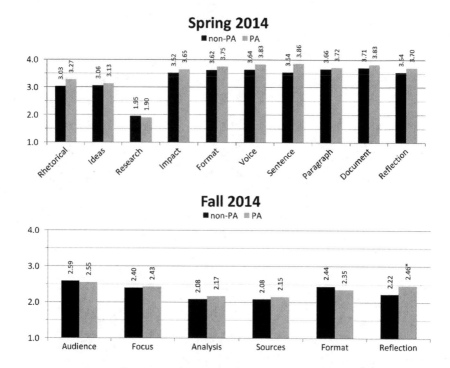

Figure 14.2. Spring 2014 and Fall 2014 peer advocate versus non-peer advocate scores on the electronic portfolio evaluation criteria. *p < 0.05

Student Qualitative Feedback

In addition to the quantitative surveys, we asked students to comment on what they found most beneficial about the program. We received qualitative feedback from 276 students from Fall 2014 classes. Overall, 81 percent of the students reported that they found the program to be helpful. Students reported that they were encouraged to connect to campus through the many events and resources shared with them and they were supported with learning both inside and outside the classroom. They appreciated being able to confide in a peer who could relate to them and felt more comfortable asking for assistance, which made their transition into college easier. Below are a few examples of student comments:

- "Since my professor was new, she didn't know a lot of specifics about campus resources or things going on, so my peer advocate was able to step in and answer any questions."
- "They can relate to the problems and concerns you may have because they are also students too."

Table 14.1. Spring and Fall 2014 Quantitative Peer Advocate Responses

Item	Spring 2014 Mean	Fall 2014 Mean
I enjoyed being a peer advocate.	4.07	4.59*
I was able to help students as a peer advocate.	3.67	4.09
I was effectively used as a peer advocate by students.	2.53	3.18
Being a peer advocate was a rewarding experience for me.	3.93	4.32
Being a peer advocate has helped my professional development.	3.80	4.32
I learned a lot from being a peer advocate.	3.67	4.18
I received the support I needed to be an effective peer advocate.	3.53	4.23*
I would recommend that other students become peer advocates.	4.33	4.45
I would become a peer advocate again.	4.00	4.05

*$p < 0.05$

- "If you had any questions, there was someone closer to you to ask without feeling embarrassed."

Peer Advocate Feedback and Experiences

Peer advocates were asked the same nine questions at the end of both the Spring 2014 and Fall 2014 semesters. Similar to their mentees, they were asked to rate the statements on a five-point, "strongly disagree" to "strongly agree" Likert scale. Overall, they reported having had a more positive experience in the Fall 2014 semester, most notably in their level of enjoyment in their PA role.

Peer advocates were also asked to give qualitative feedback on what they found most beneficial about the program. We received qualitative feedback from twenty-two peer advocates for Fall 2014. The majority of the peer advocates reported that the experience helped them improve their leadership and communication skills, build relationships with students, and learn from other peer advocates and instructors. They reported enjoying advocating for students and helping them avoid unnecessary mistakes. A few examples included:

- "I feel as though I have helped my freshmen students not make the same mistakes that I had made my first year. Being a peer advocate demonstrates to students that you don't have to be afraid of getting involved."

- "I learned how to be a voice of support for students and help them in the best way I can."
- "[I enjoyed] the network of the other peer advocates."

Challenges and Suggestions for Improvement

Although most students and peer advocates in the fall reported positive experiences, a few agreed that more support could have been provided. These students desired more of an active in-class PA presence while the PAs desired more student participation outside of class along with better collaboration with course instructors.

The challenges and concerns expressed by both PAs and their students in 2014 formed the basis for further PA improvement. In their 2015 weekly meetings and online discussions, PAs took extra steps to better define the PA role and relationship to the FYComp instructor, come up with activities that would attract more students, and better integrate PAs into the fabric of the FYComp classes.

Unfortunately, funding for the PA program has been withdrawn for the coming year since our state has been without a budget for most of a year. However, our campus-wide partnerships remain, and we have been encouraged to regroup and submit a proposal for a new mentoring program when the budget returns to normal.

FINAL THOUGHTS AND FUTURE DIRECTIONS

Although we were somewhat disappointed that the quantitative results indicated very little difference in academic improvement and retention between PA and non-PA students, we feel more assured that the program has been a success when we consider the following factors:

1. **Short duration of the PA program and research study.** The data we analyze and present here came from only one year of the PA study, and the first semester of that year was severely truncated because we were asked to put the program in place at very short notice. Thus it may have been too early to see more significant results that might become evident in a longer duration, more established program.

2. **Multiple interacting FYComp improvements.** Since the retention summit, all FYComp instructors (administrators and support staff, not just those teaching PA sections) have been working hard on retention and student success issues. Instructors spend more time in individual conferences, they use MAP-Works and other early warning systems to help students, they make more frequent referrals to support services, they encourage participation in the Showcase of Student Writing, FYComp

awards competition and electronic portfolio process, and they keep in better touch with students via Blackboard and email. Overall FYComp assessment studies—that compare retention and success rates for those who have taken FYComp to those who have not—show as much as a ten percentage point positive difference in retention for those who have taken FYComp. Could it be possible that the combination of "high touch" and high-impact practices in the entire FYComp program is making the biggest difference, not simply the PA program? In the retention and student success literature, most schools report that retention cannot be tied to a single variable.

3. **The possible mitigating effect of inexperienced teachers.** In both Spring and Fall semester 2014, the sections of FYComp that involved PAs were almost all taught by new Department of English teaching assistants (TAs). In the spring, all eighteen classes were taught by these TAs, and in the fall, twenty-two of thirty sections were taught by new TAs. We believe that we do an effective job of supporting new TAs in their teaching through our English 600 pedagogy seminar, which provides a full year of hands-on practicum training, but it could be possible that the fact that these are not our most experienced teachers had a slightly negative influence on success and retention that canceled out the positive gains of the PA program. In the future, we need to compare results from new TA and non-new TA classes to see whether there are differences. We may also break down results by rank (instructor vs. TA), gender, and years of teaching experience.

4. **Persistence is largely dependent upon factors we cannot control.** To some degree, as Pegeen Reichert Powell (2013) reminds us in a chapter of *Retention and Resistance* entitled "The Seduction and Betrayal of the Discourse of Retention," many of our efforts to prevent students from leaving "may be futile" (52), since "in fact, no one knows how to prevent attrition" (52), and even after seventy-five years of retention research, according to Braxton, Brier, and Steele (2007), retention rates have not improved nationally. Reichert Powell's point is that no matter how heroic and innovative our retention efforts, we may not be able to do much about students' persistence at our institutions unless we can come up with money for them, change their family commitments, and/ or change the entire business-oriented model of higher education.

5. **Student diversity and demographics determine retention.** In discussing retention and persistence, we need to be mindful of the diverse populations of students at our university. We serve several hundred Chicago-area special admit students whose high schools did not give them an opportunity to compete for college acceptance. We see increasing numbers of disabled students, veterans, and students who are struggling to get an education while serving

as primary breadwinners for their households or caring for disabled relatives. On this point Reichert Powell refers to Alexander Astin's (2005–2006) analysis of data from the Cooperative Institutional Research Program, which surveyed over fifty thousand students across the country "in order to identify those factors that correlate with a tendency to withdraw or persist" (65). Astin observes that "an institution's degree completion rate is primarily a reflection of its entering student characteristics, and that differences among institutions in their degree completion rates are primarily attributable to differences among their student bodies at the time of entry" (7). Since our institution enrolls many students who are at a greater risk of dropping out than students at some other institutions, we must take a careful look at how the demographics of admitted students are changing, and how those changes might have a greater effect on retention than any other factors.

In light of these mitigating factors, why do we persist in our support efforts, including the PA program? We know we can make a difference for some students. We agree with Upcraft, Gardner, and Barefoot (2005) that "Efforts to help first-year students succeed are often focused on retention rather than student learning (6), so we need to take an approach that balances retention and academic success. We persist because we owe the opportunity to succeed at university to *all* students, not just the ones who can stay at our institution. We have an obligation to teach the students in front of us, not the students we wish they could be. As Reichert Powell suggests, "recognizing how transient our students are, how unpredictable their paths through higher education, compels us to reframe our goals in terms of *kairos* [proper timing]. We need to recognize the opportunities for our students that exist right now, in our classrooms" (Reichert Powell 2013, 30). Later in her book, *Retention and Resistance*, Reichert Powell describes a *kairotic* composition pedagogy designed to engage and support the students in front of us, regardless of whether they will stay or leave, a practice that she hopes will lead to "an institution that educates all of our students" (30), not just the ones who graduate in four years.

In short, those of us involved in the Peer Advocate program and other retention initiatives are not discouraged by the preliminary results of our study; we believe that we are making progress toward providing an inclusive, engaging environment in First-Year Composition classes, an environment that does, according to most of the comments from students and peer advocates, make a difference in students' learning, engagement in class, and feelings of connection to the university. We will not be deterred by the current rhetoric of retention in higher education, which tends to view students as bodies in seats, as tuition dollars, and as consumers of a product—not individuals who deserve attention to their particular needs.

Finally, in an age of shrinking budgets, declining enrollments, and increasing demands for accountability, everyone acknowledges that colleges and universities need to change. Students crave connection: between courses, between curricular and extracurricular endeavors, and to the faculty, staff, and other students. The colleges and universities that will survive in this new age are the ones that can provide connections from day one. We believe that our PA program provides an effective model of the kind of campus-wide cooperation necessary to make lasting student-friendly changes. As Chaskes and Anttonen (2005) suggest, we were able to "recognize that timing is important in initiating change" and "build coalitions with those committed to change" (203). We seized a moment where change was not only possible, but imperative, and created a coalition that is not only grass-roots and top-down but also spread across key offices and stakeholders on campus. Based on this collaborative success, FYComp is now building similar coalitions (such as one focusing on electronic portfolio pedagogy and assessment) with administrators and offices across campus, and even beginning to work with counterparts at our "feeder" community colleges to create a supportive environment for both first-year and transfer students.

Although our funding for the PA program has been withdrawn due to the statewide budget crisis, cooperating administrators have asked us to channel our energy and expertise into future projects. Coordinators of other on-campus mentoring programs will accept applications from experienced PAs, and we will share our organizational structure, strategies, and data with those programs. We have learned that every first-year student does not need a mentor for a full year; in time, when the budget situation improves, we may choose a specific population of at-risk students for peer-mentoring at a particular juncture of the first year, such as the spring semester, when they are most at risk of leaving. Modeling a new pilot of the Peer Advocate program on the success of our school's Black Male Initiative, SPlan and OHANA minority peer-mentoring programs, we might achieve more measurable retention results by targeting those most at need at the time they are most in need.

We are encouraged by the growing attention being paid to the discourse of retention, one that balances retention and student success, by composition programs across the country, as evidenced by the growing number of publications on composition and retention and increasing

numbers of panels on retention at national conferences. We will be part-
nering with other institutions in the future to compare notes and collaborate on strategies and assessments of mentoring programs and other
retention/student success initiatives, with the goal of making FYComp
relevant and engaging, and making the university accessible, inclusive,
and productive for students from all walks of life.

Note

1.   MAP-Works is a student success and retention software system. Students take surveys
      several times during their first year of college and the results are shared with sup-
      port staff prepared to help them.

Appendix

- Self-reported learning
  - Three items answered on a 1 to 5 Likert scale ($\alpha = 0.89$)
    1. My writing skills have improved significantly this semester.
    2. This course has helped me to develop my critical thinking and
       analysis skills.
    3. This course has prepared me to write effectively in my future
       course work.

- Self-reported connection to NIU
  - Five items answered on a 1 to 5 Likert scale ($\alpha = 0.87$)
    1. I feel involved in campus life at NIU.
    2. I am glad to be a student at NIU.
    3. I feel good about my decision to come to NIU.
    4. I intend to finish my degree here at NIU.
    5. I feel a sense of belonging to the campus community.

- Self-reported academic resource use
  - Five items answered in a yes/no response format
    1. I have used the University Writing Center at least once this se-
       mester.
    2. I have used MAPWorks at least once this semester.
    3. I have used the Academic Advising Center at least once this
       semester.
    4. I have visited the instructor during office hours (not including
       required conferences) at least once this semester.
    5. I have attended an NIU lecture (outside of class) by an outside
       speaker at least once this semester.

- Self-reported extra-curricular resource use
  - Nine items answered in a yes/no response format
    1. I have been involved with Intramural sports/Sports Club at least
       once this semester.

2. I am a member of a Fraternity/Sorority.
3. I have been involved with a Student Organization at least once this semester.
4. I have attended an NIU sporting event at least once this semester.
5. I have attended an NIU music, art, or drama event at least once this semester.
6. I have visited an NIU museum exhibit at least once this semester.
7. I have visited Career Services at least once this semester.
8. I have visited one of NIU's resource centers (e.g., Asian, Latino, Gender & Sexuality, Disability) at least once this semester.
9. I have visited the Student Involvement & Leadership Development (SILD) office at least once this semester.

- PA relationship quality (peer advocate sections only)
  - Seven items answered on a 1 to 5 Likert scale ($\alpha = 0.94$)
    1. I get along well with the peer advocate for my section.
    2. I can confide in my peer advocate.
    3. I have a lot of respect for my peer advocate.
    4. My peer advocate takes a personal interest in my success.
    5. I am very satisfied with the relationship my peer advocate and I have developed.
    6. The mentoring relationship between my peer advocate and I was effective.
    7. My peer advocate and I benefited from the mentoring relationship.

References

Astin, Alexander W. 1993. *What Matters in College? Four Critical Years Revisited.* San Francisco: Jossey-Bass.

Astin, Alexander W. 2005–2006. "Making Sense Out of Degree Completion Rates." *Journal of College Student Retention* 7 (1–2): 5–17. http://dx.doi.org/10.2190/7PV9-K HR7-C2F6-UPK5.

Barefoot, Betsy O. 2005. "Current Institutional Practice in the First College Year." In *Challenging and Supporting the First-Year Student: A Handbook for Improving the First Year of College,* ed. Lee M. Upcraft, John M. Gardner, and Betsy O. Barefoot, 47–66. San Francisco: Jossey-Bass.

Braxton, John, Ellen M. Brier, and Stephanie Lee Steele. 2007. "Shaping Retention from Research to Practice." *Journal of College Student Retention* 9 (3): 377–99. http://dx.doi .org/10.2190/CS.9.3.g.

Bruffee, Kenneth A. 1984. "Peer Tutoring and the 'Conversation of Mankind.'" In *Writing Centers: Theory and Administration,* 87–98. Urbana: National Council of Teachers of English.

Brunk-Chavez, Beth, and Elaine Fredericksen. 2008. "Predicting Success: Increasing Retention and Pass Rates in College Composition." *WPA Journal* 32 (1): 76–96.

Chaskes, Jay, and Ralph C. Anttonen. 2005. "Advocating for First-Year Students." In *Challenging and Supporting the First-Year Student: A Handbook for Improving the First Year of College,* ed. Lee M. Upcraft, John M. Gardner, and Betsy O. Barefoot, 191–203. San Francisco: Jossey-Bass.

Clark, J. Elizabeth, and Bret Eynon. 2009. "E-portfolios 2.0—Surveying the Field." *Peer Review : Emerging Trends and Key Debates in Undergraduate Education* 11 (1): 18–23.

Crissman Ishler, Jennifer L., and Staci Schreiber. 2002. "First-Year Female Students: Perceptions of Friendsickness." *Journal of the First-Year Experience and Students in Transition* 14: 89–104.

Crissman Ishler, Jennifer L., and M. Lee Upcraft. 2005. "The Keys to First-Year Student Persistence." In *Challenging and Supporting the First-Year Student: A Handbook for Improving the First Year of College*, ed. Lee M. Upcraft, John M. Gardner, and Betsy O. Barefoot, 24–46. San Francisco: Jossey-Bass.

Cuseo, Joseph. 2010. "The Empirical Case for the First-Year Seminar: Promoting Positive Student Outcomes and Campus-Wide Benefits." *The First-Year Seminar: Research-Based Recommendations for Course Design, Delivery, and Assessment.* Dubuque, IA: Kendall/ Hunt.

Eynon, Bret, Gambino, Laura, and Judit Torok. 2014. "What Difference Can ePortfolio Make? A Field Report from Connect to Learning Project." *International Journal of ePortfolio* 4(1): 95–114.

Henry, Jim, Holly Bruland, and Ryan Omizo. 2008. "Mentoring First-Year Students in Composition: Tapping Role Construction to Teach." *Currents in Teaching and Learning* 1 (1): 17–28.

Hirsch, Barton J. 1980. "Natural Support Systems and Coping with Major Life Changes." *American Journal of Community Psychology* 8: 159–72.

Hossler, Don, and Douglas K. Anderson. 2005. "The Enrollment Management Process." In *Challenging and Supporting the First-Year Student: A Handbook for Improving the First Year of College*, ed. Lee M. Upcraft, John M. Gardner, and Betsy O. Barefoot, 67–85. San Francisco: Jossey-Bass.

Levitz, Randy L., Lee Noel, and Beth J. Richter. 1999. "Strategic Moves for Retention Success." In *Promising Practices in Recruitment, Remediation, and Retention*, ed. Gerald H. Gaither, 31–49. San Francisco: Jossey Bass.

Naisbitt, John. 1999. *High Tech High Touch.* New York: Broadway Books.

Natalicio, Diane M., and Maggy Smith. 2005. "Building the Foundation for First-Year Student Success in Public, Urban Universities: A Case Study." In *Challenging and Supporting the First-Year Student: A Handbook for Improving the First Year of College*, ed. Lee M. Upcraft, John M. Gardner, and Betsy O. Barefoot, 155–75. San Francisco: Jossey-Bass.

Pascarella, Ernest T., and Patrick T. Terenzini. 1991. *How College Affects Students: Findings and Insights from Twenty Years of Research.* San Francisco: Jossey-Bass.

Pascarella, Ernest T., and Patrick T. Terenzini. 2005. *How College Affects Students: A Third Decade of Research.* vol. II. How College Affects Students. San Francisco: Jossey-Bass.

Paul, Elizabeth S., and Sigal Brier. 2001. How College Affects Students: A Third Decade of Research. Vol. 2. "Friendsickness in the Transition to College." *Journal of Counseling and Development* 79: 77–89.

Paul, Elizabeth S., and Michael Kelleher. 1995. "Precollege Concerns about Losing and Making Friends in College." *Journal of College Student Development* 36: 513–21.

Reichert Powell, Pegeen. 2013. *Retention and Resistance: Writing Instruction and Students Who Leave.* Logan: Utah State University Press.

Tinto, Vincent. 1993. *Leaving College: Rethinking the Causes and Cures of Student Attrition.* 2nd ed. Chicago: The University of Chicago Press.

Tinto, Vincent. 1999. "Taking Retention Seriously: Rethinking the First Year of College." *NACADA Journal* 19 (2): 5–9. http://dx.doi.org/10.12930/0271-9517-19.2.5.

Upcraft, Lee M., John M. Gardner, and Betsy O. Barefoot, eds. 2005. *Challenging and Supporting the First-Year Student: A Handbook for Improving the First Year of College.* San Francisco: Jossey-Bass.

15

AFTERWORD
Navigating the Complexities of Persistence and Retention

Linda Adler-Kassner

Here's a hypothetical that will likely sound familiar to many readers of this collection. Southwestern Central State is a regional comprehensive university with an undergraduate population of about 18,000 students. Most of the students at Southwestern come from the home state. Admissions standards are generous, and Southwestern Central is concerned about retaining the students that it admits after a decline in persistence numbers in the last ten years. They have a sense that first-year writing can affect persistence, a point also made in many of the chapters in this collection (e.g., Garrett et al.).

Currently, students complete a placement exam developed many years ago by the writing faculty. For the exam (which is administered at the beginning of each term), students read an excerpt from a piece on a contemporary social issue and then write a response to a question based on the passage. The placement exam is scored by the writing faculty at regularly scheduled sessions using a rubric developed by predecessors, many of whom have since retired. The scoring sessions are hard but fun—faculty read, rate, and periodically discuss as a sort of informal norming. Participating in these scoring sessions is seen as a central activity of the program and has become de facto professional development.

The provost thinks the exam isn't as accurate as it might be. He knows placement is important, because it's related to students' time in first-year writing and their success at the university. His broader concerns about persistence and retention have led Southwestern Central State to sign on with a learning analytics company. A consultant from that company has suggested that the company's predictive analytics interface can do a better job with placement than the homegrown exam developed by the writing program. The company will use the institution's available data—demographic information about students, high school ratings

DOI: 10.7330/9781607326021.c015

and rankings, standardized test scores, parent/guardian income, and other data that the institution collects. This data will be put into the company's proprietary algorithm, and the results will be delivered back to Southwestern Central's advising staff via a learning dashboard, which advisors will use to talk with students.

The goal is for Southwestern Central to create a "nice clean path" (Brightspace 2016) through college that begins with first-year composition (see below for more on Brightspace and its Degree Compass, including this phrase). Beginning with that placement and looking toward a student's entire four-year degree pathway, the data provided by the predictive analytics system will recommend to students courses where they'll be more successful, rather than those where they might struggle. The data will also be fed to a research consortium of similar kinds of universities across the country interested in persistence. The consortium will make comparisons among the data generated by individual institutions, and those comparisons will become the basis for local institutional policy. The metrics generated by campuses that are part of the consortium will also become part of the accountability information provided to stakeholders— legislators, parents, students, policymakers, and others—as they seek to make decisions. Although the analytics system is expensive, its cost is subsidized by the consortium of campuses interested in persistence.

The provost has told the WPA that he would like her to consider abandoning the current placement method in favor of using the predictive analytics system for writing placement. The provost sees the proposed system as a much more objective placement method—it relies on hard numbers, the algorithms used by the analytics platform have been shown to be effective for similar purposes at other institutions, and it's more cost effective than the exam and scoring that the program currently uses. But the provost truly has presented the WPA with a choice: she doesn't have to do it, and he will support whatever decision she makes. On the other hand, he has let her know that she can use the current funding devoted to the writing placement process for other retention initiatives that she's proposed over the years, initiatives that echo many of the possibilities included in initiatives in this collection: developing a robust system of professional development (Giordano et al.; Buyserie et al.); creating a "studio" model for writing courses (Chemishanova and Snead); creating "stretch" courses with smaller class sizes (Snyder); and implementing a supplemental instruction program with writing fellows (Harris; Day et al.). She's also long proposed converting the positions of a handful of dedicated part-time faculty, excellent teachers and regular participants in the exam-scoring process, into full-time ones. Each of these efforts, the WPA has contended in memos to the provost over the last six years, would increase retention by enhancing the effectiveness of first-year composition.

Hence the dilemma. In the name of persistence and retention efforts, Southwestern Central's WPA has decisions to make about whether to use the analytics system for placement, although the institution has already made a number of decisions that precede this one. The institution will subscribe to the analytics system, and this system will recommend courses for students. The data points that contribute to those recommendations, as well as the algorithms that are used to produce them, are proprietary and will be inaccessible to the WPA and institution. Southwestern Central has already joined a consortium that will lead to comparisons made through data between institutions, and those comparisons will contribute to future decisions about all manner of things, including what the institution should target in its success initiatives and how the institution determines whether those initiatives are successful. The institution has received a grant from an outside organization to fund the analytics system; the grant comes with reporting requirements that will result in mandates outlining the provision of certain kinds of data.

But there are still choices. Should the program give up a long-established, locally developed writing placement exam? In addition to losing something homegrown and not atypical of writing placement exams, this will mean losing the scoring sessions that have become an important part of the program's bonding and professional development activities. On the other hand, if the WPA does agree to let the predictive system take over placement, she'll get some funding for one initiative, and maybe several, that she and her colleagues in the writing program have long wanted to implement.

While the choices facing this hypothetical WPA are associated with her program, the broader questions that compel her to these choices illustrate a point I've invoked before: writing is everybody's business—at least, everyone thinks writing is their business. In this case, because the administration believes that student success is in some way related to writing courses, they've decided that much rides on those courses. For that reason, placement into those courses has become a topic of interest beyond the program itself. Many have an interest in ensuring that the placement process "works." But what "working" means depends on who's defining the term, what goals are associated with it, and what actions are seen as central to the achievement of the goals. The provost is thinking of institutional goals (which, to be sure, are influenced by the goals of others outside the institution, such as legislators and policymakers); the WPA is focused on the program's goals (which, too, are influenced by the institution's goals). In the traditional formulation of choices among goals and actions—in other words, strategies and tactics—the smart WPA would keep the long-term strategy in mind, choosing tactics appropriately.

But here the strategies and tactics are interwoven and difficult to separate. For instance, if the WPA's broader strategy is to ensure that the expertise of writing program faculty is seen as central in making decisions about writing and writers, is it in her best interest to surrender decisions about program placement that, up to this time, have been based on a locally developed placement exam in favor of the use of an outside proprietary software? Is it in the program's best interest to have information about courses and student performance included in a larger research project that will be based only on quantifiable data, and which therefore might now allow for qualitative evidence or conceptualizations of writing development that aren't easily captured in systems that are machine-processed? Both of these decisions seem to contradict the WPA's broader strategy associated with expertise. But they would free up funding to create new initiatives that *do* reflect this strategy and, therefore, would advance the program's broader goals. Which ends, then, take priority over others?

As we move into the twenty-first century, questions like these are becoming increasingly common—especially when they arise in the context of institutional retention efforts. The editors rightly assert that such efforts can be opportunities for "composition to become more involved in student persistence conversations," opportunities to "flip the retention conundrum . . . to . . . center on student learning" (see chapter 1, 3). This "flipping" represents the best kind of decision-making, the kind of artful and smart balancing between strategies and tactics, means and ends, that the WPA at Southwestern Central State is facing. The chapters here also speak to the laudable efforts of WPAs and instructors to consider the contexts and cultures of both students and institutions as they make these kinds of choices, considering why students are there—often, as Reichert Powell points out in this collection, not to "complete college"—and bringing together those intentions with institutions' justifiable foci on student retention (see chapter 8).

At the same time, it's possible to identify three cautionary tales that arise from the current focus on persistence and retention that are documented in these chapters. These tales breathe reality into the dilemmas that are hinted at in the hypothetical I've posed. I'll describe these cautionary tales shortly. Previewing my intention, though, I won't end with them. Admonitions about the perils of persistence or retention efforts that draw in data, methods, or stakeholders that we find problematic, for whatever reason (like the details in my hypothetical), are useful only insofar as they lead us to productive action. Ignoring—or, even worse, dismissing—those elements of the educational landscape that we find troublesome simply isn't an option unless we hope to have no voice in that landscape at all.

CAUTIONARY TALE 1: PREDICTIVE ANALYTICS, BIG DATA, AND RETENTION/PERSISTENCE

One of the issues at the core of the hypothetical WPA's dilemma is whether to allow Southwestern State to use data from their predictive analytics system to place students in writing classes. Predictive analytics is but one use of what is ubiquitously defined as "big data," the possibility of using massive amounts of quantified information for a wide range of purposes. As Rob Kitchin (2014) defines it, big data has some defining characteristics:

- huge in volume, consisting of terabytes or petabytes of data
- high in velocity, created in or near real-time
- diverse in variety, both structured and unstructured in nature
- exhaustive in scope, striving to capture entire populations or systems
- fine-grained in resolution and uniquely indexical in identification
- relational in nature, containing common fields that enable the conjoining of different data sets
- flexible, holding the traits of extensionality (can add new fields easily) and scaleability (can expand in size rapidly) (1–2)

Big data propelled efforts, especially the use of predictive analytics systems like the one described in the hypothetical, are increasingly being used for placement and advising. Because these data are already quantified, they can be readily adapted to accountability-oriented perspectives on learning, providing quick and "easy" feedback on how many, how much, how well, and so on. Marc Scott's chapter in this collection, too, outlines the potential and some of the problematics of big data for WPAs. As Scott notes, their use might provide information that can help to "tailor interventions to meet student needs" (chapter 4, 56). At the same time, Rita Malenczyk's chapter points to some of the issues associated with these predictive uses. She cautions that "implemented uncritically, retention efforts can turn a university into a panopticon, a Foucauldian instrument of power and control that reflects a fear of the

disorder that often accompanies human agency and human development, particularly the development that occurs in the adolescence of
traditional-aged college students. The creation and marketing of programs such as GradesFirst, which enable unlimited access to student
data, feed into this fear even as they perform useful services that help
students navigate their college experience" (chapter 2, 21).

Malenczyk's invocation of GradesFirst provides the opportunity to
consider the process of one of the many predictive/learning analytics
systems circulating in postsecondary education. GradesFirst is part of
Educational Advisory Board (EAB), an organization that is emerging as
a significant player in the learning management industry. According to
EAB's own data, "78 percent of four-year students in the U.S. attend [an
EAB institution]" (EAB n.d.). EAB's proprietary algorithms are black-
boxed—that is, the means by which results are produced for and about
individual students are not visible to those who are using the results of
the data. Additionally, as with all big data analytics systems, the information that goes into the system—"testing, numbers, and [other] data
points"—are presented as objective, as are the results that are ultimately
produced. But as researchers like Rob Kitchin note, "all data provide
oligoptic views of the world: views from certain vantage points, using
particular tools, rather than an all-seeing, infallible God's eye view . . .
data are not simply natural and essential elements that are abstracted
from the world in neutral and objective ways and can be accepted at face
value" (Kitchin 2014, 4). The use of GradesFirst thus raises questions:
Might systems like this contribute to persistence? And, if so, at what cost?
Southwestern Central's WPA is facing a slightly less daunting challenge
than the one Malenczyk previews in that the predictive system is being
used for the slightly narrower purpose of writing placement—but only
slightly less daunting, because the possibilities for expanded use of these
systems is omnipresent. The possible multiple uses of such systems—that
is, expanding its use for predictive purposes related to major trajectories or career tracks or data mining to see what emerges—is literally a
mouse click away. Cautionary tale 1, then, has to do with the possibility
and perils of big data and analytics, especially as they are associated with
retention and persistence efforts.

CAUTIONARY TALE 2: RESPONSIBILITY AND
ACCOUNTABILITY IN RESEARCH AND ASSESSMENT

As the Southwestern Central WPA debates between surrendering a
homegrown assessment process for one that is linked to the use of a

predictive analytics system, she's making choices among activities that stem from different perspectives on learning. These perspectives are reflected in two ideas: *responsibility*, when professionals analyze and act upon social need through the knowledge associated with their practice, and *accountability*, when professionals act in order to "justify or account for the ways that . . . responsibilities [are performed]" (Fenwick 2016, 9). As researcher Tara Fenwick explains, accountability can lead to a "preoccupation . . . with auditing" that can "distort core commitments of responsibility" (9).

The distinction between responsibility and accountability has significant implications for implementing and studying the effects of retention and persistence efforts (and, indeed, for education more generally). In writing, especially, we tend to gravitate toward what Bob Broad (2009) refers to as "organic" work—efforts that take into account local contexts, situations, and cultures. Our study of the effects of these efforts tends to involve qualitative, grounded data, focusing on the ways that educators engage *specific* needs—of students in classrooms, in institutions. These efforts, then, extend from a foundation of research and teaching-based knowledge grounded in disciplinary expertise, reflecting the idea of "responsibility" defined by Fenwick.[1]

The suggestion that the Southwestern Central WPA abandon the locally developed placement process in favor of using the predictive analytics system, though, represents a perspective on learning that is primarily accountability-focused. In the hypothetical, the predictive analytics system is seen as more "objective" than the written exam; this invocation of objectivity reflects the idea that expert professional judgment (of writing instructors) is less reliable than that generated by algorithms analyzed by a machine. The data in the system is already quantified; it can be used to recommend as well as to easily study the quantitative effects of those recommendations. Too, the data from the analytics system is being used for the multi-institutional consortium's research, which will generate comparison. These comparisons will then become bases for new policies and processes. This represents one among many instances where data is used "to *make* policy, rather than simply as aids to decision making" (Fenwick, Mangez, and Ozga 2014, 3). The differences between responsibility and accountability and the consequences flowing from these differences have important implications for WPAs considering issues associated with persistence and retention, as the hypothetical here suggests.

The ideas of responsibility and authority can be extended to two perspectives on assessment that are also visible here. Responsibility positions "practice within a language of values and integrity, contextual nuance and relationship, and processes of situated judgment and negotiated standards" (Fenwick and Edwards 2016, 121). Many chapters here (e.g., Giordano et al.; Webb-Sunderhaus; Reichert Powell) include evidence gathered from examinations of students and/or faculty members within specific institutional contexts. This focus on the local and contextual is typical of the research in our field and, in fact, of grounded research more broadly.

But from the perspective of accountability, assessment "frames practice through economic concerns for standardized, measurable priorities and rationales and economic processes of external audit and counting" (Solbrekke and Sugrue, quoted in Fenwick and Edwards 2016, 121). Of the twelve pieces in this collection focusing on specific efforts (i.e., all chapters excluding the editors' introduction and this afterword), eight include or discuss the potential uses of quantified data—analyses of grades, rates of persistence, or other numerical information—to speak to the effectiveness of these efforts and/or of first-year composition.

That quantified data speak most powerfully to decision-makers—administrators, policy officials, and the public—is hardly news. But it's worth considering the ways in which these data reflect an accountability-oriented perspective and reify perceptions that these data are most significant because they are seen as "objective"—things that *are*, rather than judgments that *have occurred* through the multiple human, subjective decision—or that are used to compare one site to another through data (see Bowker and Star 1999, 266–67; see also Fenwick and Edwards 2016).

The need to produce such data or fixes can also obscure the complications of implementing persistence efforts that are so ably described here. Stories about retention/persistence programs developed smartly and quickly by dedicated writing faculty drawing from the most current research on both program development and retention, like that in the chapter by Day and colleagues, are expected to produce results under conditions that our research also tells us are unlikely to be as successful as they would be over a longer period of time. In the same vein, Giordano and colleagues' chapter describes the critical place of faculty professional development in retention initiatives and provides a remarkable illustration of one such program, but also points to the complications that are manifest through those programs.

Because contemporary public conversations about education focusing on accountability (i.e., the expense of undergraduate education, the likelihood of employment prospects after college, time to degree, efficiency of education, and so on) are so dominant, institutions are under often intense pressure to provide accountability data attesting to their abilities to retain students. For these reasons, the stakes attached to persistence initiatives like the ones described here—efforts that are intended to foster student success to some degree through the scaffolding of low-, medium-, and ultimately higher-stakes learning—are stratospherically high for the faculty and writing programs involved. To complicate matters even further, research conducted on efforts like the ones represented in these chapters, which provide outstanding examples of responsibility-focused imperatives, are often assessed through the lens of accountability. They are expected to provide "standardized" quantified data that attests to the effectiveness of the efforts described to move the proverbial needle and increase the percentage of students who move from one term, one year, to the next, in part to satisfy "economic processes of external audit and counting." The perspectives on assessment (and research) reflected in these expectations, though, are challenging to those invested in the local and contextual. The choices facing WPAs and writing instructors as they navigate among these are similarly challenging. The hypothetical WPA might be able to fund initiatives at the classroom level, efforts linked to the local contexts and the idea of "responsibility." But what is the tradeoff when the basis for the funding is largely required for institutional accountability? Complicated and complicating questions.

CAUTIONARY TALE 3: FRAMING PERSISTENCE

Framing is the process of outlining broad boundaries of the possible and not possible. Frames reflect and perpetuate values and ideologies, reifying particular stances.[2] The previous cautionary tale references different perspectives on professional practice; "responsibility" and "accountability" are themselves frames, lenses that shape the ways that people understand education and activities associated with education (like, e.g., teaching and learning).

The chapters in this collection demonstrate the importance of questions associated with framing and persistence: What should persistence mean, and why should we focus on it? What factors should be understood to contribute to persistence? How should those factors be considered? What stories about students, writing, and postsecondary learning are shaped within the frame? As the chapters here demonstrate, these stories now go far beyond an argument about the futility of "remedial" courses and their effectiveness to reform efforts that are attempting to address (at a structural level) larger stories: about the expense of college education, the time that students spend pursuing degrees, and seeming divergences that can complicate a trajectory through college.

Increasingly, these questions (and the responses to them) reflect an accountability-oriented perspective; as I've suggested in the previous cautionary tale, this can be problematic for faculty. Such a perspective also has implications for learners and learning. A video promoting Degree Compass, a predictive analytics program included in Brightspace/D2L, illustrates the point. The story is told by Tristan Denley, Vice Chancellor for Academic Affairs at the Tennessee Board of Regents and the developer of Degree Compass. In the video, Denley explains that

> [r]ather than higher education being a nice clean path toward a degree, for [some students] it's very much like a maze. When we look at the data that's coming from Degree Compass what we see is that when students actually follow the advice the technology provides we can take about a whole semester out of that. . . . A whole semester of not earning the salary that you get when you get the job afterwards. One of the things that we've seen from Degree Compass . . . is that it really does suggest courses in which students can be much more successful with a better than 92% accuracy. Degree Compass is able to predict whether or not a student would be successful in that class. What we're seeing is that students who take the courses that are recommended to them are 50% more likely to make an A or B than the general population. (Brightspace 2016)

Through the frame surrounding this story, the entire process of postsecondary education has the potential to become a quagmire for students. To be sure, the path through college can be problematic for some—a student, for instance, who is enrolled in three science/lab courses in a term, two of them for the second time, or another student who is pursuing a major in one discipline because of external pressures rather than an interest in that discipline. But postsecondary education has also (historically) been seen as an opportunity for students to explore new subjects, encounter new challenges, and experience a process of learning that can be messy at times. The process of intellectual and personal growth that is explored in research on writing development (i.e., McCarthy 1987; Carroll 2002; Sternglass 1997; Haswell 1991) reflects, in part, the idea that learning takes time.

But the accountability frame has the potential to obviate ideas of time—as well as those of context and embodiment—associated with learning. (For more on the intersection of time, context, and embodiment in learning see, for instance, Kreber 2009; Meyer and Land 2006; Baxter Magolda 2009.) A "nice clean pathway" might remove opportunities for exploration. It also might be tagged to data points that recommend against challenging courses of study—and, in worst-case scenarios, might reinforce biases or prejudices against particular groups that are built into the system. For instance, if data from female low-income students from underrepresented minority groups were framed as pointing to more or less success in certain courses or majors, other students who were characterized (through their data) in the same way might be advised against such courses or majors, perpetuating a frame around students ("it's not for you . . .") or courses/majors ("just not right for x, y, and z students").

Another manifestation of this frame is the creation of "guided pathways," which enroll students in "coherent majors or programs" or "metamajors" such as "STEM, health care, or social science" rather than "random, individual courses" (CCA). In its definition of these pathways, Complete College America (one of the leading promoters of the "completion agenda") explains that within the pathways "exploration outside one's major is allowed and enabled as intentional exploration, rather than aimless wandering." Based on feedback—that is, grades in "milestone courses," students are provided the input they need regarding their success and change out of the pathway in which they are participating only with the consent of an advisor. It's the data that makes decisions here, not the student and that student's experience. What, then, of the kind of students like those so richly described by Webb-Sunderhaus or Reichert Powell? Of the thoughtful programmatic initiatives like those developed and studied by Holmes and Busser, Buyserie et al., Chemishanova and Snead, Wolff Murphy and Hartlaub, Day et al., or any other chapter in this collection? Each points to the problems that arise when students are characterized through an accountability-oriented frame, which is directed toward straightforward paths. In a commentary on the "guided pathways" model, Mike Rose raised the same issues:

> Like all structural remedies, [guided pathways] runs the risk of reducing nuanced and layered human dilemmas to a technical problem, and thus being unresponsive to or missing entirely the particular life circumstances of students. So, yes, make the college curriculum more coherent, but realize that human and other material resources will be needed to meet the needs of many students, and, as well, build into your structural changes the flexibility needed to honor the range of life circumstances your students bring to college. Otherwise, the fix may create unintended negative consequences. (Rose 2016, n.p.)

MOVING FORWARD WITH CAUTION: PERSISTENCE AND RETENTION IN AN ERA OF ACCOUNTABILITY

As is so often the case, Rose's admonition points to another kind of "pathway"—one that writing instructors and WPAs like the ones included in this collection can take as we consider how to navigate the tricky options (and potential opportunities) that are presented in an era of educational accountability. As I've noted above, pretending that these options and the frames surrounding them are going to go away isn't an option.

The contributions in this collection, though, point to the ways in which WPAs and writing instructors are working hard to gain the greatest value from institutional and policy-informed emphases on persistence. Balancing means and ends, tactics and strategies, they're tipping the scales in the right direction, whether that direction is attempting to reframe first-year writing in the face of excessive emphasis on persistence (Reichert Powell), establishing correlations between writing courses and persistence (Garrett et al.), or developing innovative programs to engage faculty (e.g., Giordano et al.; Buyserie et al.) or mentor students (e.g., Chemishanova and Snead; Snyder; Harris; Day et al.). Each of these efforts points to a strategy for navigation outlined by Fenwick, who argues that "professionals need to learn to distinguish the purposes that the logic of accountability is intended to serve and what purposes actually serve . . . professional[s]" (Fenwick 2016, 50). This can help professionals to move from "survival strategies, [where] individuals develop accommodating ways of acting [that leave mechanisms largely unaltered]," to "coping strategies" that "seek more energetically to bring agency, imagination, and creativity to bear in a manner that is potentially more transformative" (50). Moving from survival to coping can mean the difference between perpetuating the ideas associated with accountability and those reflecting responsibility—and this collection provides a number of pathways toward this goal.

Notes

1. The impulse to begin articulating elements of this expertise in a relatively concise and accessible way was one of the impulses driving the development of Naming What We Know, in which experts from the discipline attempted to define and describe some of the field's threshold concepts. See Adler-Kassner and Wardle "Naming."

2. See Goffman; Reese; and Bolman and Deal for different iterations and illustrations of framing; see also Adler-Kassner and Adler-Kassner and O'Neill discussions of framing and writing instruction/writers).

References

Baxter Magolda, Marcia. 2009. "Educating Students for Self-Authorship: Learning Partnerships to Achieve Complex Outcomes." In *The University and Its Disciplines*, ed. C. Kreber, 143–56. New York: Routledge.

Bowker, Geoffrey C., and Susan Leigh Star. 1999. *Sorting Things Out: Classification and Its Consequences*. Cambridge, MA: MIT Press.

Brightspace. 2016. Predictive Analytics with Brightspace's Degree Compass. https://www.youtube.com/watch?v=20wF6SHLSWw.

Carroll, Lee Ann. 2002. *Rehearsing New Roles: How College Students Develop as Writers*. Studies in Writing and Rhetoric. Carbondale: Southern Illinois University Press.

EAB. n.d. "About Us." https://www.eab.com/about-us.

Fenwick, Tara. 2016. *Professional Responsibility and Professionalism: A Sociomaterial Examination*. New York: Routledge.

Fenwick, Tara, and Richard Edwards. 2016. "Exploring the Impact of Digital Technologies on Professional Responsibilities and Education." *European Educational Research Journal* 15 (1): 117–31.

Fenwick, Tara, Eric Mangez, and Jenny Ozga. 2014. *Governing Knowledge: Comparison, Knowledge-Based Technologies and Expertise. World Yearbook of Education 2014.* New York: Routledge.

Haswell, Richard. 1991. *Gaining Ground in College Writing: Tales of Development and Interpretation*. Dallas, TX: Southern Methodist University Press.

Kitchin, Rob. 2014. "Big Data, New Epistemologies, and Paradigm Shifts." *Big Data and Society* (April–June): 1–12.

Kreber, Carolin. 2009. "Supporting Student Learning in the Context of Diversity, Complexity, and Uncertainty." In *The University and Its Disciplines*, ed. C. Kreber, 3–18. New York: Routledge.

McCarthy, Lucille. 1987. "A Stranger in Strange Lands: A College Student Writing across the Curriculum." *Research in the Teaching of English* 21 (3): 233–65.

Meyer, Jan, and Ray Land. 2006. "Threshold Concepts and Troublesome Knowledge: An Introduction." In *Overcoming Barriers to Student Understanding: Threshold Concepts and Troublesome Knowledge*, ed. J. Meyer and R. Land, 3–18. London: Routledge.

Rose, Mike. 23 June 2016. "Reassessing a Redesign of Community Colleges." *Inside Higher Ed*. https://www.insidehighered.com/views/2016/06/23/essay-challenges-facing-guided-pathways-model-restructuring-two-year-colleges.

Sternglass, Marilyn. 1997. *Time to Know Them: A Longitudinal Study of Writing and Learning at the College Level*. Mahwah, NJ: Lawrence Erlbaum.

ABOUT THE AUTHORS

LINDA ADLER-KASSNER is professor of writing studies and associate dean of undergraduate education at University of California, Santa Barbara. Her research and teaching focus broadly on how literate agents and activities—such as writers, writing, writing studies—are defined in contexts inside the academy and in public discourse. She also examines the implications and consequences of those definitions and how writing faculty can participate in shaping them. She frequently works with faculty across disciplines on articulating threshold concepts and making them more accessible for students. She is author, coauthor, or coeditor of nine books, including *Reframing Writing Assessment, Naming What We Know,* and *The Activist WPA.*

MATTHEW BRIDGEWATER is assistant professor of Writing at Woodbury University. His work has appeared in the journals *Computers and Composition Online, Computers and Composition,* and *Kairos,* and he has presented at the *Conference on College Composition and Communication, Computers & Writing,* and *Rhetoric Society of America.* His research interests include technical and scientific writing, writing about history, and writing and technology.

BETH BRUNK-CHAVEZ is professor of Rhetoric and Writing Studies at the University of Texas at El Paso (UTEP) and dean of Extended University, which houses UTEP's online program initiative. She is a 2009 recipient of the University of Texas System Regents' Outstanding Teaching Award. Her publications have recently appeared in *WPA: Writing Program Administration, Written Communication, Composition Studies,* and numerous edited collections. Brunk-Chavez served as the writing program administrator for the first-year composition program for five years, during which time the program was awarded with a Conference on College Composition and Communication Writing Program Certificate of Excellence.

CRISTINE BUSSER received her MA in writing from Nova Southeastern University. She is currently pursuing her PhD in rhetoric and composition from Georgia State University, where she teaches first-year composition and serves as an associate director of the Writing Studio. Her research interests include writing program administration and composition pedagogy.

BETH BUYSERIE is the assistant director of Composition and assistant clinical professor at Washington State University, where she teaches both composition and English education courses. She also coordinates the Critical Literacies Achievement and Success Program, which serves both underrepresented students and their teachers via student-teacher dialogue and reflective critical pedagogy practices.

POLINA CHEMISHANOVA is associate professor and director of Composition in the Department of English, Theatre, and Foreign Languages at the University of North Carolina at Pembroke where she teaches first-year composition, professional communication, and upper-level rhetoric and composition courses. Her research interests include WAC/WID, writing program assessment, and composition theory and pedagogy.

MICHAEL DAY is professor of English at Northern Illinois University, where he directs the First-Year Composition Program and teaches rhetoric, composition, teaching of writing, technical writing, and writing for electronic media. He has presented and published widely on topics ranging from intercultural rhetoric to digital rhetoric and electronic portfolios.

HEIDI ESTREM is professor of English and director of the First-Year Writing Program at Boise State University. The First-Year Writing Program was recently awarded the Council of Basic Writing's Award for Innovation for curricular and programmatic innovations that are designed to deepen student learning and improve retention. She has published on first-year writing pedagogy, new instructor development and support, and a range of writing program administration issues in *WPA: Writing Program Administration, Composition Studies, Pedagogy*, and numerous edited collections.

BRUCE FEINSTEIN is an institutional researcher at Woodbury University. His areas of emphasis include enrollment tracking analysis and reporting and providing customized dashboards for stakeholders across the institution.

PATRICIA FREITAG ERICSSON is an associate professor at Washington State University where she directs the Composition Program and teaches undergraduate and graduate courses in rhetoric and composition. Her previous articles have appeared in *Computers and Composition* and *Kairos* as well as in several edited collections. She is the co-editor of an edited collection on Automated Essay Scoring.

NATHAN GARRETT is assistant professor of Information Technology at Woodbury University. He earned his PhD in information systems and technology from Claremont Graduate University. Nathan researches educational technology, PowerPoint, Excel, and student success. His website and open educational resources are located at profgarrett.com.

JOANNE GIORDANO is the Developmental Reading and Writing coordinator for the University of Wisconsin Colleges, at a statewide, two-year institution. She teaches reading and writing at the University of Wisconsin-Marathon County and for the University of Wisconsin Colleges Online. Her work has appeared in *Teaching English in the Two-Year College, College Composition and Communication,* and *College English.*

TAWANDA GIPSON is a research associate at Northern Illinois University where she manages various projects related to the assessment of student learning outcomes, including the University Writing Project and the Voluntary System of Accountability. She is also currently pursuing her master's in educational research and evaluation.

SARAH E. HARRIS is coordinator for Curriculum and Outcomes Assessment at the College of the Sequoias. During her time as writing program director and assistant professor of English at Indiana University East, she served as a campus team member on the American Association of State Colleges and Universities (AASCU) Re-Imagining the First Year of College project and worked closely on student success initiatives in the writing program and across the campus; she continues to research how success is defined and measured in higher education.

MARK G. HARTLAUB is professor of psychology and dean of the College of Liberal Arts at Texas A&M University-Corpus Christi. His work has appeared in the *Journal of Learning Communities Research, Learning Communities Journal,* and *The Journal of College Student Development.*

HOLLY HASSEL is professor of English and women's studies at the University of Wisconsin-Marathon County. She earned her PhD in English from the University of Nebraska-Lincoln. Her work has appeared in *Feminist Teacher, Teaching English in the Two-Year College, College Composition and Communication, College English, Pedagogy,* and other journals. She currently serves as associate editor of *Teaching English in the Two-Year College.*

JENNIFER HEINERT is associate professor of English at University of Wisconsin Colleges Online and University of Wisconsin-Washington County. She earned her PhD in English from Marquette University in Milwaukee, Wisconsin. In addition to teaching composition and literature courses, Jennifer directs the UW Colleges' Virtual Teaching and Learning Center. She is the author of *Narrative Conventions and Race in the Novels of Toni Morrison*. She also has worked collaboratively with colleagues on research, writing, presentations, and workshops related to faculty development, peer review in the writing classroom, feminized labor in composition, and competency-based education.

ASHLEY J. HOLMES is assistant professor of English at Georgia State University. She is currently working on a book-length manuscript that argues for public approaches to pedagogy and administration based on comparative analysis of three case studies conducted within writing programs. Holmes has published articles in *Community Literacy Journal, Reflections, English Journal,* and *Kairos,* and she is currently an assistant editor with the refereed open-access online journal *Kairos.*

RITA MALENCZYK is professor of English and director of the writing program and writing center at Eastern Connecticut State University. Her work on the rhetoric and politics of writing program administration has appeared in numerous edited collections and journals. With Susanmarie Harrington, Keith Rhodes, and Ruth Overman Fischer, she co-edited *The Outcomes Book* (Utah State UP, 2005); her edited collection *A Rhetoric for Writing Program Administrators* was published by Parlor Press in 2013. She is Immediate Past President of the Council of Writing Program Administrators.

CHRISTOPHER P. PARKER is the associate vice provost for Academic Outcomes Assessment and an associate professor of Industrial / Organizational Psychology at Northern Illinois University (NIU). Chris manages the Office of Assessment Services, providing technical and analytical support to NIU degree programs and their efforts to demonstrate accomplishment of their student learning outcomes.

CASSANDRA PHILLIPS is an associate professor of English at the University of Wisconsin Waukesha. She earned her PhD in rhetoric and composition from the University of Louisville and serves as the writing program administrator for the University of Wisconsin Colleges. Her research interests include faculty and instructor development, writing studies, feminized labor and composition, teaching online, and writing program curriculum and development.

ANNA PLEMONS, Blackburn fellow at Washington State University, teaches composition, rhetoric, technical communication, and creative writing in a variety of settings, including an ongoing teaching practice at New Folsom Prison in Represa, CA. She is the associate editor of *Studies in Writing and Rhetoric,* the monograph series of *College Composition and Communication.*

PEGEEN REICHERT POWELL is associate professor of English and director of the Program in Writing and Rhetoric at Columbia College Chicago. Her research on pedagogy, basic writing, and critical discourse analysis, as well as feminist mothering studies, has appeared in several journals and edited collections. Her study of the role of writing instruction in retention efforts, *Retention and Resistance: Writing Instruction and Students Who Leave,* was published by Utah State UP in 2014. She also co-edited a collection titled *Mothers Who Deliver: Feminist Interventions in Interpersonal and Public Discourse* (SUNY Press, 2010).

TODD RUECKER is assistant professor of English at the University of New Mexico. His work regularly crosses disciplinary boundaries and he has published extensively on the transitions of Latina/o writers from high school to college. He has published articles in respected composition, education, and applied linguistics journals, including *TESOL*

Quarterly, College Composition and Communication, and *Writing Program Administration.* He has published two books: *Transiciones: Latina and Latino Students Writing in High School and College* and *Linguistically Diverse Immigrant and Resident Writers: Transitions from High School to College.*

MARC SCOTT is assistant professor, former Writing Center director, and current director of Developmental English at Shawnee State University in Portsmouth, Ohio. His research interests include writing and programmatic assessment, developmental writing, research methodologies, and critical pedagogies.

DAWN SHEPHERD is associate professor of English and associate director of the First-Year Writing Program at Boise State University. She is the author of *Building Relationships: Online Dating and the New Logics of Internet Culture,* and her research on romantic matchmaking and algorithmic culture has been featured in local and international media, including BBC World and *The Times of London.* Her work has been published in edited collections as well as *The Norton Book of Composition Studies* and *WPA: Writing Program Administration.*

ROBIN SNEAD holds a PhD in communication, rhetoric, and digital media from NC State University. She is a lecturer in the English, Theatre, and Foreign Languages Department at the University of North Carolina at Pembroke, where she teaches composition and advises in a program for at-risk students. Her research interests include composition pedagogy, multimodal rhetoric, and creative processes.

SARAH ELIZABETH SNYDER is a doctoral student in writing, rhetorics, and literacies at Arizona State University, where she has also served as the assistant director and then associate director of Second Language Writing. Sarah was a co-associate chair for the 2014 Symposium on Second Language Writing, and the institute coordinator for the 2016 Symposium on Second Language Writing, and a committee member of the Writing Program Administrator-Graduate Organization. Sarah earned both of her master's degrees at Northern Arizona University in rhetoric and the teaching of writing, and teaching English to speakers of other languages.

SARA WEBB-SUNDERHAUS is associate professor of English at Indiana University-Purdue University Fort Wayne. Her research focuses on two separate areas of interest, Appalachian literacy/identity and basic writing, and her work has appeared in numerous journals and edited collections. With Kim Donehower, she is co-editor of *Re-Reading Appalachia: Literacies of Resistance* (forthcoming from the UP of Kentucky).

SUSAN WOLFF MURPHY is associate professor of English and associate dean of the College of Liberal Arts at Texas A&M University–Corpus Christi; also, she is a CompPile. org editor. She co-edited *Teaching Writing with Latino/a Students: Lessons Learned at Hispanic Serving Institutions.* Her interests include developmental and first-year writing, transfer, and faculty development.

INDEX

absolute hospitality, as productive challenge for WPAs, 136, 143, 145–49
access institutions. *See* open-access institutions
accountability: and big data, 60, 64, 158, 261; demand for, 8, 167, 182, 237, 253, 258; in research and assessment, 262–68; student, 23
Accuplacer, 40, 173
Adler-Kassner, Linda: chapter on contexts of retention, 15, 257–268; on threshold concepts, 142, 221, 229, 268(n1, n2)
advocacy, 13, 16, 155, 241
agents: mentors as, 241; students as, 141, 154, 161
analytics. *See* big data analytics; predictive analytics
Anttonen, Ralph J., *Challenging and Supporting the First-Year Student* (with Chaskes), and peer advocates, 240, 241, 244, 253
assistance: institutional, 14, 155; intrusiveness with, 233; peer advocate, 248; Student Learning (SLA), 182n3
Astin, Alexander, factors in student retention, 6, 154, 239, 240, 252
"at-risk" students: in CLASP, 154; and developmental learning communities, 222, 225, 226, 232; and faculty development, 75, 81, 82; in Georgia State University programs, 43, 51, 53n4; in peer-mentoring programs, 253; in the *PlusOne* program, 173, 183(n6); in the Stretch Program, 12, 199; and supplemental instruction, 208–10, 212, 214; tracking with GradesFirst, 23, 29, 33

basic writers, writing: with absolute hospitality, 149; in the *kairotic* classroom, 204, 205; and second language writers, 185–86; and the Stretch Program, 185–88(table), 189. *See also* Stretch Program
BDA. *See* big data analytics
big data, 57–59, 261; as panopticon, 27, 29, 261. *See also* big data analytics
big data analytics (BDA): limitations of, 61–66, 262; opportunities of, 59–61,

262; pedagogical use of, 63, 65; in Writing Program Administration, 66–70
Brunk-Chavez, Beth, "Predicting Success: Increasing Retention and Pass Rates in College Composition" (with Fredericksen), 4, 40, 41, 95, 173, 239

challenges to student persistence: financial, 10, 27–29, 41, 110(n3), 114–16, 148, 181; mental health, 117; substance involvement, 117–19; time or scheduling difficulties, 4, 46, 116, 124, 128, 224–26; transition to college, 78, 117, 169–70, 220, 228, 230; underpreparedness, 74, 75, 116, 168–69, 181, 220–21
Chaskes, Jay, *Challenging and Supporting the First-Year Student* (with Anttonen), 240, 241, 244, 253
chronological pedagogy, 136, 140, 141. *See also* kairotic pedagogy
CLASP. *See* Critical Literacies Achievement and Success Program
co-requisites, 75, 173–75, 226
Critical Literacies Achievement and Success Program (CLASP), Washington State University, 151–52; with critical composition pedagogy, 151, 156, 157; encouraging student-faculty dialogue, 155, 161, 163(figure), 164(figure), 165(figure); faculty development through, 153, 156–58; pedagogy series, 156, 157(table), 159; and retention discourse, 154, 158–60(figure), 161(figure); students as agents, 141, 154, 161

Department of Education, data and assessment, 74, 93, 115, 169
Derrida, Jacques, absolute hospitality, 15, 136, 145–48
developmental learning communities (DLCs), at Texas A&M University-Corpus Christi, 225–30; data results, 230–32(table); designing, 219, 220, 223; recommendations for, 232–33; sample week, 226(table); three previous initiatives, 221–23

developmental writers, writing. *See* basic writers
DFW. *See* grades
directed self-placement (DSP), 12, 31, 207
DLCs. *See* developmental learning communities
Downs, Doug, *Writing about Writing* (with Wardle), 32, 33, 142, 143, 228; on FYC, 48
"Dropout from Higher Education" (Tinto), 5
DSP. *See* directed self-placement

early-warning systems, 239, 250
Educational Advisory Board (EAB), 262
engagement, 4–6, 169, 170. *See also* agents
enrollment: declines in, 237, 253; increases in, 9, 50, 53(n1), 196, 207, 217(n1), 224; in multilingual sections, 193, 201; in the *PlusOne* program, 171, 174(table), 177(table); universal, 223; in writing programs, 11, 144
Estrem, Heidi, 12

financial aid, 27, 114; grants, 41, 42, 110(n3), 159; loans, 7, 68, 114, 115; scholarships, 9, 110(n3)
first-year composition (FYC; FYComp) courses: at Arizona State University, 188(table), 189–93; and big data analytics, 64, 65, 68–70; at Georgia State University, 45–52; as high-impact practice, 109, 121, 152, 170–72; and retention, 15, 39–41, 95–96, 151–54, 237; student performance in, 93–110; and student persistence, 11. *See also by various program models*
first-year learning communities (FLCs), 39, 43, 44, 53(n2), 223, 232
first-year seminars: as high-impact practice, 170, 223; and retention, 39, 208, 224, 229, 231, 238
first-year student persistence, 219–22, 239–40, 244
first-year writing (FYW) courses: as high-impact practice, 170; retention in, 11–13, 171; revising, 137, 138; student performance in, 167, 174(table), 177(table), 207, 210, 223; student underpreparedness for, 40, 79. *See also by various program models*
FLCs. *See* first-year learning communities
Foucault, Foucauldian, 21, 29–30, 36(n1), 261. *See also* panopticon

Fredericksen, Elaine, "Predicting Success: Increasing Retention and Pass Rates in College Composition" (with Brunk-Chavez), 4, 40, 41, 95, 173, 239
freshman learning communities. *See* first-year learning communities
funding: cuts in, 9, 167; formulas, 3; performance-based, 8, 58, 67
FYC. *See* first-year composition
FYW courses. *See* first-year writing courses

Glau, Gregory, and the Stretch program, 11, 12, 185–91, 196–201
grades, D, F, and withdrawal (DFW), 207, 208, 210–12
GradesFirst, 23–25, 29, 33, 262

Haswell and Haswell, *Hospitality and Authoring: An Essay for the English Profession*, 145, 146, 148
High-Impact Practices, 169, 170; learning communities as, 222–24; writing courses as, 109, 121, 152, 170–72
Hispanic-Serving Institution (HSI), 219, 221, 223, 229, 232–33
HSI. *See* Hispanic-Serving Institution

inclusion, 147, 156, 157(table), 191
involvement, 5
Institutional Review Board (IRB), 82, 96, 116
integration, 5–7

kairos, 139–41, 148, 205, 206, 215, 252
kairotic classroom, the, 214–17
kairotic pedagogy, 32, 136–41; and absolute hospitality, 145, 148, 149
kairotic opportunity, 205, 217
key concepts, in writing and rhetoric, 137–43, 148, 229

L2 writers. *See* second language writers
Latina and Latino students, and retention initiatives, 7, 221, 222, 224
learning communities. *See* developmental learning communities; freshman learning communities
Likert scale, in peer advocate program evaluation, 246, 249, 254, 255

MAP-Works, 239, 250, 254(n1)
Matsuda, Paul Kei, on second language writers, 186, 193
mentoring programs, 240–44, 250, 253–55. *See also* Peer Advocate program

minority/minoritized students, 6, 7, 9, 10; in first-year composition, 96, 97(table), 100(table); at Georgia State University, 50; peer-mentoring programs, 253; at the University of North Carolina at Pembroke, 168
multilingual writers. *See* second language writers

National Survey of Student Engagement (NSSE), 94, 122; focus on high-impact practices, 109, 152, 153

open-access institutions, 67, 74–77, 81, 82, 89–91. *See also* two-year institutions

panopticon, panopticism, retention efforts as, 25, 29, 31, 36(n1), 261
PA program. *See* Peer Advocate program
Peer Advocate (PA) program, 240–44; advocate responses, 249(table), 250; advocate roles, 244; future models of, 250, 251; impacts of, 244, 245, 247(table), 248(table)
peer mentoring programs. *See* mentoring programs; Peer Advocate program
persistence, discussion on, 4–7, 10–12, 28, 31, 251, 257–68; and big data analysis, 62; in CLASP, 151–54; faculty influences to, 126–29; first-year student, 219–22, 239–40, 244; in the *PlusOne* program, 167, 169–71, 179–81; role of writing in, 33, 121–24; and self-efficacy, 31; in the Stretch program, 188–91, 193–200; and student success, 62, 81, 109. *See also* challenges to student persistence; tenacious persister
placement: evaluating measures for, 40, 208, 212, 217(n1), 234(n7); exams, 109, 173, 223, 227, 231, 257; methods of, 12, 13, 258–63; multiple measures, 75, 82, 91(n3); policies, 149, 207; in the Stretch program, 187, 191, 192. *See also* directed self-placement
PlusOne program (University of North Carolina at Pembroke), 167, 171–75; design, 17; expansion of, 179; impacts of, 181, 182; student performance in, 174(table), 176, 177(table); student response to, 176–78
politics, institutional, 15, 25; with big data analysis, 64
politics, state/national, 14
power structures, 26, 88, 155–57, 165

predictive analytics, 257, 258, 261–63, 266; at Georgia State University, 43, 53(n6)
professional development, for faculty: and curricular redesign, 78–80; impacts of, 88, 89; ongoing, 81, 82, 86, 90, 156, 157, 258, 259; resources for, 74, 75, 77, 82; and retention, 74, 75, 264
professional development, for students: early, 116, 122, 123, 127; as peer advocate, 249(table)
program models. *See* Critical Literacies Achievement and Success Program (CLASP); developmental learning communities; Peer Advocate program; *PlusOne* program; Stretch Program; supplemental instruction model

Reichert Powell, Pegeen: chapter on absolute hospitality, 135–50; and kairotic pedagogy, 215, 217, 252; *Retention and Resistance*, 28, 31, 36(n1), 38, 40, 251, 252; and retention v. persistence, 24, 28, 31; on role of first-year writing in retention, 11, 40, 41, 95, 153, 171, 179, 220, 238; on writing program design, 32
remediation, remedial: effect on grades, graduation, 98, 102, 106, 114; reducing, 13, 84, 205
resources, for professional development, 74, 75, 77, 82, 88, 89
responsibility, 263–65, 268
retention: role of first-year writing/composition in, 11, 39, 153; role of instruction in, 74; role of WPA in, 221; role of writing in, 121
Retention and Resistance (Reichert Powell), 28, 31, 36(n1), 38, 40, 251, 252
retention efforts: mandated, 40, 41, 46; as panopticon, 25, 28–33
retention programs (Georgia State University): assessment/evaluation of, 52; collaboration with writing programs, 38–40, 42, 43, 47; and resources, 50, 51
Rose, Mike: on "guided pathways," 267, 268; *Lives on the Boundary*, 31, 35
Ruecker, Todd, *Transiciones*, 4, 229

second language (L2) writers: in basic writing program models, 185, 186; in the Stretch Program, 189, 191–93, 199
self-assessment: in faculty development, 82; in peer advocate program, 244; in student placement, 78; writing, 87
self-efficacy, 31, 151, 152, 244

Shepherd, Dawn, 12

Stretch Program (Arizona State University), 185–89; current (2012–2013) study on, 189–202; other stretch courses, 207, 258; persistence rates in, 197, 198; retention rates in, 193, 194. *See also* second language writers

student success, and first-year composition courses, 95, 96, 100, 102, 106, 107

Student Success, Office of (Georgia State University), 39, 42–52

supplemental instruction (SI) model, 208–217, 221; student performance in, 176, 177(table). *See also PlusOne* program; Stretch Program

support: academic 170, 172; financial, 179, 182; services, 224, 227, 230, 238, 250; writing, 175, 181, 192

tenacious persister, 119, 120, 122, 124, 129(n2)

threshold concepts, in writing and rhetoric, 142–43, 147, 150(n1); and curriculum, 229

Tinto, Vincent: *Completing College*, 29; "Dropout from Higher Education," 5; *Leaving College*, 28, 39; and persistence, 4–6, 154, 179, 237, 238; retention language, 5, 31; theories of dropout and integration, 5, 6

top-down retention efforts, 38, 40, 46, 48, 51

transition, student: challenges of, 117, 169, 170; and peer advocates, 243, 248; role of composition in, 220, 228, 230

Two-Year College English Association (TYCA), guidelines, 81

two-year institutions: enrollment initiatives, 9; faculty development in, 81, 87; writing program development in, 75–77

TYCA. *See* Two-Year College English Association

undergraduate mentorship program, at Northern Illinois University, 15, 237–55. *See also* Peer Advocate program

underprepared students: and development work, 67, 78–81; and learning communities, 221–23, 226; and placement, 91(n3), 220; and retention, 74, 75, 78, 81, 169, 204

Villanueva, Victor, 26, 155

Wardle, Elizabeth, *Writing about Writing* (with Downs), 32, 33, 142, 143, 228; on FYC, 48

Webb-Sunderhaus, Sara, 4, 15, 122, 186, 204

workshops: faculty development, 77, 82–86, 151; retention, 10; writing, 172

writing centers: and big data, 57, 64, 67–68; and developmental learning communities (DLCs), 228, 230; at Eastern Connecticut State University, 22, 23, 33, 34; and supplemental instruction (SI), 209

Writing Program Administrators (WPAs): and absolute hospitality, 143–45, 147, 149; and assessment efforts, 39–41, 49, 51–53; and big data, 57–59, 61–64, 66–68, 70, 261; and developmental learning communiites, 219–21, 225, 227, 228, 232–34; ethical dilemmas for, 25, 156, 258–60, 265; and first-year composition, 152; and kairotic pedagogy, 205, 206; models for, 168, 200, 205, 233; and placement, 258–65; and the *PlusOne* program, 181; roles in retention, 39, 116, 126–29, 135, 136; at two-year institutions, 76, 77

Writing Program Administrators' listserv (WPA-L), and retention, 4, 152

writing program development, strategies for, 75–77, 78

writing programs: and big data, 61, 63; collaboration with retention programs, 38–41, 47; and first-year composition, 96, 109; and kairotic pedagogy, 32, 136; and the *PlusOne* program, 179; and professional development, 89, 123, 128; retention efforts, 5, 14–16; and second language writers, 185, 186, 195, 199–201; at two-year institutions, 76

writing studio model, 167, 172, 173. *See also PlusOne* program